Euthanasia, Ethics and the Law

Euthanasia, Ethics and Law argues that the law governing the ending of life in England and Wales is unclear, confused and often contradictory. The book shows that the rules are in competition because the ethical principles underlying the rules are also diverse and conflicting.

In mounting his case, Richard Huxtable considers some familiar and topical debates, including assisted suicide and voluntary euthanasia, examining such situations as the Dianne Pretty litigation and Lord Joffe's *Assisted Dying for the Terminally Ill Bill*. The book also enters some important, but less well-charted areas, looking at the advent of 'death tourism' and the real status of involuntary and passive euthanasia in English law, in addition to clarifying the confusion that surrounds the use of powerful painkillers like morphine. Dealing with both legal and ethical issues, the text concludes that the time has come to more openly adopt a compromise position – one that endeavours to honestly recognise and accomodate the competing values, whilst also restoring a measure of coherence to the law.

Richard Huxtable is a Senior Lecturer and the Deputy Director of the Centre for Ethics in Medicine at the University of Bristol, UK.

Biomedical Law and Ethics Library
Series Editor: Sheila A M McLean

Scientific and clinical advances, social and political developments and the impact of healthcare on our lives raise profound ethical and legal questions. Medical law and ethics have become central to our understanding of these problems, and are important tools for the analysis and resolution of problems – real or imagined.

In this series, scholars at the forefront of biomedical law and ethics contribute to the debates in this area, with accessible, thought-provoking and sometimes controversial ideas. Each book in the series develops an independent hypothesis and argues cogently for a particular position. One of the major contributions of this series is the extent to which both law and ethics are utilised in the content of the books, and the shape of the series itself.

The books in this series are analytical, with a key target audience of lawyers, doctors, nurses and the intelligent lay public.

Available titles:

Human Fertilisation and Embryology (2007)
Reproducing Regulation
Kirsty Horsey and Hazel Biggs

Intention and Causation in Medical Non-Killing (2006)
The Impact of Criminal Law Concepts on Euthanasia and Assisted Suicide
Glenys Williams

Impairment and Disability (2007)
Law and Ethics at the Beginning and End of Life
Sheila McLean and Sheila Williamson

Bioethics and the Humanities (2007)
Attitudes and Perceptions
Robin Downie and Jane Macnaughton

Defending the Genetic Supermarket (2007)
The Law and Ethics of Selecting the Next Generation
Colin Gavaghan

The Harm Paradox (2007)
Tort Law and the Unwanted Child in an Era of Choice
Nicolette Priaulx

Assisted Dying (2007)
Reflections on the need for law reform
Sheila McLean

Medicine, Malpractice and Misapprehensions (2007)
Vivienne Harpwood

Euthanasia, Ethics and the Law (2007)
From Conflict to Compromise
Richard Huxtable

Forthcoming titles include:
Best Interests of the Child in Healthcare
Sarah Elliston

Values in Medicine
The realities of clinical practice
Donald Evans

Medicine, Law and the Public Interest
Communitarian Perspectives on Medical Law
J. Kenyon Mason and Graeme Laurie

Healthcare Research Ethics and Law
Regulation, Review and Responsibility
Hazel Biggs

The Body in Bioethics
Alastair Campbell

About the Series Editor

Professor Sheila McLean is International Bar Association Professor of Law and Ethics in Medicine and Director of the Institute of Law and Ethics in Medicine at the University of Glasgow.

Euthanasia, Ethics and the Law

From Conflict to Compromise

Richard Huxtable

Routledge·Cavendish
Taylor & Francis Group

First published 2007 by Routledge-Cavendish
2 Park Square, Milton Park, Abingdon, Oxon OX14 4RN

Simultaneously published in the USA and Canada
by Routledge-Cavendish
270 Madison Avenue, New York, NY 10016

Routledge-Cavendish is an imprint of the Taylor & Francis Group, an informa business

© 2007 Richard Huxtable

Typeset in Times New Roman and Gill Sans by
Florence Production Ltd, Stoodleigh, Devon
Printed and bound in Great Britain by
Antony Rowe Ltd., Chippenham, Wiltshire

British Library Cataloguing in Publication Data
A catalogue record for this book is available from the British Library

Library of Congress Cataloging in Publication Data
A catalog record has been requested

ISBN10: 1–84472–105–1 (hbk)
ISBN10: 1–84472–106–X (pbk)
ISBN10: 0–203–94044–X (ebk)

ISBN13: 978–1–84472–105–4 (hbk)
ISBN13: 978–1–84472–106–1 (pbk)
ISBN13: 978–0–203–94044–0 (ebk)

To Samuel, Genevieve and Green Gran – for the past, present and future

Contents

Acknowledgements   xi
List of abbreviations   xii
Introduction   xiii

1   Judging the end(ing) of life: conflict and confusion   1

   1   Conceptual rights and conceptual wrongs: defining 'euthanasia' 3
      1.1 Humpty Dumpty at the end of life 4
      1.2 Towards a working definition of 'euthanasia' 8
   2   Moral rights and moral wrongs 9
      2.1 The intrinsic value of life 10
      2.2 Choosing the value of life 13
      2.3 The instrumental value of life 15
      2.4 Executioners on slippery slopes 17
   3   Assessing the rights and wrongs of ending life 21
      3.1 The intrinsic value of life 21
      3.2 Choosing the value of life 24
      3.3 The instrumental value of life 26
      3.4 Executioners on slippery slopes 27
   4   Conclusion: conflict and confusion at the end of life 30

2   Not Pretty: 'mercy killing' in legal fact and legal fiction   32

   1   The mercy killer as murderer 34
   2   The mercy killer at 'breaking point' 37
      2.1 Accommodating the mercy killer 37
      2.2 Stretching a (breaking) point 39
      2.3 Diminishing the mercy killer 40
   3   The 'unique' mercy killer 42
      3.1 Before the breaking point 43
      3.2 After the breaking point 44
      3.3 The 'unique' mercy killer 45

4   *Locating the mercy killer 46*
    4.1   *When is a killing not a mercy killing? 47*
    4.2   *When is a killing a mercy killing? 48*
    4.3   *Pretty, not Pretty and the sentencing lottery 49*
5   *The mercy killer: presumed innocent? 50*
6   *Conclusion: collusion, compromise and confusion 52*

3   Assisted suicide in 'the shadowy area of mercy killing'   **55**

1   *What is assisted suicide? 57*
    1.1   *Guilty for aiding the innocent 58*
    1.2   *Publishers in peril 58*
    1.3   *Assisting, assisting an attempt, and attempting to assist in an attempt 59*
    1.4   *Pills, pillows and pistols 60*
2   *Looking for borders in 'shadowy areas' 62*
    2.1   *Stretching the borders of assisted suicide 62*
    2.2   *Assisted suicide beyond the borders: the curious case of 'death tourism' 63*
    2.3   *The classic case of providing the pills 66*
    2.4   *Left to die 68*
        2.4.1   *Passive complicity in suicide 70*
        2.4.2   *Innocent doctors and guilty relatives 72*
        2.4.3   *Left to die or abandoned to die 73*
3   *The 'unique' mercy killer revisited 77*
4   *A right to assisted suicide 79*
    4.1   *Dianne Pretty's failure: the right to die denied 79*
    4.2   *Why Dianne Pretty failed 81*
5   *Conclusion: complicity, compromise and confusion 82*

4   Get out of jail free? Double effect and doctors in the dock   **84**

1   *Double effect in English law 87*
2   *Clarifying the clinical confusion 88*
    2.1   *Clarifying the clinical concepts 89*
    2.2   *When double effect matters 89*
    2.3   *Double effect or covert euthanasia 91*
3   *No intention 92*
    3.1   *The guilty father and the innocent doctor 92*
    3.2   *Double effect or covert euthanasia (revisited) 94*
    3.3   *Double effect in the dock 96*
    3.4   *Killing by accident 99*
4   *Not a cause of death 100*
    4.1   *The guilty layperson and the innocent doctor (revisited) 100*

4.2   Not a cause in fact 101
4.3   Not a cause in law 102
5   Justified murder 102
5.1   Overstretching the judicial reach 102
5.2   The guilty layperson and the innocent doctor
      (re-revisited) 104
5.3   Get out of jail free 105
6   Beyond the boundaries of double effect 106
6.1   Dodging the dock 107
6.2   Engaging the jury's sympathy 109
6.3   Directing the jury and directing the result 110
6.4   Get out of jail free (revisited) 112
7   Conclusion: compromise or confusion? 112

5   Beyond Bland: hedging bets on the value of life?   **115**

1   Quinlan's challenge: letting die and letting
    morality in 117
1.1   Quinlan's challenge 117
1.2   Letting die as a moral matter 119
1.3   Duties, doctors and intruders 120
2   Beyond Bland: the problem of fatal omissions 123
2.1   Bland's challenge: letting the incompetent
      patient die 123
2.2   Karapetian's challenge: duties, doctors and intruders
      (revisited) 126
2.3   Diverting doctors from the dock 128
2.4   Beyond Bland: letting die as a moral matter
      (revisited) 130
3   Doctrinal difficulties: what is the value of life? 131
3.1   The intrinsic value of life 131
3.2   From intrinsic value to instrumental value 133
3.3   From intrinsic value to self-determined value 136
4   Conclusion: hedging bets on the value of life 139

**6   Euthanasia and the middle ground: from conflict
to compromise**   **141**

1   From conflict to creativity and consensus 143
1.1   Condoning conflict and confusion 144
1.2   Creativity at the end of life 145
1.3   Consensus and convergence at the end of life 146
2   The case for compromise 149
2.1   The conditions of compromise 149
2.2   Condoning compromise 151

3   *The contours of compromise 155*
    3.1   Compromise by committee 155
    3.2   Moral discomfort, justification and excuse 158
    3.3   Clarifying the compromise on fatal omissions 160
    3.4   Clarifying the double effect 162
    3.5   Clarifying the 'shadowy area' of mercy killing 165
4   *Conclusion: from conflict to compromise 172*

Bibliography   175
Index   199

Acknowledgements

The arguments in this book have developed considerably since they were first explored in a PhD thesis, awarded by the University of Bristol in 2002, but I still owe much to the examiners, Jean McHale and Rebecca Bailey-Harris, and particularly to my advisers, Julian Rivers and Richard Ashcroft. I am also greatly indebted to the University of Bristol, the National University of Singapore and the Hastings Center, New York, for supporting and hosting sabbatical studies, during which I gained invaluable advice from a range of scholars, not least Bruce Jennings and Tom Murray. I have also learned a great deal from numerous discussions with colleagues and students over the years, for which I am immensely grateful, and equally I cannot emphasise enough how vital the support of my family and friends has been to the preparation and completion of this book. I am grateful too to Sheila McLean, everyone at Routledge-Cavendish for their invaluable assistance, and to Alex, Aimee and the Barenaked Ladies for providing the soundtrack to this work.

However, the greatest thanks are undoubtedly due to those who were kind enough to comment on the manuscript at various stages. Their perceptive readings saved me from pitfalls too numerous to mention and merely listing their names here scarcely reflects how important their contributions were. Huge thanks, then, to Richard Ashcroft, Lois Bibbings, Alastair V Campbell, Chris Cowley, Karen Forbes, Mary Hodgson, Ruud ter Meulen, and, most of all, Genevieve Liveley, for her unwavering support, incisive critiques and good humour, all of which helped me see this project through to the end. If I have done them any justice at all, this book will combine the legal, philosophical, clinical and personal insights each has helped me to gain; needless to say, the final responsibility for the arguments mounted here remains with me.

Finally, I thank Sage Publishing and Jordan Publishing for permitting me, in Chapter four, to re-work and partially reproduce Richard Huxtable, 'Get out of jail free? The doctrine of double effect in English law', *Palliative Medicine*, 18: 62–68 and Richard Huxtable and Karen Forbes, 'Glass v UK: Maternal instinct vs. medical opinion', *Child and Family Law Quarterly*, 16(3): 339–354, respectively.

Abbreviations

AIDS	Acquired Immunodeficiency Syndrome
BBC	British Broadcasting Corporation
BMA	British Medical Association
CPS	Crown Prosecution Service
DF118	Dihydrocodeine
DPP	Director of Public Prosecutions
GMC	General Medical Council
GP	General Practitioner
LJ	Lady/Lord Justice
LCJ	Lord Chief Justice
MR	Master of the Rolls
mg	Milligrams
NHS	National Health Service
P	President of the Family Division of the High Court
PVS	Permanent/persistent vegetative state
QC	Queen's Counsel
RCPCH	Royal College of Paediatrics and Child Health
VES	Voluntary Euthanasia Society

Introduction

Modern medicine has triumphed over many previously incurable and chronic conditions. In the care of the dying patient, in the developed world at least, palliative medicine frequently offers a death free from painful and distressing symptoms. However, this is not a complete victory, since some patients continue to suffer and some reject the options on offer, preferring instead to receive help in securing an earlier death. Against this backdrop, patients, philosophers, pressure groups and even some healthcare professionals argue that prohibitive attitudes towards euthanasia should give way to admitting that, sometimes, killing can be a part of caring.

English law claims to forbid the practise of euthanasia, even when this is what the suffering patient desires, and it also condemns related activities like providing assistance in committing suicide. Patients such as Dianne Pretty, who had motor neurone disease, have sought to challenge the formal prohibition but have been denied what they seek (see No 2346/02 *Pretty v UK* (2002) 35 EHRR 1). Parliamentarians also, like Lord Joffe in his Assisted Dying for the Terminally Ill Bill, have failed to persuade the lawmakers that the traditional resistance to allowing the deliberate causing of death should be ousted in favour of an approach that prioritises patient choice and the dictates of mercy.

In this book I will examine all these features of the ethical debate about euthanasia, paying particular attention to how they can – and should – shape the rules that make up English law. In doing so, I strive to diagnose a problem with our recent discussions – that they are marked (indeed, marred) by seemingly irresolvable and unrelenting conflict – and to provide a different prognosis for their development.

Chapter 1 provides an overview of the arguments most commonly presented by proponents and opponents of euthanasia. The first problem I examine is that the discussants are not always necessarily talking about the same thing: robust attempts to define the word 'euthanasia' are scarce, and the plethora of (alleged) synonyms (like 'mercy killing') and distinctions (like 'active' as opposed to 'passive' euthanasia) invite misunderstanding and conflicting interpretations. It becomes apparent that the labels chosen can reflect very different underlying moral perspectives, which tend to be premised on one of three views of the value of human life.

The first, traditional, view of the sanctity or inviolability of life maintains that life is intrinsically valuable or 'sacred', such that it should never intentionally be brought to an end (e.g. Keown 2002a). Advocates of this view, nevertheless, do not feel that every effort should be taken to prolong or preserve life. The 'doctrine of double effect' condemns the intentional shortening of life, but acknowledges that death can justifiably occur where this is only a foreseen side effect of the agent's action. So, it is claimed, practitioners of palliative medicine are right to use powerful drugs like morphine and sedatives in caring for the terminally ill, even if these drugs can carry a risk of hastening death. Equally, in this view, it is not always the case that life should be prolonged: 'futile' or 'burdensome' treatment can legitimately be withheld or withdrawn from the patient.

Opponents of this position claim that such distinctions are tenuous and hypocritical, since what they really reflect is a second, very different perspective on the value of life, namely that it is only instrumentally valuable for as long as it is a life free from significant suffering or impairment and, indeed, a life that the person wants to continue living (e.g. Singer 1993). And it is not wrong, they argue, to end a miserable life, least of all when this is what the patient wants, but perhaps also when the patient is severely compromised and unable to communicate their opinion.

A third, yet more prevalent argument insists that the ethics of euthanasia turn entirely on the wishes of the autonomous (or self-determining) patient and their view of the value of life (e.g. Brock 1993). If, like Dianne Pretty, death is what they desire, then there is no cogent reason for denying them dominion (cf. Dworkin 1993a; Freeman 2002).

However, the field is not dominated by purely principled positions, since critics of euthanasia have one other major ground of opposition, which moves the debate on to more pragmatic concerns about what allowing euthanasia could – perhaps would – mean in practice. Fears of embarking on a 'slippery slope' to involuntary killing, abuse and a general devaluing of life suggest to these critics that this is neither an ethical nor a safe practice.

So familiar and entrenched are these various arguments that this summary of the contemporary debates could easily have been written as long ago as 1957 (see e.g. Kamisar 1957; Williams 1958b). Certainly, the arguments on both sides are becoming increasingly refined; however, the principal claims and main areas of contention have changed little in recent years. Each has its merits but, I will suggest, also its flaws, because their meanings can be unclear and contestable, their capacity for extension gives cause for serious concern, and they all appear rather less appealing than their proponents would admit. No serious attempt to settle the moral problem of euthanasia is going to succeed if it does not pay some heed to conflicting ideas about end(ing) life. How, then, does – and, ultimately, should – English law resolve these ethical conflicts?

In Chapters 2, 3 and 4 I examine how the law is currently responding to behaviour in three related spheres, which are, respectively: the special case of euthanasia known popularly as 'mercy killing', in which it is a relative or other loved one who ends the life of a patient; the phenomenon described by philosophers as 'assisted suicide' and by lawyers as 'complicity in suicide'; and the actions taken by doctors (and sometimes other health professionals) that might or will end life. Each of these chapters starts with a description of a real case, drawn from the law reports and popular media, which is aimed at illustrating the key themes of the chapter. Indeed, it should be noted that my sources include not only classic legal materials, such as reported judgments, statutes, and official reports and pronouncements, but also media reports covering various trials for alleged euthanasia. Mindful of the bias and inaccuracies that can come from some of these materials, I have, wherever possible, consulted more than one source and attempted to exercise caution in the conclusions that can be drawn from them.

My aim is to illustrate various trends in the law both as it is stated and as it is applied by the various legal officials, including the police, the prosecutors and the judges. Although I will, of course, include consideration of the ever-growing body of medical law, my focus is more often on the criminal law. Indeed, some of the observations I make and arguments I mount might be equally applicable to other topics and issues arising in the criminal law, but these are generally left to others to tackle. Instead, the focus of this book is euthanasia, and its uneasy relationship with a host of homicide offences including murder, manslaughter and complicity in suicide.

Chapter 2 therefore begins with an examination of 'mercy killing', which is that form of euthanasia in which someone, usually a loved one, puts an end to the patient's suffering. I start here because the operation of the law in this area provides a particularly vivid illustration of the problems with our current policies. A mercy killer, we are told, is indistinguishable from any other murderer, which implies that they will be subject to the mandatory sentence of life imprisonment. So much for legal theory; in practice, this is overwhelmingly not the case. Instead, this alleged murderer is transformed into a manslaughterer, who is said to have acted under 'diminished responsibility'. This re-casting is neither accurate nor fair, although it does say much about what the legal officials are trying to achieve. Faced with conflicting ethical norms, the legal officials strive to preserve a measure of condemnation, reflective of the intrinsic value of life, but also to achieve leniency, in recognition that a mercy killing is, by definition, benevolently motivated. I will suggest that, remarkably, the law even affords an excuse to the killer who acts against the patient's wish to live or else does not consult them on the matter.

Similarly confused messages of permission and prohibition emerge from Chapter 3, which focuses on the offence of complicity in suicide, a crime that mirrors (to some extent) the practice known as 'assisted suicide' in popular bioethical discussions. Beyond the simple claim that complicity in suicide is a crime, there is little certainty about when that crime has been committed and how the legal officials will respond if it has. The modern emergence of 'death tourism', in which the suffering patient obtains help in travelling abroad to take up the option of assisted suicide, is particularly problematic. In terms of the letter of the law, it would appear that the person who helps the patient to get to a country like Switzerland has committed an offence in this country but so far no such prosecutions have been mounted. Equally, despite arguments to the contrary, it appears that the entitlement to commit suicide afforded in the Suicide Act 1961 is not all that it seems, as people who have done nothing more than sit with a dying patient have been convicted of a crime of 'omission'. In contrast, the paradigm case of providing the pills to a suicidal individual seems to be treated differently and has a doubtful legal status: at least one defendant has avoided conviction by claiming that he 'only provided the option' of committing suicide (Gorman 1993: 3), and, despite suggestions that such assistance has sometimes involved members of the medical profession, no doctor has ever been prosecuted in relation to such conduct.

The protection awarded to the doctor under our current laws gets more comprehensive coverage in Chapter 4, in which I specifically examine the legal recognition afforded to the ethical doctrine of double effect. Close attention to the trials to date and to the evidence provided by expert clinicians shows that there is something amiss in the way that the prosecutors and judges tackle allegations against doctors whose management of symptoms have apparently shortened a patient's life. It is not even clear how the doctrine occupies English law, since none of the conventional explanations is satisfactory. The doctor's innocence cannot entirely or easily be attributed to them lacking the guilty intention to cause death: elsewhere in the law of murder, it is clear that lay-people can be convicted when they foresee that their actions are virtually certain to cause death. It is also not necessarily the case that a doctor's actions will never cause death, such that a charge of murder will fail on the ground that causation cannot be proven. Finally, it is insufficient to say that the doctor merits a special defence to a charge of murder; this might not even be welcomed by the doctors, who must, on this account, be viewed as justified murderers.

Although these three chapters detail the main problems with our existing legal responses to euthanasia and related activities, Chapter 5 includes consideration of another, particularly thorny dilemma: when life-sustaining treatment might lawfully be withheld or withdrawn. My principal aim in looking at this issue is to show how the law pertaining to the end of life more generally has arrived in its current position, in which rules are relaxed and accommodations are made to diverse and sometimes contradictory arguments. At this stage, the resultant legal patchwork begins to appear less surprising, since the chapter reveals how closely entwined the conflicts over the morality of euthanasia are with the evolution of the legal rules in this area. Each of the main arguments canvassed in Chapter 1 finds some place in English law but none is taken to its seemingly logical conclusion.

This all suggests that, before we can sort out the law, we need to achieve some resolution on the value of life. In Chapter 6 I therefore return to the underlying problem, which was canvassed in the first chapter: that of identifying an appropriate ethical framework on which to base the legal rules and processes. Here I suggest that the time has come to look beyond conflict and towards a more subtle and nuanced solution. Alexander McCall Smith (1999) has argued that the current legal position is the least worst option available; he has a point, but he underplays the need to tackle the numerous legal difficulties I discuss throughout Chapters 2 to 4. Building on the work of Lon Fuller (1969) and Roger Brownsword (1993; 1996), I argue that if it is to guide anybody, law must be clear and consistent. Because if it is not, revision is required.

Some theorists believe that we might be able to anchor any revisions in new theories of right and wrong (e.g. Battin 2005). Whilst undoubtedly a worthwhile endeavour, it is too early to tell whether there can be a workable and wholly 'new' end-of-life ethic. It is also unlikely that a suitable consensus can be reached, least of all on a practice like voluntary euthanasia. It is, however, possible to satisfy Margaret Battin's recent plea for an end to the persistent for-and-against of these debates (Battin 2005) and I believe that the way forward lies in compromise.

In Chapter 6 then, I argue that compromising on an issue like this is not only desirable but also feasible (Benjamin 1990a). In short, conflict should give way, in English law at least, to efforts to split the difference between the disputants. The focus here is indeed on the law in England and Wales and how it already does seek to achieve a compromise and how it might now do this in a more rational and defensible fashion. However, other apparently prohibitive jurisdictions faced with arguments and proposals like those advanced by Dianne Pretty and Lord Joffe might also begin to see the benefits of the middle ground.

The key proposal defended here is that English law should openly and explicitly recognise euthanasia as a distinct legal category – neither justified, as proponents argue, nor unjustified as opponents maintain, but instead (partially) excused as a lesser form of homicide than murder. A specific crime, labelled 'mercy killing' or some other suitable synonym, offers a reasonable compromise, and even has renewed currency, since the English Law Commission (2005; 2006) has recently given thought to reviving the concept. Whilst significant, such a reform in itself will nevertheless not suffice and so I will also use the last chapter to re-think the various examples of criminal and innocent behaviour arising from the earlier chapters. Both withdrawing life support and using potentially fatal drugs will remain lawful, but I will argue for numerous clarifications in these areas and, indeed, in relation to the offence of complicity in suicide. Various methods are proposed for improving the coherence of the law, whilst remaining firmly on the middle ground.

Some of the conclusions I come to are uncomfortable, and I recognise that my own views have changed, and might do so again. I believe, however, that this need not be a problem in itself, but might instead hint at a problem within the debate itself – that there are many important insights on offer but there are few people attempting to accommodate, let alone concede anything to, their opponents' views. I try to do this here, but I appreciate that this is necessarily only the beginning of a new debate and that the attempt to map the middle ground will undoubtedly invite attack from all sides. However, what we currently have does not work and what we are told should replace it will not necessarily work either. It is hoped that this book will spark real progress towards rationalising the law and moving the debate beyond an all-too-familiar impasse.

The approach taken here is primarily legalistic in nature: it operates within a framework that will be familiar to those versed in the philosophy of law (i.e. jurisprudence) and the sociology of law (i.e. socio-legal studies). However, legal concepts and theories are conveyed as clearly as possible, so that the reader is not required to be a legal scholar. Equally, whilst philosophers, bioethicists and clinicians might find some arguments more accessible than other readers, every effort has been made to clarify their claims for those who are not familiar with these areas. Indeed, the issues covered here are ones in which we all have a stake and some interest, not least because we are all likely to be patients at some point and we are all going to die. Hopefully, then, patients and their families will also find something of value in the following pages. Discussions about when and how life might come to an end are important and simply will not go away; ideally, the perspective on offer here will help opponents and proponents of euthanasia alike to see the value in one another's perspectives and some of the deficiencies in their own.

Chapter 1

Judging the end(ing) of life

Conflict and confusion

The questions whether the terminally ill, or others, should be free to seek assistance in taking their own lives, and if so in what circumstances and subject to what safeguards, are of great social, ethical and religious significance and are questions on which widely differing beliefs and views are held, often strongly.

R (on the application of Pretty) v DPP [2002]
1 FLR 268, *per* Lord Bingham, para. 2

If self-determination is a fundamental value, then the great variability among people on this question makes it especially important that individuals control the manner, circumstances, and timing of their dying and death.

(Brock 1993: 206)

If competent patients who are terminally ill should be legally able to choose assisted death because they believe that their lives are no longer worth living then should it not be possible for clinicians in partnership with families to make similar decisions on behalf of those who cannot competently choose for themselves?

(Doyal 2006: 66)

The right to refuse treatment should be regarded as a shield not as a sword. The courts should consistently hold that patients have no right to commit suicide by refusing treatment and that, whether or not doctors have a duty to prevent patients from committing suicide thereby, they certainly have a duty not intentionally to assist them.

(Keown 2002b: 239)

In April 2002, Dianne Pretty's final appeal for a 'right to die' foundered before the judges of the European Court of Human Rights in Strasbourg. Mrs Pretty had motor neurone disease, a neuro-degenerative condition that progressively attacks the sufferer's muscles, for which there is no cure. According to Mrs Pretty, she had 'fought this disease each step of the way' (Dyer 2002). She nevertheless knew that the disease would overpower her and she particularly feared the prospect of suffocating in the final stages of her life. Mrs Pretty's husband, Brian, confirmed that he would be willing to help his wife commit suicide, but only if the legal officials would in turn confirm that he would not be prosecuted. 'If I am allowed to choose when and how I die I will feel that I have wrested some autonomy back and kept hold of my dignity', said Mrs Pretty. 'That is how I want my family to remember me – as someone who respected the law and asked that in turn the law respect my rights.' (ibid)

The legal officials – ranging from the Director of Public Prosecutions (DPP), to the English Law Lords, to the judges in Strasbourg – denied that Mrs Pretty, or indeed anyone else, had a right to be helped to die. Legal backing did exist for a wide range of personal choices, including the choice to have life-supporting treatment removed, but respect for personal autonomy did not encompass or entail positive assistance in dying. To rule otherwise, thought the judges, would be to signal that life, especially a compromised life, is not intrinsically valuable, and so would undermine the respect and protection due to vulnerable patients. Less than two weeks after hearing that she had lost this battle, Mrs Pretty died.

A decade earlier, however, the Law Lords had not been so resistant to the idea that there might be circumstances in which an early death could be in a patient's interests. Anthony Bland had been trapped in the horrifying crush at the Hillsborough football stadium in 1989. By 1993 the doctors agreed that he was in what was then termed a persistent (now, a permanent) vegetative state (PVS). Mr Bland's diagnosis was amongst the most extreme there could be for this condition, since his higher brain had effectively liquefied. He would never again be able to participate in life in any conscious way. However, his brain stem was still functioning. Mr Bland was therefore, in legal terms, still alive, and medical science could ensure that he stayed alive, through, for example, the provision of nutrition and hydration via a nasogastric tube.

Neither Bland's parents nor his doctors felt that such treatment should continue, and their request that it be stopped travelled through the English court system, ultimately arriving at the House of Lords. All of the judges agreed that the nutrition and hydration could be brought to an end and that the doctors would not be committing any crime, such as murder, if they did so. This was not, they claimed, equivalent to euthanasia, and did not demolish the idea that all lives warranted equal respect and defence. It was, however, apparently clear that this treatment was not in Mr Bland's best interests, and so he should be allowed to die with dignity.

No one familiar with medical law, be it through the specialist journals or the popular press, can have failed to have tracked the debates surrounding the fates of Mrs Pretty and Mr Bland and thereafter to have formed some opinion on the rights (and wrongs) of the two rulings. To some, including our judges, these are radically different cases, requiring radically different responses. To others, the issues at stake are basically the same. What is the value attached to life, especially a life of suffering or inability, in English law? Is life intrinsically valuable, to the extent that it should never intentionally be curtailed? Or is life only instrumentally valuable, for as long as it is a 'meaningful' or 'useful' life? Or can we perhaps get around these complicated philosophical questions by turning the decision over to the individual: is it, then, for the autonomous person to judge the value of his or her life?

These are, as Lord Bingham noted, 'questions on which widely differing beliefs and views are held, often strongly'. In this book I will consider how English law has sought to answer these questions and how, in doing so, it has degenerated into confusion and contradiction, as it seeks simultaneously to stress that the value of life is intrinsic, *and* instrumental, *and* subjectively determined. This is not to say that English law has arrived at entirely the wrong place. Part of the reason why the law seems to clutch at conflicting concepts is that they all offer some important part of the moral picture of ending life. By the close of Chapter 6, I hope therefore to have demonstrated why the law is right to strive for ethical accommodation but also how it can achieve this in a manner that better realises a – perhaps the – fundamental goal of law, that is, issuing rules that can guide those to whom they apply (see Fuller 1969; Brownsword 1993; 1996).

Chapters 2 to 5 nevertheless combine to suggest that the messages sent by current legal rules and processes are rarely capable of achieving law's basic purpose: the relevant authorities are replete with conflicting and sometimes blatantly contradictory edicts, which can guide nobody. However, the philosophical debates appear to fare little better: there too, conflict is everywhere, not only over the values at stake but also over the very words used to describe the practices under examination. It is to this latter problem I will turn first in this chapter, before moving on to consider what is right but particularly what is wrong with much of our current thinking about the values brought to bear on the end(ing) of life.

I Conceptual rights and conceptual wrongs: defining 'euthanasia'

What is 'euthanasia'? This looks like the most obvious place to start in any examination of the morality of ending lives blighted by suffering, but it has been relatively neglected in recent debates (Beauchamp and Davidson 1979; Wreen 1988). Yet, this neglect might not be surprising given the disagreements that exist even over this seemingly simple issue. Theorists appear to have a tendency either to assume that we know what we are discussing or to stipulate meanings that are contestable and that rest on a particular moral position that is itself contestable. Both approaches have their risks: either the discussants will talk past one another or else a battle of values will immediately commence.

I will not try here to find a shared moral language that might help us to overcome these difficulties, although I will stipulate definitions of some of the central terms that should enable debate to occur without begging the key moral questions. However, my main aim is to show how conflict exists even at this basic level.

1.1 Humpty Dumpty at the end of life

'When I use a word,' Humpty Dumpty said, in rather a scornful tone, 'it means just what I choose it to mean – neither more or less.' 'The question is,' said Alice, 'whether you can make words mean so many different things.'

(Carroll 1982: 184)

It has not escaped notice that there are more Humpty Dumptys than Alices populating end-of-life discussions (Morgan 2001: 205; Cohen-Almagor 2000; Derse 2000). A wide variety of words are used, ranging from 'euthanasia', 'aid-in-dying' and '(physician) assisted suicide' in the academic press, to more popular phrases and political rallying cries like 'mercy killing', the 'right to die' and 'death with dignity'. Medicine and euthanasia meet in the term 'medicide', coined by America's recently incarcerated 'Dr Death', Jack Kevorkian (1991; see also Keown 2002a: 31). They may sometimes be used interchangeably (e.g. Dworkin 1993a: 3–4, 184–186) but the predicament, according to one opponent of the practice, is that none of these expressions, even 'euthanasia' itself, has any 'accepted and philosophically warranted core of meaning' (Finnis 1997a: 23).

Etymologically, 'euthanasia', derived from the Greek *eu* and *thanatos*, translates as 'good death' or 'dying well'. Unfortunately, these translations immediately threaten to beg the moral question: if euthanasia is, by definition, about achieving a 'good death', then how can the practice be 'bad'? The question can also be begged in the opposite direction. Some opponents of euthanasia emphasise that the word was used to describe the Nazi policies of the 1930s, when the preservation of Aryan purity led to the killing of 'undesirable' individuals and groups (see Davies 1997: 84). Used in this way, 'euthanasia' clearly conveys an evil practice (cf. Finnis 1997b: 53; Harris 1997c: 56).

Even if we restrict ourselves to the idea of 'dying well', this does little to clarify what we are specifically interested in examining, since one can die well from entirely natural causes without there having been any human intervention. Moreover, euthanasia is nowadays most often seen as the preserve of patients and, in particular, those suffering unbearably from disease and decline. Indeed, William Lecky is thought to be the first to use the word in this modern sense, in his *History of European Morals*, first published in 1869 (Lecky 1924: 93). Lecky was discussing those instances of suicide intended 'as an euthanasia, an abridgement of the pangs of disease, and a guarantee against the dotage of old age' (ibid). As VanDeVeer (1986: 226) points out, a basic etymological definition encompasses more than this: we might, for example, describe certain killings in self-defence or war as 'good' (justifiable) deaths. He similarly notes that the label can be applied to painful, rather than painless, killings; a common example involves the fatal shooting of a wounded soldier (see also Harris 2003: 14–15).

Perhaps mindful of the many pitfalls, modern thinkers tend instead to direct their attention to the types of behaviour that might be classed as euthanasia. This, of course, does not get round the central problem of defining the word, to which I shall return. Presently, however, it is worth noting how the debate currently focuses on a variety of categories and distinctions that have been introduced, gravitating primarily around, first, the wishes and mental competence of the person receiving euthanasia and, second, the ways in which it might be practised (e.g. Glover 1977: 182, 185, 197–199; Kuhse 1991: 296; Keown 2002a: 8–17).

The first distinction in this nomenclature centres upon the person whose life or death is at stake. She or he might want help in dying, not want help in dying, or be unable (like Anthony Bland, for example) to form or communicate any decision on the matter. These different positions are often labelled as, respectively, voluntary, involuntary and non-voluntary forms of euthanasia. But even here there is some confusion. The Netherlands, for example, has long allowed euthanasia to occur without criminal sanction, provided that certain conditions are met (see e.g. Janssen 2002). A central requirement is that the patient must want to receive help in dying. Defining and delineating the practices then becomes difficult because, to the Dutch, 'euthanasia' describes only this situation. This suggests that it is meaningless – or at least very difficult – to talk of involuntary or non-voluntary euthanasia occurring in that jurisdiction, since euthanasia is, by definition, a death that is desired.[1] The same problem has surfaced in other areas of policy-making, including in a document issued by an Ethics Task Force of the European Association for Palliative Care, which adopts a similarly narrow definition of euthanasia (2003; see Campbell and Huxtable 2003: 180–181).

This is not the only complexity that can arise with these three categories, particularly when some writers term a practise 'non-voluntary' euthanasia

---

1   This may be difficult but, as I will argue later in this chapter, it is not impossible (see Manninen 2006).

that others would classify as 'involuntary' (e.g. Gordon 1966: 149). Indeed, VanDemeer points out that more than one of the labels can sometimes be applied to the same case (1986: 227; cf. Foot 1977: 105). If, for example, Anthony Bland had been lethally injected, this might look like non-voluntary euthanasia. However, if he had previously held the view that life is sacred and that he would never want to have his life ended in such a way, then this would also be an instance of involuntary euthanasia.

The problems are even more pronounced in the second set of categories that are conventionally introduced. This time a distinction is drawn between (positive) acts (active euthanasia) and (negative) omissions (passive euthanasia). The clearest examples of each are the act of lethally injecting the patient, and, on the 'passive' (negative) side, failing to provide the patient with something necessary to sustain his or her life. Beyond this, matters become murkier, particularly around the description (and then evaluation) of an omission. No longer supplying nutrients down Mr Bland's feeding tube looks like an omission. But what about pulling out the feeding tube? This has the same effect, but starts to look much more active (e.g. Kuhse 1991: 296; Otlowski 1997: 5–7; Huxtable 2005b). So is it an act or an omission, and should the classification even matter? Some argue on moral grounds that it certainly does matter, but disputes also occur at the level of definition, as others deny that 'passive euthanasia' can even exist as a category (e.g. Gay-Williams 1979: 100). Beyond this, references to 'selective non-treatment' or 'withdrawing treatment' (e.g. Mason and Laurie 2006: 543) might be more appealing to clinicians and patients, but they do not necessarily prevent the situation from being described as one of 'passive euthanasia'.

Categorisation can be difficult but the problem with the contemporary focus on which categories of euthanasia (if any) exist and can be defended is that it downplays the importance of first agreeing upon that which is being categorised, that is, how we should understand 'euthanasia'. Unfortunately, even the most sophisticated attempts to define the term rest on concepts that can be understood in different ways. Consider, for example, the following from Wreen:

Person A committed euthanasia if and only if:

(1) A killed B or let her die.
(2) A intended to kill B.
(3) The intention specified in (2) was at least partial cause of the action specified in (1).
(4) The causal journey from the intention specified in (2) to the action specified in (1) is more or less in accordance with A's plan of action.
(5) A's killing of B is a voluntary action.
(6) The motive for the action specified in (1), the motive standing behind the intention specified in (2), is the good of the person killed.

(1988: 637–640)

Although somewhat daunting to the non-philosopher, Wreen's description undeniably captures some of the key elements of euthanasia, but it still invites conflicting interpretations.

From the outset, the differentiation between 'killing' or 'letting die' is, of course, hotly disputed. Yet, a more fundamental question might be asked: what is 'death'? Many nowadays accept, at least in the developed world, that death is the loss of brain stem function (Capron 2001; Randell 2004). A 'brain dead' body can nevertheless be sustained through, for example, the use of a mechanical ventilator. Some will still argue that stopping the machine means 'killing' the patient (see Appel 2005; Dubler 2005: s22). Others, including Peter Singer (1994), argue that life is only valuable, and perhaps might only be described as a life, when the higher brain is functioning (contrast Fisher 1999). Could we then claim that it is better to class someone like Mr Bland as dead, such that any removal of life support from his body is not an instance of 'killing' or 'letting die'?

Second, the meaning of 'intentional' conduct needs clarification. Am I only performing euthanasia when I directly aim at causing a patient's death? What if, for example, I do not deliberately want to bring about death but I do foresee that death will almost certainly (or even inevitably) follow from my removing a ventilator? Confusingly, some commentators would describe this as 'indirect euthanasia' (e.g. Otlowski 1997: 8), which prompts the question: what does the word 'direct' add to the requirement that a straightforward case of euthanasia will be 'intentional'?

Then there is the quandary of causation. When I remove the ventilator, death follows because the patient is unable to breathe unaided: it is their underlying medical condition that leads to their death. So, to borrow a phrase from elsewhere in Wreen's definition, is it enough for my conduct to be only 'a partial cause' of death? If so, how big a part must I play before I can be said to have practised euthanasia?

And when does euthanasia transform into assisting in suicide? There, the suicidal person enlists my help in dying, so I clearly play a causal role in their death, but – at least according to many current definitions – it is that person him or herself who performs the final, fatal act (see e.g. Kamisar 1997: 228–229). I have played a part, maybe by purchasing the pills that they then consumed. Is this 'only' assisting a suicide or is it instead, or even also, a case of euthanasia? And where, if anywhere, are the boundaries between the two, especially between assisted suicide and voluntary euthanasia? To these questions many more can be added, since it is also not clear whether one can be a passive assistant in suicide, a problem which again rests on the difficulty of differentiating an act from an omission (e.g. Kamm 1998: 29–30).

The final dilemma to note here concerns the motive of the person practising euthanasia, which is what gives them their reason for acting (or omitting). Wreen tells us that this arises from an urge to serve 'the good of the person killed'. The sort of 'good' that is usually envisaged involves freeing a person from such suffering as is frequently associated with some terminal or perhaps chronic illness. Dianne Pretty, for example, wanted to avoid the distressing symptoms that motor neurone disease can inflict. Ending her life would certainly seem to qualify as euthanasia, but what about ending the life of Anthony Bland, who was apparently permanently and irreversibly insensate? He, it seems, would not be able to experience any suffering, so if he had been deliberately lethally injected, one might question whether this action would more accurately be described as simply a case of murder.

More generally, clarification is required as to the sort of 'suffering' that will suffice before the killing (or letting die) can amount to euthanasia. Is a head cold sufficient? It may well make the killing look extremely morally questionable but does it prevent the label even being applied? Consider also the decision made by the British General Practitioner (GP) Dr Anne Turner, who sought – and received – assisted suicide in Switzerland. Dr Turner had the incurable condition progressive supranuclear palsy and she wished to end her life with assistance while she still could. She feared that her condition would deteriorate to the point at which she could no longer swallow the solution of barbiturates (Boseley and Dyer 2006). So Dr Turner was, in a sense, seeking pre-emptive euthanasia: is that a valid label? Indeed, is it necessarily the case that the suffering must have arisen from some disease or injury? Will old age or loneliness suffice (Huxtable and Möller 2007)? Some 'medical' problem is usually assumed in these debates, and understandably so, when they typically concentrate on whether or not people working in healthcare should be entitled to practise euthanasia. That, nevertheless, imposes an arbitrary limit on the scope of the terms, since there are occasions when non-doctors might be described as engaging in euthanasia. When such laypersons do so, however, the tendency is to describe the situation as a 'mercy killing'. Should that label be reserved for non-medical cases, with 'euthanasia' only applied to medical killings?

1.2 Towards a working definition of 'euthanasia'

Theorists, in the main, might want to identify and employ a description of euthanasia that allows the moral debates to flourish (Beauchamp and Davidson 1979: 299, 312), but, as has already been hinted, they all too often rely on concepts that will themselves 'reflect a particular moral viewpoint' (Otlowski 1997: 4). This problem is unlikely to be eradicated, so the best I can currently do is offer a working definition (see e.g. Harris 1997a: 6; Finnis 1997a: 23–24), which at least concedes the areas of complexity and quarrel.

Allow me to stipulate that 'euthanasia' involves the intentional ending of the life (whether the recipient wants this or not) of someone, who I will call the patient, which is motivated by the belief that this will be in some way beneficial for them. The motive rests on the idea of mercy, familiar from the phrase 'mercy killing': the agent practising euthanasia aims to (and does) put an end to the poor quality life that the patient is enduring or is likely to endure. The patient will typically have a medical condition of some kind, usually a severe one that is terminal or chronic in nature. Suicide, which can (at least) be described as intentional self-killing (see Daube 1972; Frey 1981; Beauchamp 1993), can be performed for the same reason, when it might be described as 'autoeuthanasia' (Humphry and Wickett 1986). Assisted suicide can be similarly motivated, although – in line with popular accounts – here it is the patient who performs the final action. As regards the person practising euthanasia or assisting in suicide, there seems to be no reason why this can only be a doctor. Instead, I will describe as euthanasia any killing (and, indeed, letting die) that satisfies the conditions noted above.

With the central term so defined, the aforementioned categories can be invoked, leading to six versions of euthanasia: active voluntary, active involuntary and active non-voluntary, as well as passive voluntary, passive involuntary and passive non-voluntary. To this list a seventh type of behaviour, known as assisted suicide, can be added. That concept too should be amenable to separation into active assistance and passive assistance. I actively provide you with the pills or I passively stand aside and let you take the pills. In either case, so long as I intend by my behaviour to facilitate your suicide, then I can be described as having assisted in it. And that leads to one final, and again brief, definition: suicide, in the autoeuthanasia sense. Here, you can intend to end your life by taking some positive action like consuming an overdose, but it seems just as accurate to say that you have committed suicide when, for example, you refrain from eating in order that you will die and so be freed from your suffering.

These concepts – and the problems with them – will resurface throughout this book, not least because what I have emphatically not done is take any clear position on the various contested terms on which they rest. The contests over what is to count as 'passive', 'intentional' and 'causal' continue to be waged, alongside arguably even harder battles over the meaning of 'life' and the meaning of 'death' (e.g. Beauchamp and Davidson 1979: 304). The possibilities are deliberately kept open (see similarly Otlowski 1997: 7) in order to see most clearly how those contests rest on deeper conflicts over the ethics of what the disputants are trying to describe and debate.

2 Moral rights and moral wrongs

The ethical dimensions of euthanasia, as well as of end-of-life decisions more broadly, have been exhaustively mapped, particularly in recent decades (e.g. Downing 1969; Steinbock and Norcross 1994; Keown 1997c). The main area of contention, and the one to which I will direct most attention, relates to patients like Dianne Pretty, who seek some positive assistance in drawing their lives to a close. This does not mean that I will completely neglect patients like Anthony Bland – and nor is that sensible, when the questions that arose in his case are so tightly intertwined with those that arose in Mrs Pretty's.

The questions posed by patients like Dianne Pretty, nevertheless, have the most currency, particularly as in various jurisdictions across the developed world the outright prohibition on euthanasia is giving way to lawful accommodation of either voluntary euthanasia or (physician) assisted suicide. The law in the Northern Territories of Australia may only have lasted one year, but similarly permissive reforms in Oregon, Belgium and the Netherlands look likely to prove more durable (see e.g. Nys 1999; Jackson 2006: 960–972). Closer to home, pressure is being exerted in Scotland, Guernsey and the Isle of Man (Purvis 2005; Policy Council 2004; House of Keys 2006), while Lord Joffe is one in a long line of Parliamentarians and pressure groups like the Voluntary Euthanasia Society (VES) to have proposed a Bill that would afford people like Mrs Pretty the 'right to die' in England and Wales. That Bill may have failed, but it cannot be long before another is brought before Parliament.

Just as the pressure for change will not go away, neither will the main ethical arguments offered in support of, and in opposition to, such reform (see e.g. Battin 2005: 17–46). The debate may have become increasingly refined, but the central arguments have changed little and are easily stated. How successful they are nevertheless remains open to question. Here, it is necessary to survey four prominent positions that tend to be taken on euthanasia. First, from opponents like Keown who opened this chapter, is the view that life should be seen as intrinsically worthwhile, such that it should never intentionally be brought to a premature end. In opposition to this view is Doyal's claim that life is (only) instrumentally valuable, for as long as it is a life worth living, alongside the argument, on which Brock's point rested, that the value of life is for the autonomous individual to determine. Opponents do, however, have one more ground of attack, which tends to be seen as a more practical warning (or set of warnings) about the effects that allowing euthanasia might have on the law, medical practice and society more generally.

2.1 The intrinsic value of life

The idea that life is intrinsically valuable is the most obvious starting-point, particularly as this 'traditional ethic' (Keown 2002a: 232) provided the spur for its critics to articulate alternative accounts of the value of life, on which to rest their pleas for allowing euthanasia (e.g. Kuhse 1987). Papal declarations, advice from the Church of England and speeches by the Chief Rabbi all strive to make the same claim: life cannot intentionally be brought to an end (see Sacred Congregation for the Doctrine of the Faith 1980; Board for Social Responsibility of the Church of England 2000; Sacks 2003). But, say its supporters, the doctrine is not the sole preserve of the theist: its presence can be detected in the pre-modern Hippocratic corpus and in modern commitments to the equal enjoyment and protection of human rights (Keown 2002a: 40–41).

Despite its secularisation, the moral instructions associated with the invio-lability of life are most clearly defended in Judaeo–Christian, and particularly

Roman Catholic, writings (see e.g. Bayertz 1996). These deserve serious consideration given their prominence in critical discussions of euthanasia and, as will become apparent, their influence on English law. The central injunction is that the intentional ending of human life is wrong, irrespective of whether this is achieved through action or omission. Why this is wrong can be explained on various theological grounds, including that life is a gift from God, which is for Him alone to dispose of, since we are merely the stewards of our lives (e.g. Gormally 1978a: 22–24; Gormally 1994).

A secular audience, however, may be more convinced by the argument that human life possesses an intrinsic dignity, which can be revealed by the exercise of reason (rather than through divine revelation) (e.g. Fisher 1997: 316; Keenan 1996: 2, 10–15; Keown 2002a: 40). Reason should show us that each life is 'sacred' or, perhaps less contentiously, 'intrinsically valuable', and that the human body exists in partnership with the mind – they cannot be pitted against one another, with the mind seeking escape from the failing body, as they are parts of an integrated whole (Finnis 1993: 334; Linacre Centre 1993: 118–119; Fisher 1997: 316–318; Keown 2002a: 221–222; cf. Campbell and Willis 2005: 103). The believer might therefore speak of the 'sanctity' of life, but the atheist can convey the same idea in terms of the 'inviolability' of life. Believer or atheist, the first of the Ten Commandments still makes the point succinctly: 'Do not kill' or, more accurately, 'Do not murder' (Linacre Centre 1982: 52).

Keown, and others associated with the Linacre Centre for Health Care Ethics, are keen to point out that the doctrine is not vitalistic. Vitalism maintains that life is an *absolute* good to which all other basic goods must be sacrificed (Keown 2002a: 39). It is sometimes claimed that the inviolability doctrine only condemns the taking of 'innocent' life and therefore can allow killing in self-defence or in a just war. However, in the present context there are two teachings associated with the sanctity of life position that best show how it does not require the preservation of life in all circumstances.

The first of these is the doctrine of double effect, which can be 'needlessly mystifying' (Linacre Centre 1982: 48). Thought to find its origins in the work of St Thomas Aquinas (*Summa Theologiae*, II–II, Q. 64, A. 5), the doctrine retains a pivotal place in Roman Catholic thinking, but, again, its appeal is not restricted to such thinkers. The doctrine requires us to differentiate between intended outcomes (or effects) and foreseen, but unintended outcomes (or side effects). Seeking to achieve a good outcome can be morally permitted, even if this incidentally involves doing some harm, provided that, on balance, it is better to do this than not. Although it can be described in different ways, four conditions must usually be satisfied (e.g. Gormally 1978a: 9–13; Gillon 1999; Keown 2002a: 19–30). First, the action itself must not be morally wrong. Second, the agent must intend to bring about the good result. Third, that good result must not be brought about by the bad result. Finally, the harm wrought by the 'bad' result must be outweighed by the benefit effected by the good result. Obviously, for it to work at all, this doctrine must rest on some prior account of 'good' and 'bad' outcomes. For this one turns to the central doctrine, the inviolability of life, which essentially sees the preservation of life as good, and the intentional truncation of life as bad. The most common (albeit, as I will explore in Chapter 4, not entirely accurate) example used to illustrate this principle concerns the use of opioid drugs in terminally ill patients: it may be acceptable to use the drug to relieve pain, even if it carries a risk of shortening the patient's life.

Sanctity of life thinking also underpins the second distinction, which distinguishes between acts and omissions. Both can be condemned as wrong, when they are intentionally aimed at ending life. However, whilst most acts that end life will be condemned,[2] some fatal omissions are allowed, a position satirised in AH Clough's famous couplet: 'Thou shalt not kill; but need'st not strive/Officiously to keep alive' (quoted in Singer 1994: 194). Clough's reference to 'officious' attempts at preserving life is better expressed as an 'extraordinary' or 'disproportionate' endeavour, since this tradition holds that such efforts are not morally required (Gormally 1978b; Keown 2002a: 42–43). These labels may be attached to such attempts when the measure in question (usually a potentially life-sustaining medical treatment) is either futile or it imposes more burdens on the recipient patient than benefits. If, however, the reverse holds, then the treatment is 'ordinary' or 'proportionate', and there is therefore a moral obligation to provide it. Writers like Gormally and Keown insist that this is not about 'heroic' or 'hi-tech' treatments and machines, as opposed to more mundane ways of caring for patients, and neither is it concerned with assessing the quality of the patient's life (Gormally 1979; Keown 1997b: 485–487; contrast Kennedy 1976a: 6). That would breach the central injunction, in signalling that compromised lives are not due the same respect as healthier lives. Instead, the concern here is only with the worth or quality of the particular *treatment* that might be given to the compromised patient.

Where then does this school of thought leave a patient like Mrs Pretty? Put simply, she should not be granted assistance in dying. She is, however, entitled to receive palliative care, including treatment that could relieve her distress, should her breathlessness prove overwhelming (which, sadly, it ultimately appears to have done) (Dyer 2002). Some drug therapies that could help patients like Mrs Pretty nevertheless carry a risk of further depressing the patient's breathing, and thereby potentially shortening life. Here, the doctrine of double effect can help the concerned clinician: provided their intention is only to relieve distress, then the drugs can be used. Alternatively, if Mrs Pretty had been receiving life support that was proving overly burdensome, either

2   'Most' because some will argue that it is acceptable intentionally to kill an unjust aggressor.

she or the clinicians could have concluded that this was a disproportionate response to her condition, and one that could be removed, even if this led to her death. What the clinicians would need to ensure, however, is that it was the quality of the treatment and not the quality of Mrs Pretty's life that they were judging. According to Keown, the Law Lords got this wrong in their decision on Anthony Bland's fate, prompting one Member of Parliament to propose a new statute, which would have outlawed the intentional ending of life by omission (see Morris 2000).

2.2 Choosing the value of life

Mrs Pretty received, and undoubtedly continued to receive, palliative care until the end of her life, but she still seemed to endure what was, for her, a 'bad' death. She was also not receiving any life supporting treatment which could have been withdrawn with the end result of granting her wish to die. Her wish was indeed to die, and to do so in a way and at a time of her choosing. 'Making someone die in a way that others approve, but [s]he believes a horrifying contradiction of [her] life, is a devastating, odious form of tyranny', argues Ronald Dworkin (1993a: 217; see also Mill 1962a: 127).

For Dworkin, Brock (1993), Doyal (see Doyal and Doyal 2001), Singer (1993) and many others, including John Harris (1985), the value of life is self-determined. Respect for autonomy has, in the developed world at least, arguably become the dominant concern in contemporary healthcare ethics. It enjoys, for example, the position of 'first among equals' in the popular 'four principles' approach proposed by Beauchamp and Childress and defended by Gillon, in which health professionals are enjoined to respect autonomy, and act beneficently, non-maleficently and justly (Beauchamp and Childress 2001; Gillon 2003).

The reasons why respect for autonomy, from the Greek *auto* (self) and *nomos* (governance), is championed as a value central to good healthcare are various, with supporters coming from a variety of philosophical perspectives. The deontologists, following Kant, will tend to argue that we all have a right to self-determination and that there is a corresponding duty to respect others' decisions and ways of being (see Paton 1991: 90–91; cf. Hare 1975; 1994; Beyleveld and Brownsword 2001). The consequentialists might, like Mill and Bentham (see Mill 1962a), espouse the value of liberty or otherwise point to the preservation of autonomy as promoting the best consequences for human co-existence (e.g. Williams 1958b: 135; Glover 1977; Rachels 1993: 59–60; Singer 1993). Virtue ethicists, meanwhile, working within a tradition most associated with Aristotle, will seek to demonstrate that the virtuous person lives life in a manner that is respectful of others' choices (e.g. van Zyl 2000).

These are not, of course, the only schools of thought that promote the idea of self-determination, as, for example, contributions from feminist scholars readily demonstrate (e.g. Biggs 1998: 295). It is no surprise, given the various foundations on which it can rest, that the terminology of autonomy also varies considerably (Hill 1991: 44). It is not uncommon to hear talk of freedom, liberty, privacy and (increasingly) dignity, where the latter concept is here interpreted rather differently than it is in the sanctity of life tradition (e.g. Dworkin 1988: 6; Browne 1989: 38; Brock 1993: 206; Otlowski 1997: 204–206). Whichever words are used, the basic claim is the same: if a person is autonomous, in at least the sense that they are mentally competent, then that person has the right to decide what should, and what should not, be done with their body (e.g. Atkins 2000: 74).

There should be little doubt how the logic of autonomy, so conceived, applies to Mrs Pretty's plea: as an autonomous agent with a clear and freely-formed desire, she should have been able to receive assistance in dying. Indeed, as her husband Brian was also apparently freely willing to provide the necessary assistance, his autonomy too should have been given due respect (see e.g. Williams 1958b: 135; Otlowski 1997: 202, 225). Dworkin (1993a) would say that Mrs Pretty's choice reflected her 'critical interests', which are those interests that express her identity as she conceived it. Keown might think that she was duty-bound to uphold the inviolability of life but Mrs Pretty was as free to hold a different opinion on the value of life as he is to cling to his. She should not, in other words, have had the right to life imposed on her as a duty to live – it is a right she was free to waive (Singer 1993: 194–196). Harris (1985; 1997a) would say the same, albeit from the viewpoint that respect for autonomy is a facet of respect for persons, which are those creatures that are capable of valuing their own existence. Killing a person, says Harris (1997a: 10, 20), is only wrong when it deprives the person of something it values: there is no such wrong if the person no longer values life.

The denial of Mrs Pretty's autonomous choice is, according to these thinkers, a throwback to the paternalistic (or parentalistic) practises of medicine and law, which, over recent decades, has gradually been replaced by the culture of autonomy (see VanDeVeer 1986; May 1991: 28–35; Brock 1993: 107–111; Beauchamp 1994). Harris and Dworkin are characteristically direct: it is 'idle and perverse arrogance' (Harris 1997a: 20) that leaves a patient like Mrs Pretty a 'narrative wreck' (Dworkin 1993a: 211). However, some feminist scholars argue that euthanasia poses particular risks for women, based on existing gender inequalities (e.g. Wolf 1996; Callahan 1996; but see Raymond 1999), and contend that the individualistic account of autonomy usually offered in support of the practice is impoverished since it overlooks such differences (e.g. Donchin 2000). Yet even some of these scholars have conceded that someone like Mrs Pretty will meet the criteria for autonomy that are usually offered, such as information, free will and reason (e.g. Tong 1997: 66–67; Parks 2000; cf. Glover 1977: 76–77; Harris 1985: 192–203). She therefore did not need to be protected from herself, and nor could it be shown that there were social interests at stake that justified frustrating her choice (Williams 1958b: 135; Singer 1993: 199–200; Rachels 1993: 59–60).

On this reasoning, a case can therefore be made for permitting both assisted suicide and (active) voluntary euthanasia (Otlowski 1997: 189). Contemporary debates are tending to focus on the former, as indeed Lord Joffe's Bill ultimately did, and this may be because assisted suicide leaves the patient in ultimate control and so arguably better demonstrates that the desire for death is real and autonomous whenever it is acted upon (Glover 1977: 182–189; Singer 1993: 176–178). However, some theorists admit that the ethical underpinnings are the same, so allowing the one should pave the way to allowing the other (McLean and Britton 1997: 22).

What is less often argued, but still occasionally so, is that an appeal to autonomy can also justify some cases of non-voluntary euthanasia, that is ending the life of a patient like Anthony Bland. Here, the reasoning goes, the patient should be entitled to issue an advance request for euthanasia, which can be activated when they lose their autonomy (Rachels 1993: 60; Dworkin 1993a: 213, 226). Alternatively or additionally, a proxy should be empowered to decide that it is in the patient's interests to die. This will be expressive of patient autonomy provided that the decision is made on the basis of a 'substituted judgement', which rests on the values that the patient held dear whilst they were competent (Glover 1977: 75–76, 193–194; Dworkin 1993a: 213, 229; Robertson 1994: 480). However, what can never be condoned is any form of involuntary euthanasia. This, according to many proponents of respect for autonomy, is simply 'murder' (McLean 1996: 51–52; Harris 1997a: 6–7).

2.3 The instrumental value of life

The next cluster of arguments used to justify euthanasia marks another departure from the view espoused by Keown. Keown believes that life is intrinsically valuable but that some *treatments* might not be worth continuing; writers like Singer (1993), Doyal (2006) and Harris (1985) believe that life is only instrumentally valuable, such that some *lives* might not be worth continuing. Various claims are made and terms invoked, which include references to the patient's 'quality of life', the need to exercise mercy (as in 'mercy killing'), and obligations to act in the patient's best interests and avoid cruelty (e.g. Williams 1958b: 134–135; Beauchamp and Childress 2001: 133–139). The triumphs of modern medicine may be numerous, says James Rachels (1993: 46), 'but the victory is far from complete'. The moral imperative to end suffering – even through ending life – will therefore remain for as long as patients continue to suffer.

As extreme as it might sound, the scholars who offer these arguments are essentially claiming that a patient enduring a poor quality existence might be better off dead. They think that, despite any initial misgivings we might have, we should agree that this can be the most appropriate ethical judgement. The judgement is essentially relative: the patient's quality of life is or will be very poor, relative to their previous good health or, sometimes, to the good health of others. The argument tends to appeal to consequentialist thinkers, who say that ending a life of suffering can be the best outcome for the patient and even for others in the community. Singer and Rachels, for example, have distanced themselves from the traditional utilitarian desire to maximise 'happiness' (Mill 1962b: 257), instead offering a utilitarian calculus that strives to maximise 'best interests' (Rachels 1993: 46–48; Singer 1993; 1994).

This modern version of utilitarianism also takes account of the rights of the person, in emphasising the need to respect personal autonomy. Singer, of course, supports voluntary euthanasia, but it should be recognised that respect for autonomy does not need to bear the entire moral load, since an appeal to a patient's best interests can shoulder some of the burden. De Haan describes this as a 'joint view' on the justifiability of consensual killing: the doctor (for example) seeks to respect the seriously debilitated patient's wish to die and should act on this because, 'since he is suffering unbearably and hopelessly, euthanasia is in his interest' (De Haan 2002: 169). The quality of life judgement will certainly be made by the patient, since it is this that activates their desire for help in dying. However, it seems that the doctor or other agent must sympathise with that assessment, and perhaps even share it, before they can be said to have a sufficient reason for providing the help (e.g. De Haan 2002: 171; Huxtable and Möller 2007).

This thinking will obviously embolden a patient like Dianne Pretty. But the same reasoning, this time without any additional appeal to patient autonomy, can also provide the justification for ending the life of Anthony Bland. To Harris (1997b: 41–42), Bland is not a 'person' in the sense that he uses the term, since Bland can no longer value his own existence. Equally, Singer continues, a young baby has not yet become a person. Neither is owed the full respect due to 'persons' and non-voluntary euthanasia may sometimes be in their interest. 'When the life of an infant will be so miserable as not to be worth living [and] there are no "extrinsic" reasons for keeping the infant alive – like the feelings of the parents – it is better that the child should be helped to die without further suffering', argues Singer (1993: 182–183; see also Hare 1973; 1994; Harris 1985). Singer cites an extreme case of spina bifida as an example of when euthanasia might be indicated. However, he also wants to preserve and protect the autonomy of those close to incompetent patients: the parents or, according to Doyal (2006) more recently, other loved ones of an adult like Anthony Bland must agree that it is better to end the patient's life before euthanasia can be undertaken. A doctor too, if it is him or her who is expected to practise this sort of 'beneficent euthanasia', also retains autonomy, in having a right not to be involved (Otlowski 1997: 203–204).

Singer thinks that the argument for non-voluntary euthanasia gains greater moral momentum when we recognise what our society already condones. It is inconsistent, he argues, for us to deny such killings when we already permit pregnancies to be terminated on the ground of foetal disability and we practise active euthanasia of ailing animals, even punishing those who fail to deal with an animal's misery (Singer 1993: 212–213). The pioneers of principlist ethics, Beauchamp and Childress, have also conceded that it can be better not to treat an incompetent patient, although these authors fall short of supporting non-voluntary euthanasia (2001: 138–139). They do, however, attempt to provide some criteria for making these decisions. What cannot be entirely determinative is the patient's medical condition, and they claim that some conditions – like mental disability and Down's syndrome – are insufficient in themselves to indicate non-treatment. More positively, they want the surrogate decision-maker to make the decision on the basis of the patient's best interests, 'as judged by the best obtainable estimate of what reasonable persons would consider the highest net benefit among the available options' (Beauchamp and Childress 2001: 139).

In this way, Beauchamp and Childress seek to reduce the arbitrariness that might otherwise result from a variety of decisions being made by a variety of proxies. Singer (1993: 200–201, 179) has also warned that quality of life thinking cannot be used to justify involuntary euthanasia, since in that case we can never be certain that our judgement of the (autonomous) patient's life is better than their own. Harris similarly criticises 'blanket' government policies that deny treatment to the seriously ill as essentially amounting to policies of non-consensual killing (Harris 1985: 83–86). Others, however, are willing to recognise the role that justice must play in the euthanasia debate. Some argue that euthanasia can be performed for the benefit of those close to the patient, who might welcome the release from having to witness their loved one's suffering (Williams 1958b: 134–135; Bliss 1990: 121; Rachels 1993: 48). The argument can also be taken further, particularly if we remember that a quality of life claim is relative. Thus, where one patient's life is markedly worse than someone else's, and they could benefit from the treatment and care that the patient is currently receiving, there may be a case for allowing euthanasia or even imposing a 'duty to die' on the patient (e.g. Hardwig 1997; Battin 2005: 280–299; cf. Huxtable 2001). However, while few doubt the importance that resource constraints have in end-of-life decision-making, these are more often placed at some distance from the euthanasia debate.

2.4 Executioners on slippery slopes

Can and should money be brought into the euthanasia equation? How much is a life worth? And would, in time, less valuable (or more costly) lives become routinely subject to euthanasia, along the lines depicted in science fiction like *Logan's Run* (Nolan and Johnson 1967)? Uncomfortable predictions are a familiar feature of these debates and they join a variety of other concerns about allowing euthanasia in presenting a so-called 'practical' basis for opposing reform.

These are not entirely pragmatic objections because the arguments can be tied to particular normative claims. Campbell, for example, objects that a policy of euthanasia offends against the principle of justice, particularly in exposing vulnerable members of society to the risk of exploitation (1998: 90–95; see also Coleman 2002). Resource limitations in particular might mean that the elderly would come to be seen – whether by their doctors or themselves – as worthy candidates for euthanasia. This is, for Campbell, related to another hazard associated with legalising euthanasia, which is that it will be difficult to specify (and limit) the candidates who will qualify for such legalised homicide. His third concern is that this sort of policy entails a dangerous, and significant, shift in the value accorded to life.

Campbell insists that his is not a 'simple "slippery slope"' objection (1998: 90), but his arguments do share some similarities with this sort of thinking (Biggar 1998: 109). The 'slippery slope' or 'thin end of the wedge' argument (Schauer 1985: 368–370; Lamb 1988) is often presented in 'practical' terms but it too can be seen to rest on a particular normative foundation, since it has a distinct consequentialist flavour: euthanasia should not be allowed in view of various deleterious consequences that might or arguably will flow from permitting it (Frey 1998: 44; contrast Hughes 2000). Thus, even if an individual plea for assisted suicide or euthanasia like Dianne Pretty's can look right, it should not be granted because it will lead to practices that are undoubtedly wrong (Kamisar 1957: 106–117; 1997).

The argument takes two basic forms: logical and empirical. The logical objection holds that there is either no difference between the apparently innocent case and the dangerous one or that the dangerous situation can only be avoided by erecting an arbitrary and flimsy boundary, which is all too easily demolished (Van der Burg 1991; McGleenan 1995: 351). So, say opponents of euthanasia, involuntary euthanasia logically follows from voluntary or non-voluntary euthanasia, since they all rest on the poor quality of the patient's life for their justification (e.g. Finnis 1997a: 24–25; Keown 1997a: 262).

The empirical objection is concerned with probabilities: we are more likely in fact to embrace the dangerous situation if we accept the seemingly innocent case (e.g. Lamb 1988: 61). Even scholars who are, in principle, sympathetic to voluntary euthanasia concede that it might lead to a more general devaluing of life and so it should be resisted (e.g. Beauchamp and Childress 2001: 144–146).

Various calamitous predictions are made and analogies drawn. Abortions have escalated in England since they were decriminalised in the Abortion Act 1967, although the statute was apparently only designed to tackle 'back-street' practices; so too, claim opponents, might instances of euthanasia increase and expand in scope (Keown 1997a: 262). An even more urgent, and arguably more proximate, warning comes from the Netherlands, where, as was previously noted, voluntary euthanasia is now routinely approved and performed. Opponents point out that euthanasia has, in that jurisdiction, evolved to encompass situations where the patient is depressed but has no physical or terminal condition (see *Office of Public Prosecutions v Chabot* Nederlandse

Jurisprudentie 1994 No 656; Griffiths 1995b; Keown 2002a: 87, 109). There is evidence also that euthanasia is being practised without the guidelines being fully observed (e.g. Fenigsen 1990; Jochemson 1994; Keown 2002a). Particularly disturbing is the finding that 1,000 (0.8 per cent) of the annual occurrences of ('voluntary') euthanasia have taken place without any explicit request from the patient. The Dutch courts, however, frequently decline to punish health professionals who breach the legal requirements and have also moved towards toleration of non-voluntary euthanasia (Keown 1997a: 289). 'For inhabitants of such a flat country, the Dutch have proved remarkably fast skiers', remarks Keown (ibid).

There is also the fear, previously noted, that our modern understanding of euthanasia shares uncomfortable similarities with the Nazi programmes of genocide and eugenics (Alexander 1949). The work of Karl Brandt and other doctors operating in the Third Reich apparently also grew from modest and well-motivated beginnings. Opponents claim that the slide from good to evil cannot be decisively discredited today, since the policies rest on the same assessment: there are some lives that are not worth living (Lamb 1988: 61; Momeyer 1995: 14; Beauchamp and Childress 2001: 145). We are therefore urged to heed Campbell's warning about revising our stance on the value accorded to life; indeed, a rip in the moral and social fabric of society could transform an apparently humane option of last resort into an inhumane policy of first choice (Fenigsen 1990: 14).

Dehumanisation is also a key feature of the next 'practical' objection, which relates to the role that doctors would have in practising euthanasia. 'Those who demand "killing on request" place the physician on the same level as a hangman' is a striking summary of this protest (Derbolowsky 1983: 197; see also Kass 1989; Momeyer 1995). Sometimes appeals are made to the Hippocratic tradition of medicine, within which doctors are healers, committed to saving and prolonging lives (St John-Stevas 1961: 275; Fenigsen 1990: 17; Momeyer 1995: 16; Gormally 1997: 117–120). Trust and confidence are the watchwords of the Hippocratic doctor and we are told that these will be irreparably damaged if the carer becomes executioner.

Neither can it be said that this is a practice which the physician *needs* to embrace if he or she is truly to tackle the suffering of some patients (Kamisar 1957: 104–105; St John-Stevas 1961: 273; Fenigsen 1990: 15–16; Twycross 1997: 164–166). Whilst far from universally available, Britain at least has made pioneering advances in palliative medicine and hospice care. Experts working in the field tell us that proper, holistic care of the patient can reduce and remove requests for euthanasia and that, even when pain cannot be completely controlled, sedation is a safe and sensible last resort (Twycross 1997: 166; O'Connor, Kissane and Spruyt 1999). As one might expect, these experts generally tend to see no need for euthanasia. Dame Cicely Saunders, who was at the forefront of providing hospice care, has reported that only five of 20,000 patients in her hospice have taken their own lives, and that those who requested death were 'almost always referring to previously unrelieved symptoms' (Saunders 1995: 44; see also Gillett 1994; Campbell, Hare and Matthews 1995). There is therefore the possibility that euthanasia will be unnecessary and premature, particularly, some argue, when we cannot know in advance what lies ahead in the final days of life. The evidence even shows that there is a good recovery rate amongst patients who 'struggle'. Allowing euthanasia looks likely to encourage surrender, and maybe prematurely so (Gelfand 1984; Browne 1989: 49).

Euthanasia might therefore foreclose such possibilities as reconciliation, reaffirmation and the realisation of important personal truths (Gillett 1988), and it does so completely and irreversibly: many will agree that there can be no going back to life from death (e.g. Kamisar 1957: 106; Fenigsen 1990: 15; Shand 1997: 44; Frey 1998: 44). And, the critics continue, too many decisions can be taken in error and ignorance to risk granting such final decisions a place in law. Some point to research involving patients with terminal cancer, who were found neither to have cancer nor to be terminally ill (Davis 1998: 21). Diagnoses and prognoses can be wrong; cures and other treatments can also become available (Kamisar 1957: 98–106; Fenigsen 1990: 15; Twycross 1997: 157–158). If euthanasia exists as an option, then what effect might that have on the development of such new treatments? Quite apart from the patients surrendering, it might be the doctors and scientists who will see no need to explore new routes to controlling pain and combating disease (Twycross 1982: 91; Lamb 1988: 96–97; Burgess 1993a).

Medicine might also be undermined in a different way, since human nature is neither infallible nor always pure. Vulnerable patients will be placed at risk of killing by unscrupulous doctors or other agents of euthanasia (Kass 1989), which a legalised system might fail to recognise or even help to conceal (cf. Campbell 1998). The insistence that euthanasia can only occur where the patient voluntarily requests this also overlooks the point that the candidates for euthanasia might be compromised by their condition, misinformed and even feel obliged to take up the option, so as to avoid imposing a burden on their carers and even society at large (Kamisar 1957: 94–96).

Jean Haslam (1980) and, particularly, Alison Davis (2002) have both written of the depression caused by their medical conditions, which led them to want assistance in dying. Ms Davis, who still suffers from pain associated with spina bifida, ultimately found comfort in religious faith, and she now campaigns against euthanasia. As she shows, some patients' preferences for death will not be stable, and might even rest on (a treatable) depression (Twycross 1997: 144–147, 155–157). Even when the proponents of euthanasia try to ensure that the wish is genuine and durable by requiring reflection during 'cooling off' periods, opponents point out that this actually undermines one of their key aims, which is to offer a quick, easy and painless death (e.g. Kamisar 1957: 91–92; Browne 1989: 48; Fenigsen 1990: 14–15).

Proponents will still say that a safe system can be created, and that appropriate qualifying criteria can be drafted and policed, but the critics remain unconvinced. In 1994, a House of Lords Select Committee agreed that the critics' case was strong, given 'the human tendency to test the limits of any regulation' (1994a: 49). In 1957, Yale Kamisar provided one of the first, and still one of the most cogent, accounts of the practical problems attending euthanasia, and he expressed resistance to the formalities that would surround the sickbed if this were to be legalised (1957: 90). More recent opponents have also noted, again making reference to the Netherlands, that doctors can easily become complacent in their observance of such formalities. In sum, we are told that there are too many practical difficulties associated with allowing euthanasia: as Keown (2002a: 281) puts it, 'abuse is the child of legalisation and cannot be prevented'.

3 Assessing the rights and wrongs of ending life

The parameters of the disputes that occur over the morality of euthanasia are pretty stable: proponents of the practice will say it is a humane response to suffering that is particularly compelling when the patient wants to escape their compromised existence; opponents, however, will say that life must be protected and that, in any case, there is no safe or just way of legalising this sort of killing.

These four positions all have something to commend them. Unfortunately, despite a long history of discussion and refinement, none of them is free from difficulty. The main problems are related but can, I suggest, be separated into three groups. The first group of concerns recalls Humpty Dumpty's assertion about the use of language: meanings can be high-jacked or obscured in these debates, and will often remain contestable. However, even if agreement can be reached about what the various arguments for and against euthanasia should mean, there are still problems with the scope of the claims. This difficulty is Tweedledee's: 'if it was so, it might be; and if it were so, it would be; but as it isn't, it ain't. That's logic.' (Carroll 1982: 157). The logic of the various claims can be taken in some rather undesirable directions and this, in turn, suggests a third area of difficulty: that the arguments can have rather less allure than their supporters claim, especially in a pluralistic society where citizens cleave to a wide variety of beliefs. This might look like a minor concern to the philosopher, who will favour reasoned arguments over intuitive preferences, but I aim also to show that there are good reasons for doubting the appeal of the main arguments offered in the euthanasia debate.

3.1 The intrinsic value of life

The claim that life is inviolable certainly appears laudable, but the key terms on which this position depends – like 'intention', 'omission', 'futility' and 'burden' – all require further moral interpretation and invite dispute. For example, the moral differentiation between intended and merely foreseen outcomes that the doctrine of double effect seeks to achieve has been criticised for relying on an incomplete account of moral responsibility. Harris complains that intention alone cannot settle the morality of the action, since a person is responsible for the 'world' which he or she creates, including through unintentional but voluntary action (1997b: 36–40). This of course fits with Harris's brand of consequentialist thinking, in which outcomes matter most, but even the non-consequentialist might be inclined towards an argument raised by another leading utilitarian, James Rachels. Rachels believes that the doctrine relies on the agent (conveniently?) describing his or her behaviour in a way that conforms to the principle, in order to 'purify the intention' (1986: 92). Sometimes, however, the two outcomes will appear so close as to be inseparable. To these critics, theorists like Keown morally load their definitions of intended and foreseen effects to secure the results they want and in doing so they beg the question as to what is the right thing to do.

This nevertheless assumes that the theorist has taken a clear view on what is right and wrong. Remarkably, Keown is ultimately equivocal about whether or not the sanctity of life tradition 'as yet' would justify the withdrawal of Anthony Bland's life support (see Keown 2002a: 232–233). If it is justified, then the dispute with Harris *et al* becomes purely terminological. Keown will undoubtedly protest that his reasoning remains radically different from Harris's, in whose work quality of life concerns come to the fore. There is, however, reason to question the scope of sanctity of life thinking.

Rachels' (1979) persuasive attack on the influential acts/omissions distinction provides a good route into analysing this problem. His famous analogy can be briefly summarised: I want to receive an inheritance from my young cousin and am determined to kill him to get it. In the first scenario I enter the bathroom in which he is bathing and hold his head under the water until he drowns. In the second, I enter the bathroom with the same intention, formed from the same motive, but I notice that the child has slipped and is lying unconscious under the water. I deliberately refrain from rescuing him. The two situations are logically and ethically indistinguishable says Rachels, and so – by extension – if some instances of letting die can instead be good on quality of life grounds, then so too can some instances of active killing.

This is a narrowly framed analogy which might appear altogether divorced from clinical experience, in which the distinction might more accurately be described in terms of allowing nature to take its course (i.e. allowing the patient to die from a disease) as opposed to lethally injecting them. Equally, the analogy does not of itself suggest how far our moral responsibility for omissions can (or should) extend. Nevertheless, Rachels' thought experiment rightly throws down a gauntlet to those who seek to defend the distinction.

Keown *et al* naturally deny the equivalence between fatal acts and fatal omissions that Rachels detects and are particularly resistant to the notion that they are judging the patient's quality of life: the question for them is 'whether the *treatment* would be worth while, not whether the patient's *life* would be worth while' (Keown 2002a: 43). Unfortunately, the concepts to which they appeal require further interpretation and can – perhaps must – extend beyond the parameters they seek to defend (see Huxtable and Forbes 2004). Keown argues that 'futile' treatment is 'disproportionate' and so need not be given. Futility can be understood in either a qualitative or a quantitative sense (e.g. Halliday 1997; Zucker and Zucker 1997; Gillon 1997; Ardagh 2000). Qualitatively, a 'futile' treatment will produce an effect but fail to 'benefit' the patient. Quantitatively, treatment may be deemed 'futile' because previous experience indicates a low probability of it producing the desired effect. In either case, however, further deliberation is required by the moral agent. As Halliday (1997) argues, the standard looks arbitrary, because we are not told how low the probability of benefit must be, and medical journals rarely publish evidence of treatment failure rates.

Some cut-off is arguably necessary – but the point is that this needs further moral debate. The sanctity of life position, and this alone, does not give us this cut-off point. Instead, the 'futility' label conceals an underlying but unarticulated moral judgement since, Halliday continues, it involves a move from an 'is' to an 'ought': the treatment *is* unlikely to have an effect and therefore it *should* be labelled 'futile' and *should not* be offered. Halliday detects various assumptions at work here, regarding the nature of medicine and the doctor–patient relationship. The body, it seems, is a machine to be treated and when it appears that it cannot be, treatment should be discontinued, regardless of what else this might offer to the patient and their loved ones (such as hope) (Halliday 1997: 340).

Critics therefore maintain that the sanctity of life position requires a prior moral assessment of the goals of healthcare and, importantly, the value of life (Singer 1993: 211; Brock 1993: 167–169, 198–199). Keown's claim that it is permissible to withhold treatment from an elderly, 'frail' and 'dying' patient (2002a: 48) evidently rests on such judgements having been made – judgements, we should note, that are usually left to the doctors (e.g. *Re A* [1992] 3 Med LR 303). They may well be the most appropriate people to make these judgements but the problem, which Price detects, is that the judge, whoever he or she is, needs to make some assessment of the patient's quality of life (2001: 643). Keown therefore confronts Singer's complaint that a veil is being drawn over what is really being judged: whether or not, in view of her condition, the patient is worth expending effort on (e.g. Singer 1993: 210). Indeed, Price sees the inviolability of life ethic as an inappropriate prism through which to view end-of-life decisions, since it concentrates on the *doctor's* moral sensibilities and intentions, rather than openly tackling the patient's plight and preferences (Price 2001).

The inviolability principle therefore appears both too narrow, in focusing on the doctor, and too wide, in smuggling in quality of life considerations. The same criticism is made of the related doctrine of double effect, which again is said to rely on the idea that death can be a benefit to the patient (Glover 1977: 86–91; Singer 1993: 210). This complaint could be overstated, but it is arguable that the latter doctrine at least signals that, on balance, death is not so bad – and even this limited concession shares something with quality of life thinking. According to Kuhse, the only way of avoiding these criticisms lies in defining the relevant terms so narrowly that the doctrine ultimately entails a vitalistic commitment to preserving all lives at all costs, an approach that Keown *et al* claim they wish to avoid (Kuhse 1987).

Kuhse might also make too much of her objection, but she – like many other critics – will still have one persuasive protest remaining, which essentially relates to the appeal of the sanctity of life position. Deliberately described here in its most theological (indeed, distinctively Judaeo–Christian) form, it is immediately apparent that atheists, and people committed to other religions, might reasonably reject the monotheistic basis of the doctrine and then all that flows from it. Even in its more secular versions, which are based on the exercise of human reason, there will be critics who argue that reason suggests, to them, that there *are* occasions on which life can be brought to a premature end. As Dworkin and Harris said, it seems 'tyrannical' to hold other people hostage to the views of a possibly dwindling minority (Dworkin 1993a: 217).

3.2 Choosing the value of life

These counter-arguments might appear to suggest that the better approach lies with Harris, Singer *et al* and specifically with the idea that the value of life is self-determined. There are, however, significant problems here too. Respecting individual choices certainly looks important – but Velleman has pointed out that the very existence of the choice for euthanasia is not unproblematic. Its presence can, he argues, exert pressure on vulnerable patients 'to request that the permission be exercised in their case' (2004: 20). Equally, regard for one individual's choice should not lead us to overlook the rights and interests of other individuals in the moral community. Kant and Mill recognised that autonomy, properly understood and exercised, has its limits; unfortunately, modern theories tend to 'reduce autonomy to some form of individual independence, and show little about its ethical importance' (O'Neill 2003: 5). O'Neill reminds us that 'Mill's version of autonomy ... sees individuals not merely as choosing to implement whatever desires they happen to have at a given moment, but as taking charge of those desires, as reflecting on and selecting among them in distinctive ways' (2002: 31). Similarly, she says, we have forgotten that Kant's autonomous agent lives a life in which duties towards others are met (2002: 83).

There are, however, signs of a backlash against the neutral, liberal account of autonomy that has taken hold. Donchin (2000), for example, attacks the atomisation inherent in modern accounts, which misconceive human agents as 'ahistorical monads' who somehow transcend time and culture and the influence these exert on 'individual' autonomy. Similarly, according to Burt, the 'autonomy focus has no substantive content' since the implication appears to be that my choices are 'good' because they are *my* choices: in other words, 'it is ostentatiously silent about whether death is desirable or undesirable, but insists only that each individual should make this value choice for himself' (Burt 2005: s13). Appeals to allegedly synonymous concepts like 'dignity' can be similarly problematic (Macklin 2003; Velleman 2004; Ashcroft 2005), particularly when their deployment in the euthanasia debate tends to lead to the same conclusion: give the patient what he or she wants (e.g. Biggs 2001; Beyleveld and Brownsword 2001). However, we should not necessarily be beguiled into thinking that 'I want' means that 'I should get', when a more comprehensive understanding of autonomy (and related concepts) might suggest that it is more respectful of autonomy to prohibit practises like voluntary euthanasia (see e.g. Gaylin and Jennings 2003).

I do not mean here to disparage the advances made in the name of personal autonomy, not least in the realm of healthcare, but in the euthanasia context (at least) some caution is advisable, particularly when the principle looks capable of great extension. If it grants the patient the right to die, then someone apparently should meet the corresponding duty (cf. Hohfeld 1964). But what if no one is willing to help? And how far does the duty extend? Lord Joffe's Bill ultimately proposed the provision of physician assisted suicide, undoubtedly in order to give patients like Dianne Pretty what they want. However, as Mrs Pretty demonstrated, diseases can and will progress beyond the point at which the patient can act, even with assistance. It then looks illogical to deny her voluntary euthanasia (where it is the doctor or some other agent who acts), since the logic of autonomy would still require her wishes to be respected. Once the case for assisted suicide is accepted, the case for voluntary euthanasia therefore looks stronger.[3]

But why even restrict assistance in dying to 'patients'? Dr Sutorius was recently convicted in the Netherlands for assisting the suicide of Edward Brongersma, who was 'tired of life' but otherwise physically and mentally well (Huxtable and Möller 2007). Although he was not formally punished, the debate over whether Sutorius's conduct was legally justified continues; ethically, however, it is implausible to claim that his actions violated the autonomy principle as currently understood. Provided that Brongersma made an autonomous request and that Sutorius also acted autonomously, then there can be no reason for preventing the action (ibid).

Brongersma's case therefore contains important lessons both for jurisdictions contemplating permissive reform and for moral philosophers in thrall

---

3   Indeed, in a similar vein, Lord Joffe himself has admitted that his 'Bill should initially be limited, although I would prefer it to be of much wider application' (House of Lords Select Committee 2005b: 53).

to the notion of autonomy. Indeed, it leads one to question the proclaimed popularity of the case for voluntary euthanasia, as premised on respect for autonomy. Practitioners of palliative medicine say that euthanasia campaigners underplay what can be done to address suffering and are ill-informed about the reasons why most people request euthanasia. Against this backdrop it is not surprising that opinion polls find up to 82 per cent support for voluntary euthanasia (House of Lords Select Committee 2005a: 125–127; Otlowski 1997: 257–259). However, support will not be hard to find when questionnaires are simplistic or biased in their phrasing and conducted at times when emotions run high, such as when Dianne Pretty petitioned the courts (Hagelin *et al* 2004; House of Lords Select Committee 2005a: 146). The question arises whether people would be so supportive of the practice if they knew more (indeed, if their autonomy was enhanced) about its possible scope and the options that occupy the ground between consensual killing and a painful or undignified demise.

3.3 The instrumental value of life

Perhaps Harris's other argument, which is essentially premised on the instrumental value of a life that is free from suffering, offers a better way of judging the end(ing) of life. Unsurprisingly it too does not entirely succeed. We might be able to agree that a life of inability and disability looks less than ideal, particularly if the person living that life sees no value in it. But we might legitimately disagree on what moral imperatives flow from such a belief. Certainly, before it can operate as a moral guide, we need to know when a life might be described as 'miserable' by Singer (1993: 182–183) and who should be entitled to make that assessment (cf. Bachelard 2002). The autonomous person will not be the only judge: the person practising euthanasia needs some reason for judging the request reasonable (De Haan 2002) and some other person will undoubtedly have to make the assessment when the patient is not, and maybe never has been, autonomous.

These problems in turn suggest that it will be difficult to define the scope of the argument. Even if one is inclined to the aforementioned view that Keown and Singer share more ground than Keown might think, this does not mean that Singer's quality of life thinking offers the way forward. In a legal case I will describe in more detail in Chapter 4, the case of Dr Arthur, a paediatrician was acquitted of attempted murder after allegedly leaving John Pearson, a baby with Down's syndrome, to die at the request of his parents. Notably the defendant's conduct was 'accepted by modern paediatric thought' ((1981) 12 BMLR 1, *per* Farquharson J, at 14). To be blunt, the doctors (then) thought that it was acceptable to leave children with Down's syndrome to die. But is that a 'miserable' enough life, to use Singer's word, to warrant euthanasia?

Suffering takes myriad forms and arises from myriad causes: why not make euthanasia available to anyone who is 'suffering' (Huxtable and

Möller 2007; Varelius 2007)? From such thinking it is but a short step to sanctioning the ending of life, not because the person no longer wants it, but because some other person deems theirs not to be a life worth living. Notice, first, how the provider of voluntary euthanasia must share or at least sympathise with the patient's judgement on the worth of their life in order to have a reason for acting, or else they become a mere automaton of the patient's will (De Haan 2002). From agreeing to help one patient with motor neurone disease, to helping a second and then a third with the same condition, it becomes less of a stretch for that agent to start thinking that life with motor neurone disease is a less than worthwhile life.

Proponents will think that this is a stretch too far, but one needs to be aware of how the arguments for euthanasia are in fact developing. According to Doyal, voluntary euthanasia has dominated discussions for reasons of 'political expedience' – because only that appears to have 'a real chance at present of legalisation' (2006: 67). Proposals for allowing (active) non-voluntary euthanasia are nevertheless on the rise (Amarasekara and Mirko 2004; see also Brahams and Brahams 1983; Gunn and Smith 1985). Although some writers have been equivocal about its appropriateness (e.g. Williams 1958b), others are much more open to non-voluntary euthanasia – and these notably tend to be the very theorists who are at the forefront of arguments for allowing voluntary euthanasia (e.g. Rachels 1986: 178–180; Otlowski 1997: 221).

So, how long will and should the resistance to *involuntary* euthanasia continue? It is not enough to dismiss this as 'simply murder' (McLean 1996: 51–52; Harris 1997a: 6–7); indeed, it is simplistic, since, strictly speaking, euthanasia *per se* is murder, as I will explain more fully in the next chapter. Once quality of life considerations come to the fore it looks harder to oppose the case for involuntary euthanasia in principle and, in practice, one should be mindful also of the law's tendency to evolve, albeit incrementally (Van der Burg 1991: 61–63; Otlowski 1997: 223–224). The possible scope of quality of life thinking therefore gives cause for some considerable concern. Given these considerations, it perhaps scarcely needs saying that euthanasia in its non-voluntary and involuntary forms is unlikely to command much – if any – serious support, as indeed the popular and professional literature readily attests (e.g. Dodd 1999; Tobias 2006).

3.4 Executioners on slippery slopes

There are evidently questions left to be answered regarding the three main principled claims made in relation to euthanasia. Examination of these claims must indeed continue, since we need some closure on these before we can contemplate the practical ramifications of adopting one view or another (cf. Battin 2005: 36). It is, however, also essential to consider the meaning, scope and appeal of the practical objections to euthanasia, especially as some believe that this set of concerns should form the focal point of our modern discussions about euthanasia (see Battin 2005: 25).

The first objection to consider concerns the method of argument deployed in many of these critiques. Quite simply, the slippery slope argument is frequently dismissed as fallacious (e.g. Smith 2005). Indeed, some argue that it is often used to camouflage the opponent's true objection – which is that euthanasia is contrary to the intrinsic value of life (e.g. Williams 1995: 214; Doyal 2006). For these sorts of critics it is not strictly the slope, or even the destination that the slope leads to, that is the problem, but instead *any* initial step onto the alleged slope (such as seeking to permit voluntary euthanasia).

On other occasions, the slope objection looks more likely to be a complaint about where the lines are drawn between the permissible and impermissible – which is, again, not necessarily an objection to the existence of the slope *per se* and does not necessarily present an insurmountable obstacle to reform (cf. Williams 1995). As Margaret Brazier puts it, 'If it is right in principle to acknowledge a right to choose to be killed, the lawyers must struggle to find appropriate means of enforcing that right' (1996: 322). Her argument obviously founders if – as it appears – the principled case for euthanasia has not (yet) been won, but one might well sympathise with the idea that some boundaries can be erected and appropriately policed (Williams 1958a: 280–281; Glover 1977: 166; Rachels 1993: 61–62).

However, there are also occasions when the slope objection is undoubtedly sincere: the opponent genuinely does fear that embracing the seemingly innocent instant case will mean future danger. Unfortunately, this can look rather like the convenient cry of the conservative (Williams 1958a: 280–281; Flew 1969: 47; Otlowski 1997: 247–248). Indeed, the Dutch data might actually support the proponents' case, especially when the 1,000 allegedly problematic deaths noted earlier were not necessarily non-consensual. The advocates of euthanasia therefore claim that it is better to be open and seek to control such practises (Griffiths 1995a; Otlowski 1997: 436–441). However, they still cannot escape the fact that the Dutch are embracing other, blatantly non-consensual, forms of euthanasia (see Manninen 2006).

The proponents of euthanasia are nevertheless on surer ground when they criticise some of the opponents' analogies as inflated and misleading. The comparison with Nazi policies certainly looks extreme: these were some distance from the more compassionately motivated proposals under investigation here (Flew 1969: 47–48; Rachels 1986: 177–178). It is nevertheless possible to concede that this sort of slope objection is more plausibly concerned with the prospect of any relaxation in our prohibitive attitudes towards taking life. However, even here the opponents need to take better account of evidence to the contrary: for example, the fact that doctors are permitted to abort disabled foetuses does not mean that they are generally willing to kill disabled patients (Williams 1958a: 281; Singer 1993: 217; Rachels 1993: 62–63; Otlowski 1997: 222). Richmond also cites the abortion example in his criticism of Campbell's arguments, which were premised on the dictates of justice rather than the slippery slope as such. For him, Campbell too easily overlooks what is already allowed and the effects this has – or rather has not had – on society, and he more generally finds Campbell's account of justice to be incomplete and contestable, and thus his objections inconclusive (Richmond 1998: 106–108).

Meanings can also get lost or obscured in some of the remaining so-called practical arguments. The eradication or minimisation of human suffering will undoubtedly feature in many definitions of the healthcare endeavour (e.g. Pellegrino 2001: 568–569; Miller and Brody 2001: 582), so it seems wrong to suggest that medicine, by definition, excludes the provision of euthanasia (Gillon 1969: 189; Farsides 1998; Burgess 1993b: 277). Those who claim that doctors, by definition, should not kill therefore need to say more about the nature of healthcare before their case can be said to succeed. Indeed, they need also to consider seriously the suggestion that we need not even turn the carer into a killer, when we can instead create a new specialty, such as 'thanatology', the business of which will be performing euthanasia (Brazier 1996: 322–324; cf. Flew 1969: 35). Obviously, this will not be a complete answer, since the thanatologist will undoubtedly need to have some medical training and to work with or within the healthcare system. Nevertheless, it is possible to see that there are areas where the opponents of euthanasia need to hone their arguments.

Similar flaws can be detected in some of the other, related claims: for example, the idea that there can be a 'benefit' in suffering needs further explanation (Otlowski 1997: 242–244), as do the rather simplistic notions that misdiagnosis is a prevalent risk and that miracle cures can arrive overnight (Flew 1969: 37–40; Browne 1989: 45; Rachels 1993: 54–55). Moreover, the logic of the practical protests can also be turned back on the opponents of euthanasia, as many of their objections appear either to be rather selective and one-sided or else to apply equally to practices that they would otherwise wish to support (Williams 1958a: 283).

Why, for example, discount euthanasia because the patient might change his or her mind? That possibility exists for all decisions, but the opponents are not generally suggesting that patients have no rights of say, and the objection also overlooks the fact that some patients *will* have a clear and constant wish to die. It is also rather convenient to criticise killing but not (some instances of) letting die, when either can be undertaken for malevolent reasons and either might be said to rely on quality of life thinking (Singer 1993: 214–217; Shand 1997: 45). Equally, it is not just killing that is irreversible: sometimes there might also be no going back from a decision to remove life support (Shand 1997: 44–45). Furthermore, if the opponents are really concerned about whether the patient is genuinely autonomous then they might have to ask this of every decision taken by any patient, as they will, by definition, be compromised in some way by their illness (ibid; Rachels 1993: 63; Otlowski

1997: 239). Finally, and particularly persuasively, the proponents of euthanasia condemn appeals to Hippocrates as selective and anachronistic: the Hippocratic doctor, it seems, should not only eschew euthanasia but also surgery, and should be pledging allegiance to a pantheon of ancient Greek Gods (Gillon 1969: 189–190; McLean and Britton 1997: 36–56). In short, the advocates of euthanasia believe that if these are all genuine 'practical' concerns for the opponents, then logic will often dictate that they must condemn much that they would currently condone.

4 Conclusion: conflict and confusion at the end of life

So how convincing are the arguments that euthanasia is, both in principle and in practice, unethical and unsafe? And how persuasive are the opposing arguments, which declare that it should be allowed and that it can be appropriately controlled? 'When the stakes are life and death', notes Solum, 'there is a special temptation to escalate the public debate to ultimate questions of good and evil' (1998: 1121). Everywhere we look in this debate there is conflict, with clashes occurring not only over the values at stake in practices like euthanasia but also over the meanings of the words used to describe them. Sometimes the conflict is all too real: Peter Singer (1993: 337–359) describes being assaulted whilst attempting to argue his position at an academic meeting in Germany and doctors too have been attacked by relatives who (erroneously) believed that they were performing euthanasia (Huxtable and Forbes 2004). Indeed, Dr Cox, whose case I will examine in Chapter 4, was issued with death threats after he was found guilty of attempting to murder a patient. Cox was not imprisoned and was allowed to continue in practice. A Mr McArthur issued the threats because he felt that the consultant had been treated 'far too leniently' as a result of a legal and medical 'conspiracy'; McArthur was imprisoned for three and a half years (*Guardian* 1995: 7).

One thing, at least, is certain: 'the euthanasia debate will rumble on' (McCall Smith 1999: 207) and it looks likely to do so along well-worn tracks. This is understandable, since each of the arguments just outlined has some merit. The problem is that they all share various deficiencies, since it is not always clear how the claims should be understood, how far they might extend, and to whom they might appeal. Some scholars believe that we do not need to revisit these arguments: instead, all we now need is more and better evidence of what allowing euthanasia will mean in practice (Glover 1977: 167; Rachels 1993: 62–63; Otlowski 1997: 222). This nevertheless looks rather optimistic (Parker 2005); in short, the principled conflicts between writers like Brock, Doyal and Keown, who opened this chapter, will continue to be waged.

Brock is, however, right to insist that we need more light and less heat if the debate is to be fruitful (1993: 203). Unfortunately, even if we can reduce the heat, it is not obvious that there will be sufficient light to find the way forward. The euthanasia debate has already been described as 'jaded' by Glanville Williams (1958b: 143). Five decades on, we are still discussing the same issues and doing so in the same contested ways. As Dubler notes, 'bioethical and legal labels may provide a platform for and encourage intellectual and emotional chaos' (2005: s23). Nevertheless, it is currently hard to envisage any future contribution that will completely eschew talk of autonomy, quality of life, the inviolability of life, and the possibility of slippery slopes. There are important lessons in all of these conflicting accounts of the ethics of euthanasia but none of them appears to provide an adequate basis upon which to rest our entire legal response.

Where can and should the law go from here? That question will be taken up in the last chapter, in which attention will be directed to how English law governing the ending of life might best develop along the lines of compromise and accommodation, rather than conflict and competition. First, it is necessary to examine where the law currently is, and this will occur over the next three chapters. As with the conceptual and ethical debates, confusion, conflict and inconsistency appear rife in the law, and the reason for this is not difficult to discern: the apparent legal incoherence can be traced back to the ethical dilemmas outlined in this chapter. This will be illustrated most vividly in the penultimate chapter, in which I will also take stock of the fragile compromise of values currently achieved in the law pertaining to euthanasia.

I start, however, with euthanasia as performed by relatives and other laypeople; in other words, with the phenomenon known as 'mercy killing'. This might seem an unusual place to begin this inquiry, when others prefer to look at when doctors might end life. It is nevertheless instructive to start here, as the current legal response to mercy killing offers a particularly powerful illustration of the ethical conflicts that recur throughout this area of the law.

Chapter 2

Not Pretty

'Mercy killing' in legal fact and legal fiction

A person who kills, with that as their clear intention and in their right mind, is guilty of murder even though they may have been motivated by a desire to end another's suffering or to give effect to their victim's clearly and honestly held wishes.

Home Office evidence (House of Lords Select Committee 1994b: 15)

Mercy Killer is Told: 'Go Home'.

Headline, *Daily Mail*, 4 December 1979

Mercy-Killing Husband, 75, Walks Free.

Headline, *The Daily Telegraph*, 2 July 1985

Husband Loses Plea on Murder Conviction.

Headline, *The Independent*, 27 May 1989

Court Frees Daughter After Mercy Killing.

Headline, *The Times*, 15 July 1989

Home Help Cleared of 'Mercy Killing'.

Headline, *The Daily Telegraph*, 28 March 1996.

Son Walks Free Over 'Mercy Killing'.

Headline, *BBC News Online*, 16 May 2003

In July 2004, 100-year-old Bernard Heginbotham was convicted of man-slaughter for the mercy killing of his wife, Ida, aged 87 (Carter and Khaleeli 2004). Mrs Heginbotham had been suffering seriously from arthritis and had received two hip replacements. Following a fall in January 2003, she was admitted to a care home; one month later, when her condition deteriorated, she was moved to another home; shortly after that she was again relocated, at her husband's request.

In March 2004 Mrs Heginbotham was admitted to hospital following another fall and she was then taken to Kepplegate care home in Lancashire. Four days later, on 1 April, Mr Heginbotham's son informed him that, in view of her deteriorating condition, his wife would have to move to a unit offering specialist care for dementia.

As was his daily custom, Mr Heginbotham visited the home that day and was left alone with his wife by a carer. After he had left, the carer returned to find that Mr Heginbotham had cut his wife's throat, using a kitchen knife he had brought from home. Mrs Heginbotham died several hours later.

On arriving to arrest the centenarian later that day, the police found that he had attempted suicide. Mr Heginbotham was charged with murder – indeed, he is believed to be the oldest man in Britain to have been so charged – but he pleaded guilty to manslaughter on the ground of diminished responsibility. The plea was accepted by the trial judge, Leveson J, who handed down a 12-month community rehabilitation order, which meant the defendant was released into the care of his family. The judge informed Mr Heginbotham:

> The killing of your wife, to whom you had been married joyously for some 67 years, followed by your attempt to take your own life, was an act of desperation carried out in an attempt to end her suffering while you were under intolerable pressure. It was, in truth, an act of love and I have no doubt that you suffered a mental disorder at the time and the responsibility which you bear is substantially reduced. It was, as you will well know, a terrible thing to do but I entirely accept the circumstances in which you did it, and your feelings of guilt and remorse have been truly overwhelming.
>
> (ibid)

Leveson further described the case as unique and warned that the sentence provided 'no benchmark or guidance' (Bunyan 2004). After the ruling, the police defended the decision to prosecute, with a Detective Inspector acknowl-edging the 'tragic' circumstances but adding that 'at the end of the day he has killed his wife' (ibid): 'I think it's right that he comes to court and the court have got the range of sentences available to decide what is to be done' (Carter and Khaleeli 2004).

A tragic and seemingly exceptional case, meriting an exceptionally lenient sentence; or, at least, so the legal officials maintain. On closer inspection, the case is undeniably tragic, but the preceding headlines reveal it is far from exceptional, in terms of the circumstances of the killing, the decision to prosecute, the plea accepted by the court, and the ultimate sentence. The legal officials insist that euthanasia – or 'mercy killing' as it tends to be dubbed when members of the public are involved – is murder and, by extension, the mercy killer should be destined to serve the mandatory term of life imprisonment. Murder may well be the charge brought against two or three such individuals a year, but the recent media carries news of only one such conviction. Instead, ways are found to ensure that defendants like Mr Heginbotham can plead manslaughter by virtue of diminished responsibility and 'walk free' with a non-custodial sentence.

Thus, the reality of the law, as will be seen throughout this chapter, bears little resemblance to the letter of the law, and it is also noticeable how neglected this legal reality is in contemporary discussions of euthanasia. Modern debates focus on whether euthanasia ought to be freely practised by doctors, but doctors are very rarely the individuals who find themselves in court. The usual proposal is for allowing some form of consensual assistance in death, such as the help in committing suicide sought by Dianne Pretty. The judges rejected her plea, and some would say inconsistently so, given the prominence generally accorded to the ethical concept of respecting patient autonomy in English medical law (Biggs 2003). The pre-eminence of the principle might nevertheless lead us to assume that cases of voluntary euthanasia and assisted suicide will be dealt with most sympathetically by the criminal courts. In fact, no such assumption can be made, as the courts do not differentiate between a case like Dianne Pretty's, who desperately wanted assistance to die, and a case like Ida Heginbotham's, who either could not or did not (as far as is known) express any such wish. Regardless of whether the euthanasia was voluntary, non-voluntary, or even involuntary, the mercy killer will 'walk free'. These are important, but often overlooked, features of how euthanasia is dealt with in English law, which merit close scrutiny if a more appropriate, and suitably realistic, legal framework for judging mercy killing is to be found.

I The mercy killer as murderer

Murder, as every practitioner of the law knows, though often described as one of the utmost heinousness, is not in fact necessarily so, but consists in a whole bundle of offences of vastly differing degrees of culpability, ranging from brutal, cynical and repeated offences like the so-called Moors murders to the almost venial, if objectively immoral 'mercy killing' of a beloved partner.

(*R v Howe* [1987] 2 WLR 568 *per*
Lord Hailsham at 581)

For some judges, mercy killing occupies the lower end of the murder spectrum. This does not mean, however, that the judiciary is willing or (apparently) able to allow mercy killings to be treated any differently from other murders. In 1993, Mr Sawyer, who had killed his terminally ill partner, was told 'the court does not and will not sanction any form of mercy killing' (*Guardian* 1993), while the judge dealing with Mr Jones, who was being tried in 1979 for the murder of his ailing mother, insisted 'I would not like it to be thought that I approve of killing in despair or in mercy' (*Daily Mail* 1979: 11). Contemporaneous media reports disclose a long history of such pronouncements, ranging from the judge dealing with Mrs King in 1953, who hoped that 'no one will think that I am lending countenance to what is sometimes loosely called "mercy killing"' (*The Times* 1953: 4) to Rodwell J in 2001 telling Mrs Marshall that 'the law does not permit mercy killing' (Jankiewicz 2001: 12).

In short, neither mercy killing specifically nor euthanasia more generally is explicitly recognised in the legal lexicon: there is no category into which the allegedly humane relative or health professional can be slotted. The legal officials – ranging from the police, to the prosecutors, to the judiciary – are therefore required to use those other categories of homicide that do exist. A raft of homicide charges is available. Murder, which essentially involves the intentional causation of death of a 'person in being', is the most serious and the only to attract a mandatory penalty of life imprisonment. However, the imposition of this penalty will not necessarily mean that the murderer will live out his or her life behind bars. The judges can recommend the 'minimum term' that must be served before the convict can be released on licence. The starting-point for this minimum term must then be adjusted according to the gravity of the offence. Only here does the concept of mercy killing gain explicit legal recognition, since Parliament has signalled that this may be a mitigating circumstance that warrants a lower term. It is for the judge, not the jury, to decide that the defendant did indeed believe that the murder was an act of mercy (Criminal Justice Act 2003, s 269, Sched 21, para 11(f)).

Lower down the spectrum are the various degrees of manslaughter, all of which have life imprisonment as the maximum sentence. Voluntary manslaughter, for example, includes both provoked killing and killing where the defendant is said to have acted under 'diminished responsibility'. These can also be raised as partial defences to murder, which – if the plea is successful – will have the effect of reducing the offence to one of manslaughter. Elsewhere there are more specific offences, such as infanticide, with which a mother might be charged if she kills her child in its first year of life (Infanticide Act 1938, s 1(1)), and various crimes surrounding, but not including, suicide (see Suicide Act 1961). Assisted suicide is of particular relevance in the context of euthanasia and this will form the focus of the next chapter. In this chapter, however, the focus is squarely on the mercy killer as popularly understood, that is, the friend or relative who performs euthanasia, which is itself to be understood in the sense described in Chapter 1.

Since mercy killing involves the intentional killing of a person and the law as formally expressed takes no account of the killer's motive, a crime has clearly been committed and the crime immediately looks like one of murder. This is indeed the message that the legal officials consistently send, and the implication is clear: a mercy killer is in theory destined to serve the life term of imprisonment. However, this destination is rarely reached and in recent decades the courts have apparently only once passed down that sentence, to Anthony Cocker in 1988 – and he was released after four years, following a campaign by the Voluntary Euthanasia Society (VES) (Clouston 1996, 2). Mr Cocker had suffocated his wife Esther, who had advanced multiple sclerosis, following months of her persistent (and sometimes violent) appeals for help in dying. The murder verdict was recorded after Cocker's plea of provocation failed; the Court of Appeal later confirmed that there was no evidence to support the plea ([1989] Crim LR 740).

It is difficult to gauge how many more defendants ought, strictly-speaking, to have received the mandatory life sentence; 'how blunt are our sociological tools for assessing the quantity of crime of any type, and in particular the crime of homicide', as HLA Hart once put it (1970, 65). Those mercy killers who do enter the dock tend, like Cocker, to have surrendered themselves to the police or hospital staff (see e.g. *Taylor* [1979] CLY 570; *Birmingham Evening Mail* 1981; Dray and Kirker 1985: 1; Clough 1989; *Guardian* 1993). While we therefore cannot know the true extent of mercy killing – the Home Office admits it does not (House of Lords Select Committee 1994b: 17) – we do know that those few mercy killers who come to light are extremely unlikely to face Mr Cocker's fate.

Sometimes this will be entirely in keeping with the letter of the law. The idea that mercy killing is murder is obviously not threatened by cases where the patient survives and so the alternative charge of attempted murder is brought. That offence carries a maximum sentence of life imprisonment and this was indeed the charge levelled at Mrs King in 1953 when her husband survived her attempt on his life, but it can also be seen more recently in cases like those of Mr and Ms Thompson, siblings who attempted to kill their hospitalised mother (Victor 1990: 5), and Mr Bouldstridge, who failed in his efforts to asphyxiate himself and his chronically ill wife (Kelso 2000: 1).

However, there are also occasions on which attempted murder is charged even though the patient died soon after the accused's alleged actions. The rationale must be that the patient's underlying condition, rather than anything the accused did, was the true cause of death. This may (but only may) explain the decision to bring the lesser charge of attempted murder against defendants like Mrs Hough ((1984) 6 Cr App Rep (S) 406), who sat with her friend until she died (apparently from suffocation using means Hough had supplied), and Ms Heath, a carer whose client died soon after she had allegedly tampered with a morphine drip (Fleet 1996: 3). In these cases the legal officials evidently felt that the accused's actions could not be proven to have caused death. However, the decision to prosecute for the lesser crime will not always withstand scrutiny. Scepticism is certainly warranted in the case of Mrs Monaghan, who was convicted in 1989 of attempting to murder her mother, at the latter's request (*South Wales Echo* 1989: 1–2). Mrs Monaghan had given her mother sleeping tablets and then smothered her with a pillow. An open verdict was later recorded at inquest, but there are still indications that murder might have been the more accurate accusation. As the Nathan Committee, which examined the offence of murder, noted, '[t]he illogical charge of attempted murder appears to have been brought in order to avoid the stigma of a murder conviction' (House of Lords Select Committee 1989: 30).

Such comments immediately create the impression that something is amiss in the administration of the law. The most urgent question is, Mr Cocker aside, where are the convictions for murder that the theory demands?

2 The mercy killer at 'breaking point'

The mystery of the disappearing murderers is easily solved: the law is geared towards ensuring that mercy killers reappear in most cases as either assistants in suicide or manslaughterers. Assistance in suicide is sufficiently complex to merit separate, more detailed consideration in the next chapter. Here the focus will be on the frequency with which mercy killers find themselves guilty of manslaughter, specifically the voluntary form of manslaughter by reason of 'diminished responsibility'.

The offence was introduced by s 2 of the Homicide Act 1957 and commentators on the Act noted that it was immediately deployed in cases of mercy killing (Williams 1960: 53; Wootton 1960: 229; Hollis 1964: 103). More recent Home Office statistics show that the trend continues, with 14 of the 20 defendants who were brought to trial between 1982 and 1991 being so convicted (House of Lords Select Committee 1994b: 18).

When one considers the circumstances of many mercy killings, such as those in the case of Mr Heginbotham, it is not difficult to sympathise with the view that these were killers whose actions were borne of immense strain and distress. However, as severe as it might sound, this alone should not suffice. Instead, the cases show that the re-branding – from an unexceptional murderer to a 'broken' manslaughterer – is more often a convenient legal fiction, designed to offer a measure of mercy whilst preserving the official line that mercy killing is murder.

2.1 Accommodating the mercy killer

'Diminished responsibility' is a curious creation, uncomfortably straddling legal, moral and clinical concepts. The defence is available to those:

> suffering from such abnormality of mind (whether arising from a condition of arrested development or any inherent causes or induced by disease or

injury) as substantially impaired his mental responsibility for his acts or omissions. . . .

(Homicide Act 1957, s 2(1))

The two key components, an 'abnormality of mind' and 'substantially impaired' mental responsibility, are said to be characteristics shared by mercy killers, at least according to some observers. The Criminal Law Revision Committee of 1980 reported that the first criterion would certainly be satisfied 'if there is medical evidence of, for example, reactive depression' (1980: 31). Its Chairman, Lawton LJ, had previously opined that such depression would be present in 'nearly all genuine cases of this kind' (1979: 460–461).

This view is lent credibility by Dell's study of 253 men convicted of this form of manslaughter between 1963 and 1977. Dell found that, amongst the ten mercy killers she encountered, there were men who 'had reached breaking point under the severe strain of looking after wives with severe mental or physical illnesses' (1984: 35–36). Mr Morrison, who was convicted in 1997, exemplifies the finding: his diary recounts the weeks of 'bad nights and difficult days' he endured while caring for his wife Bridget, who had Parkinson's disease, before he 'snapped' and smothered her with a towel (*Guardian* 1997: 5).[1] Had his neighbours not intervened, Mr Morrison himself would have died, as he had slashed his wrists and then attempted to gas himself in his car. Suicide was also attempted by a number of other mercy killers, including Mr Heginbotham, Mr Bouldstridge and a Mr Gardner, who killed both of his ailing parents (BBC 2003), and these attempts seem to reinforce further Dell's depiction of mercy killers reaching 'breaking point'.

Even assuming that the mercy killer's will is broken, it still falls to him or her to prove that this led to a substantial impairment of mental responsibility (Homicide Act 1957, s 2(2)). According to Lawton, this second requirement is 'vague and woolly' (1979: 460); or, as Griew less kindly puts it, 'elliptical almost to the point of nonsense' (1986: 19), albeit perhaps no less so than the first (Wootton 1978a: 141). In any case, the option is open to anyone accused of murder to argue that their responsibility was impaired to some degree (see *Byrne* [1960] 2 QB 396), and so it would seem appropriate this is also available to the mercy killer. It is therefore entirely conceivable that a mercy killer will satisfy the nebulous statutory formulation and as such be appropriately diverted from a murder conviction.

1   This aspect of Mr Morrison's case recalls Mr Cocker's failed plea of provocation. Williams suggests that it should be possible, legally, for this plea to succeed (2001b). Conceptually, however, there may be some difficulty in arguing that one can be provoked into performing a mercy killing. If, as the word conventionally suggests, there is a sense in which a provoked killer has 'snapped', then this might cast doubt on the extent to which he or she was genuinely (and voluntarily) prompted to act from merciful motives.

2.2 Stretching a (breaking) point

Whilst there will be some mercy killers who are rightly considered to have acted under 'diminished responsibility', closer inspection of the available evidence frequently suggests the opposite and reveals a gaping chasm between the law-on-the-books and the law-in-action. In truth, the clause has been adopted as a *de facto* defence, albeit a partial defence, to the charge of mercy killing.

To start with, the reactive or situational depression one might find in a mercy killer is not strictly the type of 'abnormality of mind' that Parliament intended the section to cover. Citing the fact that the inept formulation arose from an attempted reconstruction of two previous drafts, Griew notes how this part of the Bill was meant to encompass the borderline insane (1988: 77–78). The words in parentheses – 'whether arising from a condition of arrested development or any inherent causes or induced by disease or injury' – were, according to Meakin, proposed to limit the defence 'to states of mind recognised as pathological by psychiatrists or neurologists' (1988: 409). Reactive depression might arguably amount to one of the 'mere emotional states' (ibid) that Parliament expressly excluded, and, in any case, it could hardly be said to arise from 'inherent causes' (Griew 1988: 80; Williams 1983: 693; Hamilton 1981: 434). Indeed, the precise cause of the depression is also open to question. As Dell points out, the diagnosis can only occur after the crime (1984: 36), giving rise to the suspicion that some such conditions might actually have been triggered by the mercy killer's *subsequent* grief or remorse.

This all assumes, however, that there is some degree of mental disorder, and that assumption finds little support in the available data. Roughly one-third of those mercy killers studied by Dell were found to be mentally 'normal' at the time of diagnosis – but the doctors *inferred* mental abnormality at the time of the offence (1984: 36; 1986: 30). Wootton has observed how the diagnosing doctor will be aware of the circumstances of the offence and she believed that this must influence the diagnosis (1960: 230). Dell adds that psychiatrists tended to disagree only when diagnosing borderline, milder conditions (1984: 28–29), of which reactive depression is presumably one (see Hamilton 1981: 434). It is therefore remarkable how infrequently that diagnosis has been challenged in relation to a mercy killer. Dell draws these trends to their seemingly logical conclusion: mercy killers, as a class, tend to display a 'total lack of mental disorder' (1986: 30).

So much for the application of the first criterion; does the second fare any better? It is not surprising to learn that it does not, although once again this is partly attributable to the imprecision of the phrase 'mental responsibility'. Described in an official report as 'a concept of law or a concept of morality; it is not a clinical fact relating to the defendant' (Home Office, Department of Health and Social Security 1975: 242), the judges have still tried to express the idea in quasi-clinical terms, as concerning:

the ability to form a rational judgment as to whether an act is right or wrong, [and] the ability to exercise willpower to control physical acts in accordance with that rational judgment.

(Byrne [1960] 2 QB 396, *per* Lord Parker CJ, at 403)

The ambiguity of the concept has certainly allowed the judges to exercise their imaginations in cases they deem deserving (Leng 1982a: 77). One, nevertheless, needs a very powerful imagination to see how some mercy killers can have been considered 'irresponsible' in the relevant sense.

Consider the early case of Mr Johnson, who was convicted in 1960 for killing his three-month-old son (see Williams 1960: 53; Wootton 1978a: 143; 1981: 77; Meakin 1988: 409). The boy had Down's syndrome, and his father undertook extensive study of the condition before concluding that it was not in his son's interests to live. The court noted the considerable premeditation, but this in itself could not destroy the plea (*Matheson* [1958] 1 WLR 474), and nor should it, when premeditated killing by a mentally abnormal defendant still involves a mentally abnormal defendant. Nevertheless, its presence in this case led Leng to conclude that Johnson:

> could hardly be said to have diminished capacity for responsibility in the legal sense of having impaired ability rationally to control his actions. In his particular circumstances Johnson viewed his responsibilities as different from those prescribed by law and acted accordingly.
>
> (1982a: 77)

The same can be said of more recent mercy killers, including Mr Jones, who explicitly asserted his lack of remorse (*Daily Mail* 1979: 11), and a Mr and Mrs Houghton, who again felt they were right to have acted on their son's pleas to help him die (*The Times* 1985). All of these defendants were found to have diminished responsibility. It is hard to disagree with Wootton's judgment that:

> the terms of Section 2 are stretched to a point at which ... the offender, far from any diminution of responsibility, appears to have acted from excessively responsible motives.... Although it might be thought that this action was morally wrong, it would be difficult to argue that it was not responsibly motivated.
>
> (1978a: 143; see also Blugrass 1980: 10)

2.3 Diminishing the mercy killer

Although the ill-defined parameters of s 2 are amenable to stretching in various ways, it seems that they are particularly elastic in cases of mercy killing. The various legal officials can be criticised for sending a decidedly mixed message, since they perpetuate the myth that euthanasia is murder, but it is also they who ensure that this is rarely the result.

The process starts with a sympathetically minded psychiatrist (Blugrass 1980: 9). Giving evidence to the Nathan Committee, one such professional, Dr Wright, noted how an initially 'grey' psychiatric report could be transformed by the adversarial nature of criminal proceedings (House of Lord Select Committee 1989: 676–678). He nevertheless argued that a sufficiently alert psychiatrist could interpret and present virtually any behaviour or psychological reaction as an 'abnormality of mind', through 'textbook' citations of a 'cocktail' of alleged symptoms and psychological attributes.

However, Wright felt that the success of the plea was less attributable to the report and more reliant on the sympathy of the jury, the skill of the defence lawyer, and the apparent integrity and experience of the expert. Yet, whilst these will be important features, they do not convey the whole story. The whim of the jury certainly cannot be the most significant factor (contrast Williams 1960: 46), when the overwhelming majority of pleas in mercy killing cases are accepted by the judge. Of the cases considered here, only Mr and Mrs Houghton had the jury to thank for the lesser conviction. A more accurate view is that all of the legal officials – including the judges and prosecutors – work together to engineer the result. Remarkably, judges, psychiatrists and lawyers do not deny this, and they invariably describe the reality of these cases in the same terms: an 'understanding' is reached through willing 'collusion' (e.g. Lawton 1979: 461; Blugrass 1980: 11; Griew 1988: 79). After the sympathetic psychiatrist has converted stress into 'a medical sounding' condition (Griew 1988: 79) and the prosecutors are satisfied that they are dealing with a genuine mercy killing, nobody examines the statutory language too closely, even though the judge 'knows that a few short questions would probably topple the evidential house of cards' (Lawton 1979: 461).

As Mr Cocker's failed plea of provocation demonstrates ([1989] Crim LR 740), hard questions will still occasionally be asked, but Cocker's legal team would have better served their client by investing in s 2. Such is the collusion that the process has reached the point that the verdict of diminished responsibility is 'rubber-stamped' on these sorts of cases (Davies 1998: 349). If any final proof of this is needed, one needs look no further than *Blackstone's Criminal Practice*, a primary reference point for criminal lawyers, which explicitly states:

> 'Mercy killing' can ... be dealt with as manslaughter, where the dilemma which has caused the accused to kill can be said to have given rise to depression or some other medically recognised disorder which can be said to be the cause of an abnormality of mind.
>
> (Murphy 2007: 157)

As the entry puts it, these things usually 'can be said', but they can only be heard if nobody scrutinises the reality behind the words.

Despite the problems, in 2005 the Law Commission provisionally proposed that mercy killings be brought explicitly within the purview of s 2, at least in cases where 'there is clinical support for the existence of an abnormality of mental functioning' (2005: 215). This was only one aspect of their wider recommendations on the law of homicide and (in line with their other revisions) it would have meant that the defendant would be convicted of 'second degree murder'. By 2006, however, the Law Commission withdrew the suggestion, noting that the issue required a more comprehensive consultation (Law Commission 2006: 145–155).

The Law Commission proposal certainly travels in the right direction, in openly acknowledging what is already occurring in the law, but it seems to alight at the wrong stop. Clinical support for the relevant diagnosis will probably not be hard to find, given what has been considered above. Why is it appropriate to stretch the defence further when so few mercy killers appear even to have the relevant 'mental abnormality'? Is it really fair or accurate to label all mercy killers as acting under 'diminished responsibility'? Critics of the proposal have made similar complaints and the Commission itself has tentatively conceded that it might be more appropriate to create a distinct legal category of 'mercy killing' (2006: 155). Making the covert overt does indeed offer a more honest way forward, and it is an idea to which I will return in Chapter 6. For now, it is possible to conclude, with Ashworth, that there is something to be said for the legal officials approaching s 2 with 'compassionate pragmatism rather than with the rarefied verbal analysis too frequently encountered in English criminal law' (2003: 282) but that such compassion can only damage the contours of the legal landscape.

3 The 'unique' mercy killer

The landscape looks even more distorted once the sentences passed down to convicted mercy killers enter the picture. Even Mr Cocker's treatment as a murderer was not as harsh as it might have been, because he was released after four years, while others convicted of this offence around the same time could have expected to serve sentences two or three times longer than this (House of Lords Select Committee 1989: 673). The clemency is, of course, much more manifest when the judges are freed from the shackles of the mandatory penalty and instead there is a conviction for manslaughter or some other, lesser form of homicide. However, undoubtedly mindful of how feeble the claim that 'mercy killing is murder' is in such cases, the judges nevertheless still strive to emphasise that mercy killing involves a serious offence, warranting a serious punishment: when sentenced for manslaughter, Cecilia Maxwell's daughter, Doreen Marshall, was told 'I have to pass a sentence of imprisonment to mark the gravity of this offence' (Jankiewicz 2001: 12), while Mr and Mrs Houghton heard that 'virtually every case' demanded a prison term (*The Times* 1985). However, once the message of condemnation has been conveyed, the judge is free to issue a penalty that indicates how grave the law really considers these cases to be: a suspended prison sentence in the case of Mrs Marshall and probation for Robert Houghton's parents.

Legal scholars have long commented on the leniency of the courts (e.g. Kamisar 1957: 85; McLean and Maher 1983: 54–56), but there appears to have been little attempt made to compile detailed data. Whilst a comprehensive picture cannot be painted, it is possible to fill in some of the detail. This is an important endeavour, since the way forward can realistically only be discerned after discovering where the law currently is. And the legal process is, and has long been, used to excuse the mercy killer, even (remarkably) in cases where the patient did not want to die. What this might mean for the mercy killer in the future remains to be assessed; I start, however, by considering some mercy killers of the past.

3.1 Before the breaking point

Mrs Brownhill was the main carer for her 30-year-old son Denis, a man described as an 'imbecile' enduring 'a living death', who was 'hopelessly incapacitated' to such an extent that his mother did everything for him 'as if he were a baby' (*The Times* 1934a; *The Times* 1934b). Concerned that there may be no one to care for him as her own health was failing, Mrs Brownhill took what she felt was the 'merciful' step of drugging and gassing her son (ibid). After immediately notifying her family doctor, Mrs Brownhill found herself charged with murder, which at that time (1934) carried the mandatory death penalty. On conviction, however, the jury added 'the strongest recommendation for mercy' and within two days the Home Secretary had recommended a reprieve (*The Times* 1934c). Three months later, Mrs Brownhill was pardoned and released from prison (*The Times* 1935).

Although the outcomes of the stories carried in the media of the day are not always revealed (see e.g. (1812) *Annual Register* 96; *Simpson* [1915] 84 LJKB 1893), Mrs Brownhill was evidently not alone in evading capital punishment. For example, 12 years after her reprieve, the Home Office commuted Mr Long's penalty to one of life imprisonment, after he had initially been sentenced to death for pleading guilty to the murder of his 'imbecile' seven-year-old daughter (*The Times* 1946a; *The Times* 1946b).

The trend did not escape the notice of the 1953 *Royal Commission on Capital Punishment*, which was instrumental in shaping the reforms to come. In practice, 45 per cent of all those convicted of murder from 1900 until the Commission met had had their capital sentences reduced to terms of life imprisonment. The Royal Commission could only guess at the Home Office's reasons, although it recognised there were cases where 'a reprieve is a fore-gone conclusion'. Among these were situations 'calling more for pity than censure – those, for instance, of what are commonly known as "mercy killings"' (1953: 11), where 'there can be no question of exacting the extreme penalty' (1953: 63). Indeed, the penalty was likely to be much less extreme for the mercy killer, with an early release 'ordinarily granted to such persons' (1953: 227). Even before the introduction of diminished responsibility, the legal officials made sure they had means of softening the law for the mercy killer.

3.2 After the breaking point

Once the Homicide Act came into force, however, the lawyers quickly took the opportunity to filter the mercy killer out of the category of murder and into the category of manslaughter, by way of the partial defence of diminished responsibility. As Hollis has noted, prison terms were passed down, but these were usually short (1964: 103), and available accounts show that a one-year sentence, such as was received by the aforementioned Mr Johnson, was not unusual (Blom-Cooper and Morris 1964: 61–64, 135–136, 146). In time, however, even these would begin to look like particularly harsh disposals, for in the years after 1957 and, indeed, 1965, with its abolition of the death penalty, the judges moved to routinely issuing non-custodial sentences.

Despite fitting the legal definition of 'murder' and contrary to what the judges and other legal authorities say, the mercy killer is hardly a murderer, but some rationality (and credibility) might be restored to the law if the sentences received by these manslaughterers resemble those given to other convicted manslaughterers. It appears, however, that they do not. Generally, manslaughter by virtue of diminished responsibility tends to attract a prison term, usually of between three years and life (e.g. Walker and Padfield 1996: 134–135). Contrast this with the Home Office statistics, which show that 14 of the 20 mercy killers avoided prison terms (House of Lords Select Committee 1994b: 18), and with most of the disposals considered in this chapter: a conditional discharge for Mr Jones; probation for Mr Morrison; rehabilitation orders for Mr Gardner and Mr Heginbotham; and so the list goes on. There is a similar dissonance between the usual penalty of imprisonment expected for attempted murder and cases like that of Mrs Monaghan, who was placed on probation (e.g. Walker and Padfield 1996: 134–135). This does not mean that imprisonment is never imposed but even where this does happen, the judges admit to leniency, with Farquharson J once marking the 'serious violence' done by one mercy killer 'with what in any normal case of manslaughter would be a purely nominal sentence of 12 months' imprisonment' (Roland 1989).

The disposal arguably also exposes the sham of diminished responsibility. Of the defendants just mentioned, apparently only Mr Morrison was to be provided with psychiatric care. However, mercy killers previously looked like the individuals most likely to have genuinely satisfied the statutory criteria and therefore, one might assume, to have been in need of such support.

Similarly notable is the infrequency with which hospital orders are issued to such defendants, although there are very occasional reports of this occurring. Mr Morris was an early example, having been convicted in 1961. Although the prosecution found greater evidence of mental abnormality than the defence, the judge prevented insanity being raised, since he felt the Home Office would send Mr Morris 'to the right place', by which he undoubtedly meant Broadmoor (Walker and McCabe 1973: 86–87). More recently, in 2004, Mr McAuley was detained under the Mental Health Act, after shooting dead a terminally ill man he had been providing care to on an informal basis (BBC 2004). Described as a mercy killing, Mr McAuley's action was apparently linked to the schizophrenia from which he suffered.

These are, of course, extreme cases, arguably closer to the original Parliamentary intent, which was to provide for the borderline 'insane' killer. It is worth conceding also that other mercy killers might not need any support by the time that the trial has concluded, even if they might genuinely have been depressed at the time of the killing. Nevertheless, it is still worth remembering how infrequently the mercy killer who pleads diminished responsibility finds themselves disposed of in such ways. The suspicion remains that the mental responsibility of more typical mercy killers is far from 'diminished'.

3.3 The 'unique' mercy killer

Although their actions convey a common approach to mercy killing, the courts appear to resist the idea that the 'typical' mercy killer even exists. Whilst understandably constrained by the need to examine only the case before them, the judges seem rather too keen to emphasise how the particular case is 'unique' and therefore deserving of 'unique' treatment.

One way of achieving this is to appeal to the 'public interest', sometimes in order to pass down a more severe sentence than might otherwise be expected (e.g. *Hough* (1984) 6 Cr App Rep (S) 406; *Sweeney* (1986) 8 Cr App Rep (S) 419), but more often to justify the opposite decision. One should recall the stern words spoken to Mr and Mrs Houghton and how the words rather lost their power in the ensuing probation order. French J nevertheless clothed his decision in appropriate legal robes: 'the public interest does not require you to receive any further punishment' (*The Times* 1985). Sentencing conventions can certainly aid the mercy killer, since most cases of mercy killing contain features that will often be taken in mitigation, such as the submission of a guilty plea, the advanced age and good character of the defendant, and the improbability of re-offending.[2] But it is in the nature of mercy killing that there will also

---

2   As was noted earlier, the term served for murder can be reduced where the killing was believed to have been merciful. However, my concern here is with sentencing for the other homicide offences, since – as has been argued throughout this chapter – the mercy killer is very unlikely to be convicted of murder.

be features that would otherwise tend to aggravate the penalty, not least the frailty of the victim and their dependency on the defendant. That the sentences remain uniformly light suggests that there is a missing ingredient, and it is not hard to locate: the fact that this is a mercy killing will be mitigation enough.

The judges, of course, strive to avoid leaving the impression that there is any unwritten rule in operation and instead, as I have suggested, much is made of the 'uniqueness' or the extreme nature of the case. Placing Mrs Wise under probation for 12 months, Jones J felt that she had 'acted, although wrongly, in what you considered the child's best interests. This is an extreme case among exceptional ones. You have suffered enough already' (Pratt 1974). The same terms are used repeatedly, although this is at least understandable in cases where a prison sentence is to be suspended, as the statute dictates that the judge can only exercise mercy where the circumstances are 'exceptional'.[3] There is therefore some justification for a comment like that from McNeil J, who suspended the term for Mr Doran because 'the mitigating circumstances are as great as they ever could be' (Jack 1985). However, no matter which disposal is chosen, the mercy killer will still be greeted with this doubtful discourse of 'uniqueness' and 'exceptionality' (see e.g. *Birmingham Evening Mail* 1981; *Western Mail* 1982: 2; *The Times* 1985; *Eastbourne Gazette* 1990: 1; *Cambridge Evening News* 1990).

Tata has observed the 'axiom of judicial rhetoric on sentencing that every case is unique', but rightly goes on to point out that 'similarity must be detectable or else the notion of uniqueness is barren' (1997: 397). The key similarity in the cases under consideration here must be that they are all mercy killings; different from other killings, but, within their own class, far from exceptional and rarely unique. With the merciful circumstances of the killing effectively – and very significantly – operating as a mitigating circumstance, the mercy killer can apparently nowadays expect the court to show 'the greatest mercy' (*Daily Mail* 1979: 11).

4 Locating the mercy killer

If mercy killers are to expect mercy from the courts, they first need the judges to recognise these killings as 'mercy' killings. Here one encounters a new problem with the official line. Aware of the courts' tendency to issue light penalties, in 1976 the Criminal Law Revision Committee proposed a new offence of consensual 'mercy killing', which would be subject to a maximum of two years' imprisonment. The proposal was dropped after it met with a barrage of criticism. One of the usual objections to such a proposal is that the law cannot easily discern and judge *why* the defendant pursued his or her particular aim (see e.g. Law Commission 2006: 146). Certainly, criminal

---

3   Powers of the Criminal Courts (Sentencing) Act 2000, s 118(4).

lawyers are better versed in the intricacies of intention, that is, in considering *what* the defendant aimed to do. It is nevertheless manifestly wrong to claim that the legal officials cannot and do not identify, and distinguish between, different motives. The vast majority of cases under consideration here show that a sympathetic disposal will follow if the case resembles a paradigm of mercy killing that the judges have quietly constructed. Some judges are louder than others, explicitly noting the features that mark the homicide out as a 'mercy killing', but the construction work can also be located in those hearings that end in more punitive disposals.

4.1 When is a killing not a mercy killing?

Patterns begin to emerge from those few recent mercy killings that have ended with the killer being confined to the cells. The first recurring feature is that the killing is unlikely to have been as 'merciful' as the concept might require. The case of Mr Sawyer provides perhaps the most extreme example, as he had hit, strangled and then drowned his partner. 'No one could view this as a mercy killing because of the substantial physical violence', stated Kay J, who ordered Sawyer to serve 30 months' imprisonment (*Guardian* 1993). Although he too had acted at his loved one's request, Mr Ambrose was also incarcerated, and this may again have been due to the fact that he had bludgeoned his mother with a hammer (Roland 1989). Similar stories feature in the media and even the law reports, and it is notable also how a suspended sentence – rather than probation or the like – might also be preferred in cases where weapons feature (e.g. *Morning Telegraph* 1975).

Although it is arguably the defendant's motive, rather than the means employed, which should be most pertinent to dubbing a killing 'merciful', the judges do seem to be more comfortable with instances of suffocation and overdose. They are also more inclined to clemency when the patient's affliction is terminal or, at least, chronic and somatic: mercy killings motivated by the victim's mental disorder tend not to be viewed so sympathetically. Thus, we learn of Mr Wallis ((1983) 5 Cr App R (S) 342) and Mr Sweeney ((1986) 8 Cr App Rep (S) 419) having prison sentences upheld for their parts in the deaths of two depressed individuals (cf. Durham 2001: 12).

The presence of mixed motives will also give the judges reason to pause. Sometimes a decidedly unmerciful motive can be detected, as in the case of Mrs McShane ((1977) 66 Cr App Rep 97), who not only wanted to end her mother's suffering but also sought access to a much-needed inheritance. That case will be considered again in the context of assisted suicide, but for now it is important to note that her two two-year prison terms were upheld on appeal. Financial considerations, albeit of a rather different type, can certainly cause the judges difficulty. Mr Heginbotham, whose trial featured at the outset to this chapter, was concerned at the future care arrangements for his wife and this is a not infrequent feature of mercy killings (see also e.g. *The Times* 1934b;

Daily Telegraph 1985). The relevance of monetary constraints to this debate is best left to others to ponder; what must be recognised, however, is how this might occasionally have inclined the courts towards more severe penalties.

4.2 When is a killing a mercy killing?

In the regrettable absence of robust data on mercy killing, it would be unwise to draw concrete conclusions from the few cases just cited.[4] There is, nevertheless, enough of a pattern to infer that the judges are most content to dub a killing merciful, and accordingly exercise their own mercy, if the method of killing is suitably gentle, the victim was physically suffering, and the accused wanted only to put an end to that suffering.

The inference is supported by at least one expert in sentencing trends (Thomas 1984: 46; 1985: 249) and is undeniably strengthened when one examines cases that do exhibit the relevant characteristics. Thus, it is not uncommon to hear the judge explicitly labelling the case a 'mercy killing', and drawing attention to the plight of the victim and the bond between victim and killer. A good example of this is provided by Rodwell J, who dealt with Mrs Marshall:

> It is, I think, common ground between prosecution and defence that your mother's existence was absolutely wretched beyond belief....I am quite satisfied on the evidence before me that what you were attempting is sometimes described as a mercy killing.
>
> (Jankiewicz 2001: 12)

Evidently, the judges can and do recognise a mercy killer, and will be minded to deal with them in a manner quite distinct from other killers. Then, however, the law starts to look even more uneven, because Mrs Marshall was actually one of the defendants who received a harsher sentence, at least when compared to other mercy killers:

> What your motive was, was one of mercy and consideration for your mother. The law does not permit mercy killing. That is the law, there are very good reasons for that law, but I have to pass a sentence of imprisonment to mark the gravity of this offence.
>
> (ibid)

The 12-month sentence may have been suspended for two years, but many other mercy killers will not receive even this penalty. Clearly, then, mercy killers still face something of a lottery when they come before the courts.

---

4   I am mindful of the possibility that the media will concentrate on extreme cases, and particularly those that result in light sentences (see O'Connell and Whelan 1996).

4.3 Pretty, not Pretty and the sentencing lottery

The inconsistency and uncertainty in the application of the law to the mercy killer is readily apparent. Mr Masters, who had ended his wife's life at her request, was convicted of manslaughter, which is not unusual; what is remarkable, however, is that he was sentenced to 125 days' imprisonment (*Daily Telegraph* 1985). This might be due to the fact that he was not only motivated to end Mrs Masters' suffering, but he was also fearful of her future should he predecease her. It might also have been the most logical disposal available to the judge, as the term equalled the time that the defendant had already spent in custody whilst on remand. However, this still does not sit well with the roughly contemporaneous case of Mr Jones: he too was convicted of manslaughter for acting on his mother's plea to die, but he was conditionally discharged. Elsewhere there are defendants who might, on previously noted trends, have expected a harsher penalty but who found themselves freed by the courts: Mr Killick, for example, had used a hatchet against his wife and then strangled her, but he was convicted of manslaughter by reason of diminished responsibility and placed on probation, with an order to undergo psychiatric treatment (*Leicester Mercury* 1986).

The media reports do not suggest that Mrs Killick had asked to die. This leads to a very significant inference: the sentencing patterns might be rather uneven, but this is not because the courts distinguish between mercy killings that were consensual and those that either were not, or, by virtue of the patient's incompetence, could not be. In Chapter 1 I considered how the conceptual distinctions, if any, between voluntary, non-voluntary and involuntary forms of euthanasia have long been debated in the bioethics literature, but there is one issue on which most theorists appear to agree: the involuntary killing of a competent individual cannot be tolerated. The sentences passed down in such cases, however, suggest that the judges are not so squeamish. Mr Killick's fate obviously contrasts sharply with that of the unfortunate Mr Cocker, who had acted at his wife's insistence but was convicted of murder.

And Mr Killick's is not the only such case.[5] Among many other examples is the case of Mr Fox, who attempted to suffocate his wife, who had terminal cancer, after telling her: 'You are dying of cancer, whether you know it or not. They all die of cancer. You will die of sheer, screaming agony' (*Daily Express* 1975). She managed to pull the pillow away and go to a neighbour's house. When convicted of attempted murder, the judge acknowledged that Mr Fox had acted 'with the mistaken motive of help' (ibid). Fox was placed on probation, thus allowing him to be with his wife, with whom he was reconciled, until her death.

5   Other examples are reported in (Blom-Cooper and Morris 1964: 61; *Birmingham Evening Mail* 1981; Oldfield 1984; Clough 1989).

Equally, no distinction appears to be drawn between the killing of a competent person and the killing of someone who is incompetent by reason of age or impairment. Mrs Wise was placed on probation after ending the life of her seriously ill baby daughter; so was Mrs Monaghan, who had attempted to grant her mother's wish to die. To proponents of voluntary euthanasia, the well-publicised plight of Dianne Pretty (outlined in Chapter 1) meets the ethical gold standards, in that this was a clearly competent patient, who desperately wanted help in escaping her condition. To the judges, however, it seems to matter little whether the mercy killing was *Pretty* or it was not: if such an assisted death takes place they will state that any such killing is illegal, but they will be sure to find a suitably humane disposal for the perpetrator, albeit one that cannot easily be predicted in advance.

5 The mercy killer: presumed innocent?

Stern warnings that mercy killing is murder, convenient re-classification as manslaughter, and uniformly light, if somewhat unpredictable, sentences: what might these trends mean for future mercy killers? Although it may seem unlikely to happen in practice, the logical end-point – the bottom of this particular slippery slope, perhaps – must be that mercy killers will be filtered out of the courts altogether. This seemingly radical result would not even require Parliament's intervention, because current practices and guidelines can already accommodate the shift.

The relevant guidelines exist in the *Code for Crown Prosecutors*, which requires the Crown Prosecution Service (CPS) to ensure both that the evidence is sufficient to offer a 'realistic prospect of conviction' and that a prosecution is in the 'public interest' (see CPS 2004). The public interest assessment clearly involves factors that will weigh in favour of the pursuit of mercy killers. Thus, where there is premeditation, the victim was vulnerable, and the defendant was in a position of trust or power, prosecutors are advised to proceed. Commentators believe that the Code is biased in favour of prosecution (Sanders 1985: 17), with Ashworth and Fionda drawing attention to its insistence that a prosecution 'will usually take place' in 'cases of any seriousness', unless there are compelling reasons why this is not in the public interest. They feel that public interest factors will nevertheless assume less significance, 'the more serious the offence' (1994: 898). Homicide, of course, comprises the most serious offences in English law, so there is reason to believe that a mercy killing must be prosecuted.

However, the same guidelines could be used to stay proceedings against any mercy killer; or at least any whose actions fit the paradigm constructed by the courts. Every Attorney General since 1951 has confirmed that suspected offences should not 'automatically be the subject of prosecution' (HC Deb Vol 483, Col 681, 29 January 1951). Amongst the factors that weigh against proceeding are the advanced age and ill health of the accused (seemingly common traits amongst mercy killers) and, most significantly, the likelihood of 'a nominal penalty' (CPS 2004: 10). Quite what a 'nominal' penalty will be is left to the prosecutor's discretion, but experience suggests that this is a fitting description of the punishments meted out to most mercy killers. Is it not logical to conclude that mercy killers ought uniformly to be filtered out of the courts by the prosecutors?

Such filtering does already occur to an extent, and it is instructive to note that four of the 24 cases compiled by the Home Office for the 1994 Lords Select Committee ended in terminations (1994b: 18, 25). The Home Office explained that it was not in the public interest to proceed against two of the accused, and this does seem to be the decisive criterion, even in those cases where evidential concerns are said to have stayed the prosecutors' hands. Journalist Derek Humphry has become a renowned campaigner for voluntary euthanasia in the United States, where he founded the organisation *Hemlock* and authored the suicide-manual *Final Exit* (1991), but his association with the issues began in England, when he and an unnamed doctor allegedly assisted in the suicide of his terminally ill wife (see Wootton 1978b: 177–178). Humphry not only declared that he would plead guilty if prosecuted but he also published his account of events in *Jean's Way* (1978). Although investigated by the police, the Director of Public Prosecutions (DPP) announced that Humphry would not be prosecuted. The absence of sufficient evidence looks unlikely to have been the real reason for this decision. Instead, as Wootton has suggested, a trial might have been a 'farcical waste of public money', since, even if he was convicted, Humphry looked likely to receive a light sentence (1978b: 178).

Humphry's is not the only case where the evidence was said to be lacking. In 1994, Mrs Blakemore avoided prosecution for her alleged attempt on her mother's life (*Nursing Times* 1994; *Nursing Times* 1995). After confessing to a doctor, the ensuing police investigation reportedly concluded that she had boosted her mother's morphine intake. An inquest nevertheless found that the patient had died from natural causes. Although she was issued with a warning by her employers, Mrs Blakemore was not charged and she was permitted to return to her work as a nurse. The fact that this was a healthcare professional allegedly tampering with an opioid drug may have exerted some considerable influence over the decision to stay proceedings, for reasons that will be explored in Chapter 4. In any case, it looks most likely that it was the public interest rather than evidential deficiencies that stayed proceedings, for what evidence there is indicates that attempted murder might feasibly have been charged.

Although evidential shortcomings continue to be raised (e.g. Dyer 1996), there have also been occasions on which the legal officials have more openly acknowledged that it was not in the public interest to proceed. One of the more intriguing examples was also revealed in 1994, when the CPS declined to pursue an unnamed man who was allegedly implicated in the death, from acute morphine poisoning, of his terminally ill wife. *The Observer* perhaps tellingly described the situation as: 'the first identified case where the CPS has declined to prosecute an alleged killer *because* they believe that if the victim was killed it was on compassionate grounds' (Nelson and Murphie 1994, emphasis added). The suspicion that a morphine drip had been tampered with can of course lead to homicide charges being brought, but the 1996 case of Ms Heath shows that an appeal to the public interest can still bring a halt to proceedings once they are underway. In Ms Heath's case, the prosecution offered no evidence after Ognall J – who also presided over the infamous case of Dr Cox ((1992) 12 BMLR 38), a case due for consideration in Chapter 4 – indicated that he was considering a 'nominal sentence' in the event of conviction.

Ognall did, however, commend the decision to prosecute, warning that prosecutors who failed to do so would be in dereliction of their duties (see Biggs 1996: 878). The message from the Bench is nevertheless decidedly mixed, as other judges have expressed dismay at the decision to prosecute a mercy killer. Few have been as openly sympathetic as Branson J was in 1927, when he observed that had an animal been suffering as much as the patient in question, the defendant would have been punished for *not* 'putting an end to its suffering' (*Lancet* 1927). Yet, even today there are judges who will tell the defendant he should not have found himself in court (*The Times* 1980), and who will single out the CPS for criticism. Turner J, for example, berated the prosecutors for hiding behind 'legalese' when trying to justify their decision to proceed with a charge of attempted murder against Mr Bouldstridge, who had failed in his efforts to kill himself and his chronically ill wife (Kelso 2000: 1).

The message is therefore very confused. The CPS maintains that homicide offences will 'virtually always' come to trial (House of Lords Select Committee 1994c: 83), and this does at least chime with the official rhetoric that mercy killing is and remains murder. Yet, the sympathetic disposals passed down by the judiciary along with the outright resistance to prosecution displayed by some of their members pull the law in the opposite direction, implying that there is a route available for diverting the mercy killer from the courtroom.

6 Conclusion: collusion, compromise and confusion

Logic aside, and short of legislative intervention, it currently remains highly likely that someone in Mr Heginbotham's position will be summoned to the dock. He or she will be told that mercy killing is murder; they will be warned that the law makes no concession to the allegedly merciful circumstances of the crime; but they will almost certainly walk free from the courtroom, having been judged to have acted under 'diminished responsibility'. As Guido Calabresi so perceptively puts it:

> As a result we can have it both ways by both forbidding euthanasia and freeing mercy killers. It is, of course, a lie because we want, and get, what

formally we deny we wanted. But it is a lie that works well because juries work reasonably well.

(1985: 89)

In the English context at least, the jury is rarely in fact required to utter the lie, for the whole process is engineered to securing the desired result. Put simply, juries seldom need to exercise their independence. Instead, it is the lawyers, the expert witnesses and, in particular, the judges who ensure that these defendants are re-labelled as 'exceptional' manslaughterers who do not deserve serious punishment.

I believe that the clemency shown in the courts, and particularly the use of non-custodial sentences, is often appropriate. There is, however, still work to be done in this area. The appropriation of diminished responsibility is particularly questionable, as is the recurrent mantra that mercy killing is murder. Neither quite captures the lived, and legal, reality of mercy killing. Calabresi rightly cites this as a 'tragic conflict', which has required the law to make a 'tragic choice' between competing ethical norms. On the one hand, the process strives to preserve a measure of condemnation, undoubtedly reflecting the belief in the intrinsic value of all human lives to which English law still holds.[6] On the other hand, the process seeks also to recognise these killings as somehow less heinous than others, insofar as the defendant was acting from merciful motives. This latter thinking is more in line with the belief that life might only have value for as long as it is enjoyed without suffering. The chosen solution, as Calabresi describes it, is one that is designed to 'cover the difficulty and permit us to assert that we are cleaving to both beliefs in conflict' (1985: 88).

Can English law coherently cling to the sanctity of life, whilst simultaneously conceding that it might not be so bad to end a life of poor quality? I will argue that it can, and that a better way of articulating this compromise of values lies in the creation of a reduced offence, such as was advanced by the Criminal Law Revision Committee, and more recently considered by the Law Commission. The seeds for this sort of legal response have already been sown: combatants over the ethics of euthanasia seem to invest all their energies in the notion of *justification*, but the law is seeking to mediate a middle way, premised on the idea of *excuse*. Of course, as the 1976 Committee found, any explicit proposal to enable mercy killings to evade the full rigour of the criminal law is likely to be criticised from all angles. Opponents of euthanasia will think that this marks a further devaluation of human life; proponents, meanwhile, will think that the reform does not go far enough. These charges will be answered in the final chapter. For now, it must suffice to say that defence of the compromise is worthwhile, but that there is still work to do in crafting, and then applying, a clearer and more coherent legal framework.

6   See further Chapter 5.

That work must wait until we have a more complete picture of mercy killing as it is depicted in English law. Attention here has been focused primarily on the mercy killer as manslaughterer. This is not the only label available to such defendants, for the distinct offence of complicity in suicide has largely become the preserve of mercy killers. This offence warrants separate attention, because – it should be no surprise to learn – the law in this area is no more coherent than that which has already been examined.

Chapter 3

Assisted suicide in 'the shadowy area of mercy killing'

A person who aids, abets, counsels or procures the suicide of another, or an attempt by another to commit suicide, shall be liable on conviction or indictment to imprisonment for a term not exceeding fourteen years.

Suicide Act 1961, s 2(1)

It is a crime, whether you pigeon-hole it under attempted murder or assisting a suicide. In terms of gravity it can vary from the borders of cold-blooded murder down to the shadowy area of mercy killing or common humanity.

Hough (1984) 6 Cr App Rep (S) 406 *per*
Lord Lane CJ at 409

I have 'aided, abetted and counselled' one suicide, and I am involved in possibly three future suicides. But, as the suicide occurred, or perhaps will occur, abroad, am I guilty of committing a crime in this country? It seems that no one currently knows the proper legal answer.

(Irwin 2004a: 1440)

On 20 July 1997, *The Sunday Times* sparked a national debate on assisted suicide and euthanasia, which ultimately led to the prosecution of a GP, when its cover carried the headline 'Doctor Admits Killing 50 People' (Austin 1997: 1). The accused GP, Dr David Moor, had not actually initiated the furore. Moor's trial resulted from incautious comments he had made in support of the featured doctor, Michael Irwin. Irwin was, at that time, Vice Chairman of the VES, and he had also previously practised as a GP and then more recently as a Medical Director of the United Nations and World Bank.

Dr Moor was not convicted, apparently because the jury accepted that his intention had been only to kill pain, not his patient, an issue which will resurface in the next chapter. Irwin too had spoken of giving pain-relieving drugs like morphine to terminally ill patients, but he claimed to have had a rather different aim: 'the intention of my actions was to end their lives and not only ease their suffering' (Murray 1997a: 1). Mr Irwin also admitted to having helped a number of his patients to commit suicide. According to Irwin, he would provide sedatives and a customised plastic bag, which could be sealed over the patient's head after they had taken the pills, so that they would suffocate while they slept. He confessed to having done this at least once in the past six months, although he denied having placed the bag in position himself.

The British Medical Association (BMA) urged for Irwin to be both charged by the CPS and disciplined by the General Medical Council (GMC), but despite a police investigation no formal proceedings ensued. Action was to be taken, however, after Irwin once more publicised his experiences of offering assistance in suicide (Wainwright 2003: 11). On this occasion, Irwin was much more explicit about his intended role in the death of Patrick Kneen, a fellow euthanasia campaigner who was dying of prostate cancer. Irwin had travelled to Mr Kneen's home in the Isle of Man, equipped with a large dose of sedatives. However, by the time he arrived, Mr Kneen was no longer capable of swallowing the pills, and died a few days later, after being sedated by his GP. Both the retired doctor and Mr Kneen's wife Patricia were questioned by Manx police on suspicion of conspiring to assist in suicide. Although Irwin claimed he had furnished the police with ample evidence of his intentions (Irwin 2004), no charges were brought. The publicity surrounding Mr Kneen's plight nevertheless prompted a legislative review of the issues by the House of Keys (2006).

Back in England, Irwin faced further official scrutiny, which initially resulted in a police caution for possession with intent to supply temazepam, a class C drug. This time the GMC took note, and disciplinary proceedings were initiated in 2005 (Dyer 2005). The panel concluded that Irwin had abused his position as a doctor and he was struck from the register as unfit to practice. Irwin was criticised for stockpiling temazepam and falsely claiming the tablets were for his personal use in relieving jetlag, with the panel further noting that it was a criminal offence to have written the prescription in his own name, when the drugs were intended to help Mr Kneen to die.

The following year Irwin was brought back in for police questioning, this time over the death of May Murphy (Dyer 2006: 256). Mrs Murphy had committed suicide in Zurich, with the help of the organisation Dignitas. Having accompanied her on the flight from Scotland, Irwin had been present when Mrs Murphy took the fatal dose of barbiturates. This was the first time he had travelled with someone to the clinic, although he had previously admitted to helping and advising five other British citizens who were considering making the trip.

In 2003, in the midst of investigations, Irwin had resigned from his position with the VES and, in an echo of events two decades previously, the organisation soon changed its name, this time to Dignity in Dying.[1] In 1981 the society had shed the moniker EXIT, after former General Secretary Nicholas Reed was sentenced to 18 months' imprisonment for his role in facilitating assistance in suicide. Then, as now, the organization insisted that its aim was to achieve a change in the law, not to operate outside its current boundaries.

In order to operate within the boundaries of the law, the members of Dignity in Dying, no less than any other citizens in this jurisdiction, will need to be aware of where those boundaries lie. Unfortunately, while it is clear that assisting in another's death looks likely to amount to a crime of some sort, it is difficult to predict in advance when and how the law might be called into operation. Mr Irwin's alleged activities amply illustrate the ambiguities. When will providing the pills amount to the offence of complicity in suicide? If Irwin had fixed an 'exit bag' in place, would this have transformed his act from one of assistance in suicide to one of murder? Is it illegal to offer advice and support to a seriously ill individual who is contemplating suicide? When is it unlawful to be involved in so-called 'death tourism'? And what about merely knowing that someone intends to commit suicide, which they subsequently do, albeit without any advice or assistance from you?

As the opening quotations show, this is an area of the law rife with uncertainty. Of one thing we can all be reasonably certain: assistance in suicide is currently a crime. This was unambiguously confirmed in the rulings denying Dianne Pretty's claim that she had the right to be helped to die by her husband. Quite how long this barrier will remain, however, is open to question, particularly when some commentators detect a relaxation in the prohibition on 'death tourism', and in view of increasing pressure to change the law (e.g. De Cruz 2005: 266). Nevertheless, the basic prohibition on helping someone to die in this country still stands, although its foundations look rather misshapen. This chapter will demonstrate how complicity in suicide offers the legal officials an alternative category to 'diminished responsibility' for dealing with the mercy killer. Familiar problems of partiality and empty rhetoric resurface but the central concern here is that the answers given to the questions just posed tend to be confused and, on some occasions, blatantly contradictory.

I What is assisted suicide?

Apart from the disputes that persist over the ethics of (physician) assisted suicide, the concept of 'assisted suicide' is itself susceptible to conflicting interpretations. That uncertainty has spilt over into the legal domain, in the confusion that surrounds the offence of complicity in suicide. An individual who 'aids, abets, counsels or procures' another's suicide or suicide attempt

---

1   Irwin was, however, quickly co-opted onto the Council of the Scottish euthanasia society FATE (Friends At The End) (see Irwin 2004b).

risks imprisonment for up to 14 years and the DPP must consent to prosecutions for this offence (Suicide Act 1961, ss 2(1), 2(4)). Beyond this, however, there is very little that is clear or uncontroversial about this offence.

1.1 Guilty for aiding the innocent

The first curiosity is that the offence even exists at all, since the Suicide Act decriminalised suicide (s 1). Whether this afforded a right or liberty to commit suicide will be considered later. Assisting a suicide nevertheless remained illegal, and this legal obstacle has prompted some patients to act alone, while they still could (e.g. Anonymous 1997: 20), one of whom made legal history after she suffocated herself with a plastic bag. The coroner recorded the verdict as: 'taking her own life as a believer in euthanasia'. Derek Humphry, whose 'suicide manual' *Final Exit* (1991) detailed the method, praised the verdict as a 'sign of great progress. Let's hope it starts a trend' (*The Times* 1994).

Humphry would undoubtedly prefer there to be no prohibition on assisting in suicide. The offence certainly looks unusual, and 'the seeming inconsistency of outlawing the assistance or encouragement of a lawful act' has not gone unnoticed (Price 1996: 271). Debating the Bill, Lord Denning, amongst others (see HC Deb Vol 644 Col 843, 14 July 1961; HL Deb Vol 229 Cols 536, 549, 9 March 1961), remarked on the oddity of committing complicity in suicide when 'logically' it was no longer possible to 'commit' suicide (HL Deb Vol 229 Col 265, 2 March 1961). Denning welcomed the Bill, however, and he tentatively conceded the need for such an offence (HL Deb Vol 229 Cols 265–266, 2 March 1961). The Law Lords recently took a similar view, basing it upon the need to uphold the sanctity of life and protect the vulnerable (*R (on the application of Pretty) v DPP* [2002] 1 FLR 268). Yet, if the prohibition is to succeed as a legal rule its parameters need to be clearly defined.

1.2 Publishers in peril

The first case that sought to clarify the boundaries of the offence was *Attorney General v Able and Others* [1984] 1 QB 795, in which Woolf J was asked to consider the legality of a booklet that contained information on methods of committing suicide (see Smith 1983). Aware that the booklet was implicated in a number of suicides, the Attorney General sought a declaration that its supply constituted an offence; the suppliers of the booklet, the VES, at that time headed by Nicholas Reed, argued to the contrary.

No declaration was issued. Woolf ruled that the VES would be guilty of complicity in suicide if it knew that suicide was contemplated, it approved of or assented to the act, and it in fact encouraged the suicide or suicide attempt. The necessary intention to assist was essential (see 809A–G, 810D–E, 812D–E, 812G–813B). The judge did, however, leave open the possibility of some 'exceptional circumstance which means that an offence is not established' (812G).

The ruling prompted the VES to stop circulating the booklet to its members. Significantly, the ranks of the Scottish VES soon swelled, as the ruling did not apply in Scotland – where it is doubtful that there even exists an offence of complicity in suicide (Mason and Laurie 2006: 611). Nowadays, however, books like the aforementioned *Final Exit* can be found in English bookshops, and advice also exists on the internet, including from such figures as Dr Philip Nitschke, who had practised voluntary euthanasia in the Northern Territory of Australia during the brief period when this was legal (see Austin 1998). There have nevertheless not been any prosecutions of publishers or suppliers, which suggests that the possibility is now more apparent than real (Freeman 1999: 220).

1.3 Assisting, assisting an attempt, and attempting to assist in an attempt

Woolf's ruling also went beyond the specific issue of advice, since he sought to provide more general clarification of the terms of the offence. The *mens rea* (or mental component of the offence) settled as 'intention', Woolf proceeded to examine the phrase 'aid, abet, counsel or procure' (s 2(1)). He cited Hale and Coke as authorities for the proposition that both 'aiding' and 'abetting' could apply to accessories who provided assistance at the time of or before the act in question (i.e. suicide) (at 808G–H). The other two terms seemed to relate exclusively to assistance given before the act was performed. Woolf J further relied upon Lord Widgery CJ's statement that '[t]o procure means to produce by endeavour' but he failed to define the remaining words (*Attorney General's Reference (No 1 of 1975)* [1975] 2 All ER 684, at 686). The judge felt that he did not need to say too much, as he concluded that the phrase was best considered as a whole in ascertaining whether an offence had been committed (at 809A).

Further guidance might nevertheless be needed, so as to distinguish the criminal from the innocent. Judging by the general principles of accomplice liability, 'aiding' and 'abetting' require more than mere non-accidental presence: an actual agreement, encouragement or assistance is needed (e.g. *Clarkson* [1971] 1 WLR 1402; *Wilcox v Jeffrey* [1951] 1 All ER 464). If I help you take the tablets that are intended to end your life, I might be said to have aided or abetted you in your suicide. To 'counsel', the defendant and the victim must have reached a consensus, where mere contact between the two can suffice (e.g. *Giannetto* [1997] 1 Cr App Rep 1). This might be where advice fits in: if you have purchased some pills and I advise you about the quantity to take in order to end your life, I might be said to have counselled your suicide. Finally, 'procuring' does not require consensus but there must be a causal link between the defendant's procurement and the commission of the offence (*Attorney General's Reference (No 1 of 1975)* [1975] 2 All ER 684, at 687). Here one might think of me purchasing the pills that you intend to take in order to end your life.

There nevertheless remain issues to be settled. One issue that was clarified, in fact before Woolf J ruled, concerned attempts at assisting suicide (see Ash 1982). Secret video surveillance recorded a Mrs McShane, who was in financial difficulty, advising her mother on how to consume an overdose ((1977) 66 Cr App Rep 97). McShane instructed her mother that her daughter's part in the suicide must remain secret or else she would be denied an inheritance. McShane's appeal against her conviction for attempting to counsel or procure her mother's suicide was dismissed. Orr LJ ruled that every *attempt* to commit an offence was an offence, notwithstanding that the crime itself was defined in 'the nature of an attempt' (at 103). Mrs Mott did not need to have formed an intention to commit suicide: it is, therefore, possible for an accomplice to be guilty of attempting to assist a suicide that is never attempted.

This all still leaves open the thorny question of what state of mind I must have in order to be judged a criminal. In 1998, the House of Lords confirmed in the case of *Woollin* [1998] 4 All ER 103 that I can be found to have intended a result where I foresee that result as a virtually certain consequence of my action. The case concerned an allegation of murder, involving a father who had thrown his baby against a wall – and we are apparently to assume that the principle applies equally to the crime of complicity in suicide. So, if I purchase a large quantity of lawfully available pills and store them in the home that I share with my ailing and suicidal relative, am I implicated in their overdose even if I did nothing further? Was this 'intentional' or merely reckless on my part – and, if the latter, will or should that suffice (Freeman 1999: 220)? Some of these ambiguities will be revisited throughout the remainder of this chapter.

1.4 Pills, pillows and pistols

It should already be clear that the offence of complicity in suicide can be committed in a variety of ways, and the courts have certainly dealt with a diverse range of conduct. Supplying the pills tends to be seen as the 'classic' case, and I will return to this, but another common example involves the assistant helping to suffocate the suicidal patient. Recent years have seen the convictions of Mr Jackson, Mr Francis, Mrs Jennison, Mrs Pratten, Mr Holden and Mr March, each of whom helped to secure a plastic bag or pillow over the head of their loved one (see *The Times* 1980; Mills and Winsper 1991; Stokes 1998; *Daily Telegraph* 2000; Teeman 2002; Horsnell 2006). Mr Beecham and Mrs O'Donohoe, meanwhile, connected hoses to the exhaust pipe of the car in which their relative sat (see Horder 1988; *The Times* 1988; Jones 1991; De Ionno 1991).

There are, however, cases that less obviously resemble the scenarios usually depicted in bioethical debates on assisted suicide. The courts have, for example, found that you can assist in a suicide by helping your loved one to drown, as Mr Young did; to hang, as Mr Ridler did; and even to shoot herself, as Mr Pitman did (see *Liverpool Daily Post* 1982; (1984) 24 *Med Sci Law* 304; Woodcock 1984; *Guardian* 1984; De Bruxelles 1997: 7). Furthermore, unlike the concept of assisted suicide in bioethics, the offence does not appear to hinge on the consent of the victim. On even the most basic definition of 'suicide', the suicider must will an end to his or her life (e.g. Price 1996: 275). One might also think that assistance in suicide requires the consensual participation of both parties; yet, complicity in suicide does not. The much-publicised case of Nicholas Reed and 'Doctor' Lyons provides a good example of this.

Reed, the General Secretary of the VES, had put patients in contact with self-appointed 'Doctor' Lyons, who would visit them equipped with his 'suicide kit'. The circumstances of the case are obviously remarkable – the VES was later keen to distance itself from Reed's behaviour (Rusbridger 1981d: 1) – and the trial contains some bizarre features. Lyons, for example, took three hours to tell the court that he was controlled by a 'puppet master', who was millions of years old and who resided in a tiny hole in the top of Lyons' head (Rusbridger 1981c).

One can only guess at what such revelations were meant to achieve, but, in the event, both men were convicted. Reed was found to have procured assistance in suicide, and his appeals to the Court of Appeal ([1982] Crim LR 819) and to the European Court of Human Rights (App. No. 10083/82 *R v United Kingdom* [1983] 6 EHRR 140) were roundly rejected. Lyons was also found guilty on a number of counts of complicity in suicide, but it is notable how some of his activities seemed to fall outside the terms of the offence altogether. Indeed, some look more like attempts at involuntary euthanasia, since a number of patients reportedly tried to stop him in his actions. One woman, who changed her mind about committing suicide, was told by Lyons that he didn't want any 'bloody arguments' the next time he came to help her (Rusbridger 1981a: 3). The court heard a recording of Lyons saying 'you stupid bitch, why should you lead me on a wild goose chase?' (Rusbridger 1981b). Another man changed his mind after he began to feel 'doubtful about the set-up'. Indeed he went so far as to comment that 'I felt it was more like murder than anything else' (ibid). In other cases, despite welcoming the assistance, the patient appeared to play no active role in bringing about their death, which, on the definitions considered in Chapter 1, suggests that a label like 'voluntary euthanasia' might be more accurate. Of course, euthanasia – whether voluntary or involuntary – is more readily described in law as an act of murder. The prosecutors did at least appear to recognise this in Lyons' case, by additionally charging him with murder, of which he was acquitted.

Clearly, then, the offence of complicity in suicide can include a range of activities. The problem, however, is that it is still not always clear whether a particular action will amount to this crime, some other crime (like murder), or no crime at all. It is to this difficulty I now turn.

2 Looking for borders in 'shadowy areas'

At the outset of this chapter Lord Lane CJ described complicity in suicide as an offence that can encompass cases which range 'from the borders of cold blooded murder down to the shadowy area of mercy killing'. This is in the nature of the criminal law, which can cover various actions and has a range of related offences available for exchange as the circumstances require. Unfortunately, the numerous 'shadowy areas' surrounding complicity in suicide threaten to destabilise the legitimacy of the law and leave mercy killers in genuine doubt as to when and how they might be called to account. This can be seen in the way that similar cases attract divergent legal responses and particularly in three situations where no clear lead has been provided by the lawyers: the recent development known as 'death tourism', the not-so-straightforward case of supplying the pills, and the remarkable case of assisting a suicide by omission.

2.1 Stretching the borders of assisted suicide

As the previous section suggested, Mr Lyons' conduct shows that the s 2 offence can cover cases that might more accurately be described as murder or some other form of homicide. It did not escape Parliament's notice, during the passage of the Suicide Bill, that the proposed offence could prove useful in cases of mercy killing (see HC Deb Vol 644 Col 843, 14 July 1961). This is not objectionable in principle; what is problematic is that one cannot always foresee how a particular mercy killing will be characterised and treated by the lawyers.

The case of *Robey* (1979) 1 Cr App Rep (S) 127 exemplifies the lottery. Here, a man was convicted of complicity in suicide, after helping his wife to stab herself. Mrs Robey had inserted the knife into her chest, but not far enough to prove fatal; Mr Robey assisted by driving the knife further in. Glanville Williams described this as an example of 'a case of consent-killing occasionally reduced to one of [complicity in] suicide' (1983: 580).

Mr Robey had actually been charged with murder, and he was fortunate that the jury returned the lesser verdict of complicity in suicide, since the judge had refused to accept his plea. However, the court has accepted such a plea in numerous other cases, including those of Mr Francis, Mr Jackson, Mr Pitman and Mrs Jennison. Counsel for Mrs Jennison detected a 'perilously fine line' between murder and complicity in suicide (Stokes 1998: 5), but it seems the reason why the lesser charge succeeded in her case was because this was deemed a mercy killing. This would explain, for example, why the judge felt that the higher charge would have been inappropriate given (again) the 'exceptionality' of the case, and why *The Times* reported that the lesser charge was brought against Mr Pitman 'when the details emerged' (De Bruxelles 1997: 7). Mr Pitman had held a shotgun in his mother's mouth, so that she could pull the trigger.

This type of legal manoeuvre should be familiar: the mercy killer, unlike other killers, is not a murderer, but is instead legally reconstructed as a manslaughterer or, now, an assistant in suicide. The difficulty is that no one can predict in advance how the mercy killer will be dealt with. In 1978, Mrs Lyons was charged with murder, after helping to hold a knife to her 'depressed and ill' mother-in-law's back, as the latter pushed her body back onto it (Hill 1978). Mrs Lyons' plea of guilty to manslaughter by reason of diminished responsibility was accepted. But why was complicity in suicide not charged or substituted as occurred with Mr Robey and, more recently, Mr Pitman?

The case of Charlotte Hough exacerbates the confusion ((1984) 6 Cr App Rep (S) 406). Mrs Hough provided sleeping tablets and a sealable plastic bag to her friend, who took the overdose unaided. Mrs Hough later secured the plastic bag over Mrs Johnson's head. The initial charge was murder, but this was reduced to attempted murder when doubt was raised as to whether the bag had actually caused the death. Hough was convicted and sentenced to nine months' imprisonment. What Mrs Hough did shares some resemblance with the activities of Mrs McShane, Mr Jackson and Mrs Pratten, all of whom were convicted of complicity in suicide. In the Court of Appeal, Lord Lane CJ accepted that the case 'fell to a great extent within the terms of the Suicide Act 1961, s 2' (at 409). To add to the confusion, Thomas' quasi-official manual, *Current Sentencing Practice*, includes the case in that category.

Too much fluidity threatens the conceptual clarity of the criminal law. However, this is more than a matter of fair labelling (Ashworth 2003: 89–92). Of more practical importance is the disposal that the mercy killer might expect. A murder conviction will lead inevitably to the mandatory life sentence of imprisonment; manslaughter and attempted murder have this as the maximum penalty; complicity in suicide, meanwhile, means no more than 14 years' incarceration. We know, however, and will see again, that the mercy killer should not expect a harsh disposal. Nevertheless, being branded a murderer, with all that entails, looks an altogether different prospect from being branded an assistant in suicide.

2.2 Assisted suicide beyond the borders: the curious case of 'death tourism'

It should, at least, have been obvious to Mr Robey and Mrs Lyons that what they were doing was in some way prohibited. On other occasions the legality or illegality of an action is entirely unpredictable. The modern phenomenon of 'death tourism', in which Michael Irwin was allegedly a participant, is a good case in point. Here, a friend, relative or a doctor helps a patient to travel abroad, currently to Switzerland, where they will be assisted in their suicide. Is helping the patient to get there an offence? And if so, what sort of help is innocent and what sort of help is blameworthy?

Michael Irwin asked these questions of the prosecutors in his case but no clear answers have been forthcoming. Death tourism is nevertheless on the rise. To date, at least 54 British citizens have travelled to Switzerland to receive help from the organisation Dignitas (Minelli 2006). The Swiss policy appears to be unique. In jurisdictions like the Netherlands, Belgium, Oregon and, previously, Australia's Northern Territories, assisted suicide can only be sought by a resident and performed by a doctor (see e.g. Nys 1999; Jackson 2006: 960–972). These restrictions are absent in Switzerland: Article 115 of the Penal Code only condemns assistance in suicide where this is motivated by selfish reasons. In the circumstances of a mercy killing, where the patient autonomously wishes to die, there will be no prosecution, even if the patient is a foreign national and the assistant has no medical qualifications (Hurst and Mauron 2003).

Although some organisations like Exit Deutsche Schweiz have distanced themselves from the practice of helping suicide tourists (Bosshard, Ulrich and Bär 2003: 316), Dignitas has seen its membership rise to 2,500 (Avery 2003) and has helped at least 619 members to die (Minelli 2006). Founded on 17 May 1998 by retired journalist and lawyer Ludwig Minelli, the non-profit organisation requires confirmation from a doctor of the patient's condition before it will facilitate the suicide. Although at least one Swiss hospital has decided to allow the practice to occur on its premises (Chapman 2006: 7), Dignitas currently books an apartment in which the assistant, often a nurse, will provide a fatal dose of barbiturates, which have been prescribed by a Swiss doctor.

The first high profile example of a Briton employing the services of Dignitas involved 74-year-old Reginald Crew. Mr Crew, who was paraplegic and in constant pain, travelled to Zurich with his wife, daughter and a documentary film crew in January 2003. He was actually the second Briton to have made the trip, but his suicide became particularly newsworthy when it emerged that his wife Win, 71, was under investigation by Merseyside police officers (Dyer 2003). In the end, no charge was brought against her.

Given what is known about the requirements imposed by Dignitas, one must assume that a doctor had prepared the necessary report on Mr Crew's condition. So, did the doctor, the Crew family and the documentary makers commit any offence in this jurisdiction? First, consider their intentions. Mr Crew's family members, presumably, at least intended to help him to get to Switzerland; furthermore, they might well have intended to help him to get there in order that he be assisted to die. The doctor and the film crew might not have intended to help him in this way. However, they look likely to have known of Mr Crew's intentions: why else prepare the report and film the trip? Here the *Woollin* ruling must be brought to bear: if they knew that their parts in the process were virtually certain to facilitate Mr Crew's suicide, then did they not (legally) intend to bring about that result?

The intention to assist in suicide will undoubtedly be present in some of these types of cases. The problem, however, is that the act occurred outside this jurisdiction. Does this render any intention to assist or even any preparatory acts (such as booking the flights or researching options) innocent? In response to Irwin's queries, Charles Foster, a barrister, concluded that 'it is at least arguable that the intended site of the suicide, and the lawfulness of the suicide in that jurisdiction, are irrelevant to the lawfulness of the aiding, abetting, counselling or procuring' (2004). Foster cited legal authorities, which, for example, show that unsafe driving is unsafe driving whether in this jurisdiction or elsewhere (*Cox v Army Council* [1962] 2 WLR 950), blackmail is blackmail whether in this jurisdiction or elsewhere (*Treacy v DPP* [1971] AC 537), and a creditor is a creditor whether in this jurisdiction or elsewhere (*R v Smith (Wallace Duncan) (No 1)* [1996] 2 Cr App R 1). By extension, suicide is suicide, and it matters not that the final act occurs abroad: one can be in this country and still assist that act. In addition, if some elements of the (preparatory) assistance take place in England, then the argument that an offence has been committed here becomes much stronger.

Foster, nevertheless, felt that the arguments needed to be tested in court: 'Dr Irwin has thrown down the towel to the Crown Prosecution Service. They should take it up' (2004). Irwin was indeed investigated, but even before this occurred death tourism managed to find its way into an English courtroom via a different route, in the case of *Re Z (Local Authority: Duty)* [2005] 1 WLR 959. Mrs Z, who was 65, had the degenerative brain condition cerebella ataxia. Although she lived at home with her husband, she required extensive support from her local authority. Mrs Z began to express the wish to die, which her family came to accept. She made an advance directive refusing life supporting treatment, but also wished to travel to Switzerland to be assisted in her suicide. Mr Z arranged the trip for his wife, whom he intended to accompany. The local authority, on being informed of this by Mr Z, argued that Mrs Z was a 'vulnerable person' and so obtained a temporary injunction restraining Mr Z from moving his wife from the jurisdiction. A psychiatrist was called upon, who confirmed that Mrs Z was legally competent to make her own decisions and that the decision to travel had been hers alone.

The case was brought before Hedley J in the High Court, who discharged the injunction. Focusing upon the duties of the local authority towards vulnerable persons, the judge held that the main task was to ensure that the decision was reached competently, voluntarily and on the basis of sufficient information, as he found it had been in this case. The local authority could call on the High Court for assistance in making these assessments, but if, like Mrs Z, the patient was found to be autonomous, then no further obstacle could be placed in their way.

The VES immediately latched onto the ruling as signalling 'that the Suicide Act is on its last legs' (Rozenberg 2004: 1), and it does seem to suggest that death tourism involves no violation of the law, despite the authorities just consulted. Hedley J, however, was sitting in a civil court and he did not feel it was his place to clarify the criminal law (para 21). 'The position of Mr Z', he noted, 'is much less clear', but he did feel it 'inevitable that by making arrangements and escorting Mrs Z on the flight, Mr Z will have contravened section 2(1)' (para 14).

This looks like a clear enough direction: participating in death tourism can involve an offence. But the decision as to whether or not Mr Z and others like him ought to be prosecuted will be left to the criminal justice agencies, as Hedley J stated (para 21). Since complicity in suicide can only be charged with the consent of the DPP, it seems the answer must lie with the holder of this position. No DPP, however, has agreed to issue any guidance on the policy in this area. Is death tourism an offence? Perhaps – but it seems no one who engages in it can know in advance whether the weight of the criminal law will be brought to bear.

2.3 The classic case of providing the pills

The next situation should be more familiar: the seemingly 'classic' case of supplying the pills. This looks like the clearest example of complicity in suicide: I aid, abet, counsel or procure the suicide by purchasing the medication, advising on the amount to take, or helping someone to take the overdose. Yet, even here the law is not clear in its application and scope.

Some such cases have indeed resulted in a guilty verdict. Mrs McShane was convicted after providing pills to her mother (as we saw previously) and there are various other examples, sometimes involving a mercy killing, as in the cases against Mr Wallis, Mr Loughran and Mrs Jennison, and sometimes not, as in the cases against Ms Hudson (*The Times* 1975) and Mr Osborne ((1991) 13 Cr App Rep (S) 225). But one then encounters the case against Mr Chard, who had purchased medication for his suicidal friend Martina Reeve. Chard was acquitted after Pownall J directed that there was no evidence to support the prosecution case that he had assisted in suicide. 'He only provided her with an option of taking her own life by buying for her the paracetamol tablets and that is not enough' (Gorman 1993: 3).

This is a curious direction, as the Court of Appeal did not doubt the validity of the charge in relation to Mrs McShane, Mr Wallis and Mr Osborne. It might nevertheless be argued that one can make sense of the acquittal by focusing on the defendant's *mens rea*. Perhaps, as the law then stood, the defendant lacked the requisite intention to assist in the suicide.[2] But would this necessarily be the case today, following the direction in *Woollin*, in which the Lords

---

2   See the next chapter for further discussion of how the legal definition of 'intention' has shifted, specifically over the issue of so-called 'oblique' intention, where the actor might foresee an outcome as virtually certain to occur as a result of his or her action.

confirmed that foresight of a consequence could amount to intending that consequence? Mr Chard reportedly told the police: 'She wanted me to buy her the paracetamol. It was her wish to have the option to take her own life' (ibid). He might not have directly intended that his friend take an overdose. Were I to purchase pills for my friend, I too might not directly intend that my friend take them. However, knowing her current feelings, I might at least be said to foresee that my supplying the pills is likely – perhaps even virtually certain – to result in her overdosing. Would I be guilty as an accomplice?

We lack a clear answer to this question. If the prospect of conviction is real, then there must be some injustice in a system that allows one defendant to walk free while another could emerge with a criminal conviction. Unfortunately, the system appears even less just when we consider the types of cases usually canvassed in the bioethics literature. There, the person depicted as supplying or leaving the pills is not a friend or a relative, but a physician (e.g. Jackson 2004). Leaving aside the case of the self-appointed 'Doctor' Lyons, what happens when a doctor is involved?

It cannot realistically be claimed that doctors never supply medication to their patients in the knowledge that they will use this to end their lives. As the next chapter will show, robust data can be hard to come by, but there are at least indications that physician assisted suicide is a reality in this jurisdiction. A study by the *BMA News Review* in 1996 revealed that 22 of 750 GPs had offered some form of assistance. That same year, McLean and Britton's (1996; 1997) study of 1,000 health professionals concluded that 4 per cent had assisted in death, while in 1998 *The Sunday Times* found that one in seven of 300 GPs had helped in some way (Norton 1998).

These findings can be coupled with revelations from individuals like Michael Irwin, who featured at the start of this chapter. Others too claim to have breached the law. One unnamed GP in *The Sunday Times* admitted to leaving painkilling drugs with the relatives of his patients. He would warn them of the dose that would prove fatal: 'I know full well that before I have gone round the corner they will have given him that extra dose' (Norton 1998: 14). Similarly surreptitious activities have been remarked on in the past. The 'Brompton mixture', for example, was a lethal combination of analgesic drugs that would apparently be left at a patient's bedside. The patient would be advised that consuming the cocktail would be lethal – with predictable results (Williams 1983: 579).

However, to date, no doctor has been convicted of or even prosecuted for complicity in suicide. Why might this be the case? Prosecutors may, of course, fear that the trial will be a waste of public money. Moreover, it may be even concluded that a prosecution might not be in the public interest, given that the jury will be drawn from a population apparently in thrall to the idea of assisted suicide (House of Lords Select Committee 2005a: 125–127). This is an issue that will arise again in the next chapter. It might also be that there has never been sufficient evidence to warrant a trial.[3] Alternatively, the professional and legal obligation to maintain confidentiality might present an insurmountable barrier. Doctors could indeed be wary of disclosing their actions for fear not only of facing a criminal trial but also of breaching their obligation to their patient (Otlowski 1997: 134–135). There is an analogous precedent in the case of Russel Ogden, a Canadian student who investigated mercy killings of patients with AIDs. He successfully argued before a coroner that he could not reveal the identity of his research subjects (Lowman and Palys 2000; see also Ogden 1995).

However, the need to preserve confidentiality might not be a complete explanation for the absence of proceedings against doctors in this jurisdiction. A major exception to the obligation is where disclosure is warranted in the public interest, for example in order to prevent serious crime (e.g. *W v Egdell* [1990] 1 All ER 835). Homicide, one might think, is a serious crime. On a more practical level, it is worth noting that the alleged incidents revealed in, for example, *The Sunday Times*, occurred in hospices and hospitals. Teamwork is a fundamental feature of the modern NHS. Certainly, and despite legislative changes, there will undoubtedly remain some resistance on the part of health professionals to 'blowing the whistle' on their colleagues (Quick 1999). Nevertheless, the alleged prevalence and location of these activities suggest that some, at least, could have been discovered, investigated and brought before a court.

Not only is the law uncertain about whether providing the pills will amount to an offence, it is also apparently unfair, since the layperson looks more likely to face charges than the doctor. Such inconsistency is not only present in this context, however. Our next group of cases shows that the doctor is also unlikely to breach the criminal law when he refrains from rescuing an apparently suicidal patient. The layperson, however, confronts the prospect that, in similar circumstances, he or she may be deemed a 'passive' assistant in suicide.

2.4 Left to die

Sue Lawson was diagnosed with multiple sclerosis at the age of 34 and by the time she was 48 'she had got to the end of her tether and wanted to die', according to her brother Graham (BBC 2005a). 'No one else could do it for her, she had to do it herself', he explained, and on her eighth attempt she succeeded in ending her life by suffocating herself with a plastic bag. The police initially suspected that Mr Lawson had played an active role in her suicide. However, five months after his arrest, no charge was brought, as the investigators appeared satisfied that he had done nothing more than watch his sister take her final action.

---

3   Mr Irwin was, however, very sceptical about this claim (see Irwin 2004b).

Suicide, of course, is not unlawful and so failing to prevent a suicide might also appear to fall outside the prosecutor's purview. There are, indeed, other situations resembling Sue Lawson's which did not result in prosecution. Thirty years earlier, in 1977, a Professor Whiteley was not charged for refraining from attempting to revive his wife or summon medical assistance after she had taken a deliberate overdose ((1977) 17 *Med Sci Law* 224). A few years afterwards, Dr Jordan went a little further than Professor Whiteley, in twice turning ambulance men away from her home, after her husband's overdose (1983 *General Practitioner* (9 September)). Mr Jordan had Parkinson's disease and had attempted suicide on three previous occasions. This time he had left a note instructing: 'do not resuscitate me'. The coroner confirmed that Dr Jordan bore no responsibility in her professional capacity as a doctor, but he urged the jury to consider her duty as a wife. An open verdict was recorded and no proceedings ensued. Another doctor, Dr Dean, also avoided prosecution when the DPP refused to instigate proceedings against him in relation to the death of Reginald Kennard ((1984) 24 *Med Sci Law* 304). Mr Kennard's home help had summoned the GP after finding the pensioner unconscious following an overdose. Mr Kennard had also left a note: 'let me die'. According to Dr Dean, 'I respected his wish'.

So far, so clear, one might think: although it will undoubtedly be difficult to do so, we are entitled to respect the wish of a loved one or a patient who has chosen to end their own life. Unfortunately, any apparent clarity in the law evaporates when one considers two cases of suicide that occurred in the late 1980s. In the first case, a Mr Cooper turned away a district nurse who was conducting a routine visit to his son-in-law, David Taylor, who, like Ms Lawson, had multiple sclerosis (*The Times* 1990; Cole 1992: 34–36). Upstairs, as Mr Cooper knew, his daughter was administering an overdose of 70 analgesics and tranquillisers to her husband, following his repeated requests that she help him to die. Also present in the family home at the time were Mrs Cooper and Mr Taylor's parents. Everyone present was charged with *attempting* to aid a suicide, as it was found that bronchial pneumonia, brought on by Mr Taylor's condition, had caused his demise and thus he was not found to have died as a result of the medication. Mrs Cooper and Mr Taylor's parents denied committing the offence, and were acquitted. Mrs Taylor was convicted and placed on probation, a result one might well expect given the trends noted in the previous chapter. What one might not expect is that Mr Cooper was also convicted and disposed of in the same way.

The second case again involved a patient with multiple sclerosis, 23-year-old Sara Johnson (*The Independent* 1989). Her parents had returned to their home, where Sara occupied an annexe, to find her unconscious after consuming three bottles of painkillers and tranquillisers. She had twice attempted suicide before, and had, after the first attempt, been admitted to a psychiatric unit for treatment. Knowing her frustration at failing in her previous attempts and that she was firmly opposed to them intervening or summoning medical intervention, Ms Johnson's parents sat with her for eight hours as she lay dying. Ms Johnson had typed a note stating, 'my illness and the psychiatric problems have reached the point which I simply cannot bear' (ibid). The Johnsons were both convicted of complicity in suicide and, passing probationary sentences, Garland J acknowledged that they were guilty of 'purely negative conduct': 'If you had taken any positive steps to assist her, it would have been my painful duty to impose a custodial sentence on you both' (ibid).

2.4.1 Passive complicity in suicide

The findings in Chapter 2 suggest that a custodial sentence would have been unlikely but whether *any* sentence should have been passed down to Mr and Mrs Johnson is also doubtful. One thing seems certain: merely being present at the suicide attempt should not be enough to imply complicity in suicide. The courts have confirmed, albeit in quite different scenarios involving alleged accomplices, that it is unacceptable 'to convict a man on his thoughts, unaccompanied by any physical act other than the facts of mere presence' (*Allan* [1965] 1 QB 130; see also *Bland* [1988] Crim LR).

Leading commentators have also doubted that there exists, in law, such a creature as 'passive complicity in suicide'. Glanville Williams certainly thought not: he once presumed that, since a bare omission could not lead to accomplice liability, one could not be prosecuted for failing to prevent a suicide (1983: 579), and his view is echoed elsewhere (e.g. Meyers 1990: 280). However, Andrew Ashworth has more recently argued that passivity can be culpable, and he goes so far as to claim that the usually cautious approach to omissions liability has been 'abandoned' in the sphere of complicity (2003: 442).

Although Ashworth does not explicitly tackle the offence in the Suicide Act, his analysis might still offer some explanation for the convictions of Mr Cooper and Mr and Mrs Johnson. He initially notes that an act of encouragement, intended to encourage the principal offender (the suicidal patient in our situation), could be blameworthy (*Coney* (1882) 8 QBD 534; *Clarkson* [1971] 1 WLR 1402). This might at least offer an explanation for Mr Cooper's conviction, as he had turned away the district nurse; 'keeping a look-out', as Ashworth notes, can amount to abetment (2003: 416). Mr Cooper's conviction may therefore be deemed reasonably straightforward, but Mr and Mrs Johnson, by way of contrast, did nothing so active – although one might still concede that their behaviour was not discouraging of their daughter's suicidal action.

The second situation to which Ashworth refers is one in which the accomplice was under a legal duty to act. Here, there might be parallels between Mr and Mrs Johnson's case and the established authority in *Stone and Dobinson* [1977] QB 354. There, a couple was found to have undertaken responsibility for the victim, and to have breached their duty to her when they failed to prevent her from starving herself to death. The couple was convicted of manslaughter. Sara Johnson, the media reports reveal, was residing with her parents and was reportedly 'incapable of doing anything for herself'. As such, the Johnsons might similarly have acquired a duty to care for her, rendering them legally obliged to save their daughter's life.[4] Indeed, if they had acquired this duty, they might not merely have been accomplices: instead, this might have rendered them *primarily* liable and therefore open to a different homicide charge, such as murder or manslaughter. In theory this looks possible, but ascertaining when and whether such a conviction will ensue is, again, difficult (see Stokes 2005).

Finally, there are what Ashworth terms the 'control cases' (e.g. *Du Cros v Lambourne* [1907] 1 KB 40; *Tuck v Robson* [1970] 1 WLR 741; *JF Alford Transport Ltd* [1997] 2 Cr App R 326). These are cases, according to Ashworth, in which a new class of public duty has been created – for example, involving home owners who have failed to exercise a legal power to control the behaviour of their guests. Glanville Williams did not think that these cases could be relevant in the context of suicide (1983: 579) but it is notable that Sara Johnson committed suicide in an annexe to her parents' home. Again, they could have been duty-bound to try to prevent her actions.

Perhaps, then, the three convictions can be seen, or made, to cohere with general principles of accomplice liability. The law does not emerge unscathed, however, because recourse to the Parliamentary debates on the Suicide Bill shows that Williams' scepticism was not without foundation. The Lord Chancellor, for example, referred to the proposed offence as involving some 'clear, positive element' of assistance (see HL Deb Vol 229 Cols 544–548, esp 547, 548, 9 March 1961). Consider also the words used by the Law Lords in their more recent consideration of Dianne Pretty's application, to which I will return (*R (on the application of Pretty) v DPP* [2002] 1 FLR 268). In that case, the judges noted the government's view that assistance in suicide should remain a crime and that 'the decriminalisation of attempted suicide in 1961 was accompanied by an unequivocal restatement of the prohibition of *acts* calculated to end the life of another person' (para 28). The Lords also approved a Council of Europe recommendation 'that a terminally ill or dying person's wish to die cannot of itself constitute a legal justification to carry out *actions* intended to bring about death' (ibid).

In fairness, their Lordships were only considering the prospect of Brian Pretty offering his wife some positive help in achieving her wish to die, so they arguably had no need to contemplate the notion of passive assistance. Nevertheless, it seems telling that their discussion framed complicity in suicide in purely active terms. It looks increasingly difficult to criticise the view that Williams would undoubtedly have taken on the findings against Mr and Mrs Johnson; namely that their convictions should have been impossible in theory and overturned in practice.

4   It should be noted that, had Ms Johnson been a minor, her parents would have more obviously been under a legal duty to preserve her life (e.g. Children and Young Persons Act 1933, s 1(1)).

2.4.2 Innocent doctors and guilty relatives

The Johnsons' convictions look even more problematic when they are contrasted with other cases that have not led to the courtroom. Graham Lawson sits with his sister and he is not prosecuted; the Johnsons sit with their daughter – who was, it should be noted, not a minor – and they acquire a criminal record. The unevenness of the application of the law then becomes particularly pronounced when one compares the position that seems to obtain for (some) relatives with the position that obtains for health professionals.

Here one should distinguish between two scenarios. In the first, the victim intentionally and positively acts to end her life, and the defendant intentionally refrains from rescuing her. This is basically what happened in the case of the Johnson family. In the second scenario, the victim intentionally refrains from taking the necessities for life, and, again, the defendant intentionally refrains from rescuing her. Consideration of the second scenario should help us to see why the first scenario is legally awkward.

Initially it must be asked: can and should the second scenario be described as one of assistance in suicide? Might not it even be dubbed '(passive?) voluntary euthanasia' (Huxtable 2002b: 353)? Suicide by omission is an area that is fraught with philosophical difficulty and legal scholars also appreciate the complexities (e.g. Price 1996; Wheat 2000). It might be possible, in theory, to distinguish between a situation in which a patient refuses life-supporting treatment *in order* to die, and a situation in which the person's intention is only to free themselves of an unwanted intrusion, although they do envisage that death will follow. The first refusal certainly looks suicidal (Linacre Centre 1982: 65); the second, such as arises when a Jehovah's Witness patient refuses a blood transfusion, arguably does not. There is reason to think, however, that both could be termed 'suicide' in English law. With the first refusal, the intention is to bring about death; with the second, if death is foreseen as a virtual certainty, then *Woollin* tells us that having such foresight can amount to having the relevant intention. So, in both cases, the law should say that the self-killing was intentional and thus one of 'suicide'. In fact, the opposite view was taken by the Law Lords in the Anthony Bland ruling: neither type of refusal of treatment amounts to 'committing' suicide. According to Lord Goff, 'in cases of this kind, there is no question of the patient having committed suicide, nor therefore of the doctor having aided or abetted him in doing so' (*Airedale NHS Trust v Bland* [1993] 2 WLR 316, at 367H–368A).

This principle has been criticised by those who wish to uphold the sanctity of life since the judges seem to allow too much (Keown 2002b: 238). However, it was firmly re-stated in the case of 'Ms B', who was granted the right to have her ventilatory support withdrawn (*Re B (Adult: Refusal of Medical Treatment)* [2002] 2 All ER 449). Ms B herself was concerned that her loved ones might view her wish as suicidal. One of the reasons why the clinicians were reluctant to grant her request was that they too saw this as 'killing the patient or assisting the patient to die and ethically unacceptable' (para 97). Butler-Sloss P sought to reassure both the patient and the professionals that these were not valid concerns, at least from a legal standpoint. This does, however, again look out of step with the ruling that a foreseen and virtually certain consequence can be deemed intentional. In Ms B's case the evidence suggested that she 'would have a less than 1 per cent chance of independent ventilation, and death would almost certainly follow' (para 38). Even if she does not directly intend the result, if the doctor who pulls the plug knows (or strongly suspects) that death will ensue, why is he or she not an assistant in suicide?

The answer must rest on the maxim that the doctor's duty to save life is trumped by a higher duty: the duty to respect the patient's autonomous wishes. In fact, the doctor might be branded a criminal if she does *not* grant the patient's wish that unwanted medical treatment be removed. Ms B successfully claimed damages in the tort of trespass to the person for not having her request honoured; clinicians can also be considered to have assaulted or battered their patients if they persist in providing treatment in the absence of consent. This is the case, irrespective of whether the patient refuses the treatment contemporaneously or in advance of it being given, through an advance directive or so-called 'living will'. The latter expressions of patient autonomy have long been accepted by the judges and they find renewed legal support in ss 24–26 of the Mental Capacity Act 2005 (see also e.g. *Re AK (Medical Treatment:Consent)* [2000] 1 FLR 129).

Although there is some tension in the law over the vexed question of intention, the courts' logic seems to direct us to two conclusions: when an individual refuses treatment in order to die, the doctor is neither lawfully *permitted* to intervene nor *liable* for failing to prevent the patient's death. So much for the second scenario. But is it really so different from the first scenario, in which the passive participant still refrains from saving life, when the patient has this time *acted* to end her life? Provided of course that the second party knows of the patient's wish, then in both scenarios the patient can be said to have 'committed' suicide, the second party's omission can be causally relevant, and that person might legally be said to have intended the result. Why then was Dr Dean not prosecuted? It seems hard to avoid the conclusion that the second party who is neither entitled to intervene nor liable for failing to do so can only be a health professional who is, Dr Jordan aside, acting in their professional capacity. Laypersons like the Johnsons appear instead to be duty-bound to call in the doctors or else risk prosecution. And it is this key feature, the duty that the passive participant owes to the patient, which requires amplification.

2.4.3 Left to die or abandoned to die

So, why is the relative bound to call in the doctors and what does this say of the legal attitude to the suicidal patient? The short answer must be that it is only agents of the state who have the power to legitimise and thus allow a suicide attempt. And, taken to its logical extreme, this signals that the suicidal person must let no one know of their intention: they must be abandoned to die.

The inquest into the death of Gertrude Haynes is illustrative here. The coroner praised a paramedic's attempts to resuscitate Ms Haynes, who had used a plastic bag to suffocate herself, apparently following instructions in Derek Humphry's *Final Exit*. Ms Haynes had, however, left an explicit note declining any efforts to save her life, which included the threat of legal action. The coroner reportedly declared that people 'were wrong to believe they could prevent treatment by leaving notes' (Jones 1997: 3).

As JC Smith once observed, 'the duty to intervene can hardly be greater than in the case of suicide' (1979: 253). What is the basis for this duty? Skegg has suggested that there might be a duty to intervene in order to ascertain the durability, and therefore the sincerity, of the patient's wish to die (1974: 524–525). This nevertheless seems out of step with the current law, since it is nowhere stated that the autonomous patient must have durable desires (but see Huxtable 2002b: 347–348). Indeed, the desire can apparently rest on a fleeting whim, since the competent patient can refuse life-supporting intervention for reasons that may be rational, irrational, or even entirely absent (see *Re T (Adult: Refusal of Medical Treatment)* [1992] 4 All ER 649). The better view must therefore be that the principle of necessity justifies intervention: it is necessary to attempt to save the suicidal patient's life (see *Re F (A Mental Patient: Sterilisation)* [1990] 2 AC 1).

How necessary is this? It is well settled that state bodies like the police, prisons and psychiatric units owe a duty of care towards mentally incompetent individuals who appear suicidal (e.g. *Reeves v Commissioner of Police of the Metropolis* [1998] 2 All ER 381; *Knight and Others v Home Office and Another* [1990] 3 All ER 237; *Selfe v Ilford and District Hospital Management Committee* (1970) 114 SJ 935). These bodies may thus be found negligent if they fail to prevent that person from attempting or succeeding in their attempt at suicide. Note, however, how this appears to turn on the competence of the individual. It certainly appears that the principle of necessity can only be invoked where the patient is not competent and has not left any valid direction as to what their wishes are. If some second party can intervene as soon as the patient becomes incompetent, regardless of their prior wishes, then the notion of respect for autonomy becomes redundant (Williams 1983: 268).

Autonomy seems then to become the primary issue. Is a suicide note an autonomous direction? Can it, in other words, amount to a valid advance refusal of life-saving treatment? In theory it seems there is no reason why it cannot, provided that the note was made freely when the patient was competent and informed, and that it applies to the situation that has arisen (cf. Hewson 1999; Mumford and Mumford 1999). Sara Johnson's note certainly looked clear and applicable; furthermore, in answer to Skegg's point, she evidently had a settled desire to die, given her previous attempts at suicide.

However, advance directives are rarely straightforward, even leaving aside
– momentarily – the issue of suicide notes. It is, for example, not always clear
whether an advance refusal of life support is applicable to the clinical team.
Research shows that even relatively detailed, written statements are amenable to
quite different interpretations, any of which can appear reasonable (Thompson,
Barbour and Schwartz 2003). The directives can also take quite different forms.
Is a verbal directive sufficiently compelling (see e.g. *W Healthcare NHS Trust
v H and others* [2004] EWCA 1324)? What of the pensioner who had 'not for
resuscitation' tattooed on her chest (see Polack 2001; Behan, Veasey, Higson
and Sulke 2005)? Was that a sufficiently specific, enduring and considered
refusal of treatment? Finally, to whom is the directive directed and where and
when does the direction apply? Should a paramedic, called out to a patient's
home or travelling by ambulance to the hospital, honour an apparently binding
instruction not to revive a patient (see Biggs 2001: 137–138)? Can the directive
only apply once it has been confirmed by a doctor? And, this brings us back
the Johnsons, can the directive apply to (mere?) laypersons?

The Johnsons' convictions would indeed seem to suggest that the directive
only has legal weight once its validity has been confirmed by a doctor. The
reason for this is not hard to discern: the state wants to ensure that the directive
is a true expression of the patient's autonomy, as that concept is understood
in law. A key component of autonomy is competence, and this may be the
sticking point. It should not be forgotten that Sara Johnson had a history of
psychiatric problems.[5] It might therefore be appropriate to ask whether the
suicidal individual was competent when they decided to commit suicide and
refuse any attempts at saving their life. Again, in legal theory, this must be
possible. The test for competence is functional in nature, and purports not to
involve any consideration of the nature of the choice that the patient is making
(Jackson 2006: 192–193). Provided, then, that the patient has considered the
relevant information and has used it to arrive at a choice to die, then that is a
competent decision – and it matters not that it is a decision to die.

Of course, this raises the nebulous spectre of the rationality of the choice,
because we are contemplating decisions to die (see Sullivan, Ganzini and
Youngner 1998). However, purely in terms of the common law, the rationality
or irrationality of the choice is irrelevant. Indeed, the judges have insisted
that even a mentally disordered patient can be considered competent to make

---

5   Without wishing to delve into whether a suicidal person is (by definition or otherwise)
    'irrational' or even 'mentally disordered', it might be worth noting that Ms Johnson's
    psychiatric difficulties appeared to persist beyond her treatment at a psychiatric unit. *The
    Independent*, for example, reported that she 'continued to suffer from horrific hallucinations'
    (*The Independent* 1989). However, it is difficult to discern from the media reports how
    distinct these were from the suffering Ms Johnson experienced due to multiple sclerosis,
    although she herself seemed to distinguish between the two in her suicide note ('my illness
    and the psychiatric problems have reached the point which I simply cannot bear') (ibid).

some, even life-threatening, decisions (e.g. *Re C (Adult: Refusal of Treatment)* [1994] 1 WLR 290). Strictly speaking then, Sara Johnson's psychiatric history might therefore be irrelevant to her competence. Hedley J's decision in *Re Z* is also instructive, since he confirmed that Mrs Z was competent (paras 8, 12). Competence is decision-specific, so he must have been agreeing that Mrs Z had made a competent decision to commit suicide with the assistance of another. This, nevertheless, all depends on some agent of the state – a doctor usually, but maybe a judge – confirming that the decision was competently made. This was not, it seems, a decision for the Johnsons to make.

It therefore appears that the relative has no right to conclude that they must honour their loved one's wish to die, even if this seems to have been an autonomous decision. The legal necessity to call in the doctors is two-fold: doctors are 'installed as gatekeepers at the threshold of patient self-determination' and are also the people able to save the non-autonomous patient's life (Harrington 1996: 359). The principle of necessity is given substance by an assessment of the best interests of the patient, which, according to the courts, involves an examination of both their medical interests and any other pertinent interests, be they spiritual, familial or cultural (*Re A (Male Sterilisation)* [2000] 1 FLR 549). The family of the incompetent patient, equipped with knowledge of who the patient is (or was), increasingly plays an important role in making this assessment (e.g. Mental Capacity Act 2005). However, the Johnsons apparently could not only rely on their knowledge of Sara's wishes and assumed interests, as they lacked the relevant medical viewpoint.

In sum, the doctor is not entitled to save the life of a patient who (autonomously) does not want to be saved. The doctor will also not be liable for refraining from intervening in this situation. The relative, however, is not only entitled to intervene but could be branded a criminal if they do not summon the doctors and, presumably, the paramedics. This shows some equivocation over when autonomous wishes must be respected. Even more troubling is the message the Johnsons' convictions sends to the suicidal individual. If you wish to die, you may be allowed to do so in a treatment setting, like Ms B, provided that the doctors are satisfied that your wish was competently formed. But if you wish to commit suicide, you must do so in the knowledge that the doctors should be called in, even if you have left a clear statement declining medical intervention. This might at least settle an old debate over what the decriminalisation of suicide means: it does not confer a right to commit suicide but, at best, gives you some liberty or, in the words of Hedley J in *Re Z*, the 'freedom' to do so (para 12).

The Suicide Bill was partially intended to remove the 'odour of criminality' from the suicidal individual and replace it with compassion for that individual (see HC Deb Vol 644 Cols 833–834, 14 July 1961; Col 1423, 19 July 1961). What could be more compassionate than saving an apparently vulnerable person or at least ensuring that death is really what they wanted? Some moral philosophers similarly believe that we owe a duty to frustrate a suicidal act, at least until we are sure that death is genuinely desired (Gewirth 1978: 265; Huxtable 2005a).[6] And yet what if death *is* genuinely and autonomously desired? In such a case, the Johnsons' convictions issue a rather less humane warning: one must commit suicide unassisted, alone and without informing loved ones, or else they will be exposed to the 'odour of criminality'.

3 The 'unique' mercy killer revisited

An assistant in suicide looks increasingly unlikely to know when they will be tainted with criminality, but there is still some reassurance available, since they are very unlikely to serve prison time. The previous chapter examined how the mercy killer who is convicted of manslaughter is constructed and dealt with by the courts, and the same trends resurface in the context of complicity in suicide.

What is immediately notable is how infrequently the charge is brought (Williams 1983: 579; House of Lords Select Committee 1994b: 18) and how, when it is, it is usually in the context of a mercy killing. This chapter has referred to 21 accomplices who were convicted for agreeing to play a part in a suicide, apparently from a merciful motive. To this group should be added some of those much rarer assistants whose actions are not amenable to being described as mercy killings. Ms Hudson was acquitted (*The Times* 1975). Mr Osborne was not so fortunate. He had entered into a suicide pact with Mrs Sheldon, with whom he was conducting an extra-marital affair ((1991) 13 Cr App Rep (S) 225; see also *England* (1990) 12 Cr App Rep (S) 98). Both overdosed in a hotel room, but Osborne survived and was charged with the s 2 offence. Even more unusual, although not unique (see *Glenn Paul Wright* [2000] Crim LR 928), is the case against Mr McGranaghan, a prisoner who convinced his physically disabled cell mate to hang himself, with McGranaghan's assistance ((1987) 9 Cr App Rep (S) 447).

Croom-Johnson LJ, presiding over McGranaghan's appeal against sentence, recognised that he was dealing with 'a very rare offence', for which he detected 'no established pattern of sentencing practice' (at 449). McGranaghan's 'appalling' conduct meant that his sentence of eight years' imprisonment was upheld (at 450). Osborne also received a prison term, although his initial sentence of five years was reduced to three on appeal, in view of his reactive depression and the stress that precipitated his uncharacteristic behaviour at the time of the offence.

Unsurprisingly, these sentences are the highest to have been passed down to accomplices in suicide. Only one 'merciful' assistant, Mr Robey, received a comparable disposal: three years' incarceration. Others have received prison

---

6   It might be questioned whether one could perceive a need to intervene in *every* suicide attempt, since the circumstances of each attempt will never be identical, even if the difference is only temporal.

terms but, in a recurrence of a theme identified in the last chapter, this seems to be due to the presence of aggravating features that meant the cases strayed from the paradigm of merciful killing. Mr Wallis was issued with a one-year sentence; the fact that he had helped his depressed, but otherwise well, partner to die may provide the explanation. Mrs McShane, of course, was found to have acted from mixed motives, including her desire to inherit. She was sentenced to serve two years for this offence. Mr Reed, meanwhile, must have gone too far in essentially operating an assisted suicide service. He was convicted of two counts of aiding and abetting suicide, plus two counts of conspiring to assist in suicide, and was sent down for 30 months, which was reduced to 18 on appeal (see [1982] Crim LR 819).

Reed's co-conspirator, Mr Lyons, managed to avoid the cells, despite being convicted of five counts of aiding and abetting suicide, plus the two counts of conspiring to assist in suicide. He had already been in custody while awaiting trial but his actual sentence, of two years' imprisonment, was suspended for two years. The trial judge, Lawson J, warned Lyons: 'If you get into trouble during the next two years you're going to cop it. Keep to young girls.' 'No I prefer the old ones' was Lyons' reply (Rusbridger 1981d). Of the more usual cases, only four of our 21 accomplices have received this sort of disposal. Mr Beecham, Mr Pitman, Mr Holden and Mr March all acquired prison terms of up to one year, all of which were suspended.

This leaves us with 12 convicts and the results are not unexpected: nine were placed on probation, while the remaining three were conditionally discharged. Croom-Johnson LJ may not have been able to locate any pattern for dealing with someone like McGranaghan but that does not mean that there is no pattern in sentencing, at least when the accomplice is a mercy killer. The overwhelming message, again, is that the mercy killer will not be sent to the cells. The judge did acknowledge that the charge is usually brought 'in the context of a mercy killing of some kind' (at 449), and it seemed that, when debating the 1961 Bill, Parliament also anticipated this and that there would be a measure of clemency in such cases (see HC Deb Vol 644 Cols 834–835, 14 July 1961). Nevertheless, such disposals hardly uphold the idea that mercy killers are indistinguishable from other killers.

The judges still strive to maintain that the offence is 'very serious' (*Robey* (1979) 1 Cr App R (S) 127, *per* Browne LJ, at 129). When the Bill was under consideration, the government included the requirement that the DPP consent to prosecutions, because it wished to mark the gravity of the crime (see HC Deb Vol 644 Col 835, 14 July 1961). Nowadays, however, that requirement might be viewed in a different light. In the 'death tourism' ruling *Re Z*, Hedley J opined that such a 'provision is rare and usually found where Parliament recognises that although an act may be criminal, it is not always in the public interest to prosecute in respect of it' (para 14). Commenting on Hedley's judgment, De Cruz detected a slight relaxation in the legal attitude to assisted suicide, at least insofar as the injunction restraining Mrs Z from leaving the jurisdiction was lifted (2005: 266). To this should be added the observation that a prosecutor might be disinclined to pursue proceedings where a light sentence is anticipated, as this may not be in the public interest. Are we again faced with the prospect that the merciful assistant in death will be written out of the criminal law altogether?

4 A right to assisted suicide

In truth, there are likely to remain one or two convictions a year for complicity in suicide – that is, unless the law is changed. It is difficult to predict how likely that is to occur, but many jurisdictions, including England and Wales, are indeed reconsidering their position on assisted suicide. In 1994, a House of Lords Select Committee firmly opposed any permissive reform; by 2005, however, the Lords were not so emphatically opposed. The later Committee was convened to consider the Assisted Dying for the Terminally Ill Bill, promoted by Lord Joffe, a Bill which began life embracing voluntary euthanasia but was diluted to encompass only physician-assisted suicide.[7] The committee concluded that the issue deserved further parliamentary consideration, but time ran out without the Bill finding favour amongst the majority of parliamentarians.

The issue, of course, will not go away, and we can expect to see more such Bills in the coming years. We can also expect to see the plights of patients paraded across the newspapers, as they seek a legally enshrined right to die. The rulings in the case of Dianne Pretty nevertheless confirm that nothing short of statutory reform will do away with the terms of the Suicide Act (*R (on the application of Pretty) v DPP* [2002] 1 FLR 268, *per* Lord Steyn at paras 57 and 68).

4.1 Dianne Pretty's failure: the right to die denied

Mrs Pretty, who featured at the start of this book, sought confirmation from the DPP that her husband Brian would not be prosecuted if he assisted her in her suicide. Mrs Pretty had motor neurone disease, and did not want to endure the suffering that might follow as her life drew to an end. Mr Pretty was willing to help his wife to die. The DPP, however, refused to issue the undertaking sought, whereupon the courts were called upon (see further Huxtable 2005a).

Although Mrs Pretty had an arguable case, the Queen's Bench Division and the House of Lords (*R (on the application of Pretty) v DPP* [2002] 1

---

7   The Committee examined the second version of the Bill (HL Bill 4, 53/4) that encompassed both assisted suicide and voluntary euthanasia (House of Lords Select Committee 2005a: 104–113; see also HL Bill 17, 53/3). The third, narrower Bill (HL Bill 36, 54/1) was effectively defeated on 12 May 2006.

FLR 268) rejected her claim.[8] Not only did the DPP lack the power to confer immunity prospectively, but there was also nothing in the European Convention on Human Rights, recently incorporated by the Human Rights Act 1998, to support the right that Mrs Pretty sought. The Lords examined in detail Arts 2, 3, 8, 9 and 14, on which Mrs Pretty relied, but their decision essentially rested on two propositions: life is intrinsically valuable, meaning no one has the 'right' to commit suicide whether assisted or alone, and the need to protect others in society, such as more vulnerable patients, prevented any diminution in its defence. Thus, the right to life (Art 2) did not entail a right to die, and while the State was obliged to deal with Mrs Pretty's suffering under Art 3 (freedom from torture and inhuman or degrading treatment), it was not the cause of her suffering and was not obliged to offer assistance in suicide. Art 9, freedom of thought, conscience and religion, was quickly dispensed with, as the applicant's right to believe in the justifiability of assisted suicide did not require her husband to be immune to prosecution for undertaking it. The 'parasitic' Art 14 (freedom from discrimination in the enjoyment of the Convention rights) was also of little assistance since Mrs Pretty's other claims had failed and, in any event, it was not the case that she was being denied a 'right' to commit suicide enjoyed by able-bodied citizens.

Article 8 (the right to respect for private and family life) looked more useful, in conveying the principle of respect for personal autonomy. The Lords, however, felt that this was not engaged and, even if it was, it could be limited. The European Court of Human Rights, to which Mrs Pretty then appealed, agreed that the right could be limited by the State, given its margin of appreciation in determining how such activities should be dealt with, but it notably accepted that the right *was* engaged (No 2346/02 *Pretty v UK* (2002) 35 EHRR 1). Otherwise, all of the judges were in agreement: Mrs Pretty did not have the right to be assisted to die by her husband and the DPP was not required to issue his policy on prosecution. The DPP could issue guidance but there was certainly no duty and not necessarily any right to confer immunity prospectively in an individual case, where there had not even been any indication as to how the proposed crime would be committed (*R (on the application of Pretty) v DPP* [2002] 1 FLR 268, at paras 38–39, 65–66, 95). Indeed, Dianne Pretty might really have needed voluntary euthanasia, rather than assisted suicide (Doyal and Doyal 2001: 1080).

Lord Steyn had concluded with the hope that Mrs Pretty would receive a sufficient standard of palliative care 'to make a little more tolerable what remains of her life' (para 69). She died shortly after the failure of her final appeal, reportedly enduring the very breathing problems that she had sought to avoid (Dyer 2002).

8   The first two hearings are: *R (on the application of Pretty) v DPP (Permission to Move for Judicial Review)* [2001] EWHC Admin 705 (unreported)) and (*R (on the application of Pretty) v DPP* [2001] EWHC Admin 788 (unreported).

4.2 Why Dianne Pretty failed

Should Mrs Pretty's application have succeeded? There are obviously many competing moral dimensions to the case but, on a purely legal level, some believe that the opposite result could have been reached (e.g. Tur 2003; see also Coggon 2006). Certainly, the European Court's stance on the right to respect for autonomous choices sows the seeds for a quite different legal response. But, as that Court also recognised, the discretion afforded to the State in question helps explain why the case seemed destined to fail. A survey of the European case law reinforces this conclusion.

It seems the first person to challenge the illegality of assisted suicide under the Convention was actually Nicholas Reed (App No 10083/92 *R v United Kingdom* (1983) 6 EHRR 140). After failing in his appeal against conviction, Reed approached the European Court, complaining of an unfair trial (contrary to Art 6), and interference with his private life and right to free expression. The Commission, which then operated as a mechanism for filtering out ill-founded claims before they reached the Court, rejected the application.

The Commission's comments on Art 8 may, nevertheless, have offered some hope to Mrs Pretty. The Commission denied that Mr Reed's rights were engaged but noted that Art 8 'might be thought to touch directly on the private lives of those who sought to commit suicide' (para 13). Such hopes should, however, have been dashed by the following opinion, which was that acts intended to assist a suicide 'are excluded from the concept of privacy by virtue of their trespass on the public interest of protecting life as reflected in the criminal provisions of the 1961 Act' (ibid). The same limitation, including the need to protect the vulnerable, prevented Reed from arguing successfully that he was entitled to offer advice on how to commit suicide (para 17). As Mrs Pretty later found, the margin of appreciation afforded to the UK implied that, so long as the State held to its stated prohibition, the European Court would not be able to help British citizens seeking a 'right to die'.

A decade on, Ramon Sampedro, a Spanish patient whose story formed the basis of the film *Mar Adentro* (*The Sea Inside*, dir. Amenabár 2004), also failed to have his plea for assisted suicide admitted by the Commission (App No 25949/94, *Sampedro Camean v Spain* (1994)). Like Mrs Pretty, he claimed that the right to life entailed a right to die, but his claim was actually rejected on the basis that he had failed to exhaust domestic remedies (see Nys 1999: 218). Despite the attention that her undeniably difficult case attracted, Dianne Pretty's inability to secure a right to die was not without precedent.

There is, however, a postscript that must be added to this ruling, which is prompted by what is known of the legal reality of complicity in suicide. In 1994, Sue Rodriguez sought to convince the Canadian Supreme Court that she had a legal right to be helped to die. She too employed rights-based arguments and she too failed to persuade the judges (*Rodriguez v Attorney-General of Canada and Others* (1994) 107 DLR (4th) 342). After the ruling, however, an unnamed doctor granted Ms Rodriguez's wish (Martel 2001: 165). No prosecution followed. Ramon Sampedro also managed to commit suicide, through a complicated plan in which he divided tasks amongst his friends and distributed 11 copies of the keys to his home, so that it would be difficult to trace whoever assisted him (Gooch 1998: 3; Nash 2005: 20). After sufficient time had passed that she could not be prosecuted, one of Mr Sampedro's friends confessed to providing him with the means to commit suicide and to making a video recording of his death, which was later broadcast on a local television channel in Madrid. One can only speculate as to what would have happened in this jurisdiction had Brian Pretty, or some other individual, provided Mrs Pretty with what she wanted.

5 Conclusion: complicity, compromise and confusion

Dianne Pretty's case provided a battleground for three competing ethical injunctions: there is a right to be assisted in suicide, premised on an appeal to patient autonomy, and maybe a corresponding duty to help; there is a need, perhaps a duty, to uphold the sanctity of life; and there is a need, again perhaps a duty, to eradicate suffering. It is clear which injunctions emerged victorious, and that part of the reason for Mrs Pretty's failure was the weight accorded to a fourth argument: that allowing euthanasia might place us on a slippery slope to permitting more obviously objectionable practices. However, as De Cruz detected in the death tourism hearing, Mrs Pretty's defeat does not mean that autonomous choices are wholly relegated beneath other societal interests.

Once more, the law in this area discloses a compromise of values. The accomplice in suicide, if he or she is even recognised as such, might hear stern pronouncements on the value of life, but they will be unlikely to spend time in the cells. Like manslaughter before it, the offence in the Suicide Act offers a gentler way of dealing with the mercy killer, although, unlike manslaughter by reason of diminished responsibility, the 1961 offence is virtually the sole preserve of the mercy killer. Sometimes it will be entirely appropriate for the mercy killer to be categorised in this way; however, sometimes we do not know how the alleged killer will be labelled and treated by the criminal lawyers.

This chapter has canvassed a wide range of situations in which the law is unclear, incoherent or simply inconsistent. When is helping someone to die murder and when is it a lesser offence? The answer, it seems, hinges on the whim of the court. Is advising on methods of committing suicide criminal? In theory, yes, but suppliers of suicide manuals have not been prosecuted, suggesting that, in practice, no. Is helping someone to obtain assistance in suicide abroad an offence in this country? Again, in theory, yes, but there have been no convictions to date. Is providing the pills to a suicidal patient a crime? Perhaps; but perhaps not. What of merely respecting a suicidal person's wish to be left to die? Again, this might result in conviction, but that seems to depend on the discretion of the legal officials, and, to some extent, on whether or not you are a health professional. And finally, although proponents call for the legalisation of physician-assisted suicide, are doctors willing to help their patients in this way? According to the law reports, they are not and do not do so. Other evidence, however, suggests that the reality might be different.

Many of these difficulties might be eradicated or at least minimised once a better general legal response to mercy killing is formulated, which should include consideration of not only cases where the assistant performed the final fatal act but also situations where the patient did so. But even after the basic legal position has been clarified, there will undeniably remain an urgent need to deal with the problems just detailed. Before this can be attempted, the picture of mercy killing as it appears in English law needs to be completed. Differences have already emerged in this chapter in the ways that the lawyers deal with doctors as opposed to laypersons. The main reason for this, at least as the law is written, is that doctors tend to use painkilling pills rather than pillows and pistols, and so they have been afforded what amounts to a form of defence. That defence will apparently only succeed where the court accepts that the accused doctor's primary intention was to relieve their patient's suffering. It was for this reason that Dr David Moor, mentioned at the outset of this chapter, was acquitted of murder. However, the principle on which Moor relied is not without its own difficulties, and these form the main focus of the next chapter.

Chapter 4

Get out of jail free?

Double effect and doctors in the dock

Easing the passing of a dying person is not all that wicked. She wanted to die. That can't be murder. It is impossible to accuse a doctor.

Dr John Bodkin Adams, reported in *The Times*,
27 March 1957

Dr Adams Acquitted on Murder Charge.

Headline, *The Times*, 10 April 1957

Women Cry 'Thank God' as Dr Arthur is Cleared.

Headline, *The Times*, 6 November 1981

Doctor Cleared of Murdering Patient with Pain-Killing Jab.

Headline, *The Times*, 16 March 1990

Tears as Mercy Doctor Found Guilty.

Headline, *The Sunday Times*, 20 September 1992

'Caring' GP Cleared of Murdering Patient.

Headline, *The Electronic Telegraph*, 12 May 1999

GP Cleared of Patients' Murders.

Headline, *BBC News Online*, 14 December 2005

On 14 December 2005, Dr Howard Martin was acquitted of murdering three of his patients, thus ending the 'eight weeks of hell on earth' the 71-year-old GP reportedly endured throughout the trial (Wainwright 2005b: 8). Martin had allegedly administered overdoses of the opioid painkiller morphine to Frank Moss, 59, Harry Gittins and Stanley Weldon, both 74. The prosecution could find no motive, but argued that the evidence demonstrated beyond reasonable doubt that the GP intended to kill, and in fact did kill, the three men.

Each patient had received 60 mg of morphine as intramuscular injections which, according to an expert in palliative medicine, was five or six times above the dose recommended for such patients. Moreover, only in 'very rare' cases would these injections be given directly into the muscles (BBC 2005b). The court heard that Martin carried these pre-prepared syringes of morphine with him, something an expert in general practice had not witnessed elsewhere and would not recommend.

Mr Weldon, who had severe dementia, was given the morphine in response to breathing difficulties he was experiencing. The fact that the drug could further suppress the patient's respiratory function was, claimed the prosecution, something the GP would have known. Mr Moss, meanwhile, had been undergoing hospital treatment for lung cancer, which was later found to have spread to his brain. Although his prognosis was judged to be short, the patient's family did not expect his demise to be so rapid. His daughter revealed how she found it odd that her father was given a 'top-up injection' when he had not awoken from the first of three that the GP allegedly provided (Wainwright 2005a: 5). Three members of Mr Gittins' family expressed the same surprise at the decision to provide him with a third injection. When they thought they heard Mr Gittins rising from his bed, the doctor was said to reply 'he won't be getting out of bed again' (BBC 2005c). The family disagreed with Martin's assessment that Mr Gittins was dying, pointing out that he appeared to be recovering well from surgery for oesophageal cancer undergone only days before. Martin, however, claimed to have a letter to the contrary from the treating oncologist; the oncologist informed the court that he could find no record of such a letter (ibid).

Counsel for the defence, Anthony Arlidge QC, had successfully defended Dr David Moor previously in very similar circumstances, and, as in that case, he sought to argue that the prosecution had failed to prove that Dr Martin had intended to kill, nor had it established that his actions were causative of the patients' deaths. Although Martin declined to take the stand, there were glowing tributes from a former nursing colleague and a number of patients, one of whom commended him as 'a straight-talking man' who 'tells it like it is' (BBC 2005d). Expert medical evidence was also adduced, which might have proven particularly persuasive in the case of Mr Moss. A pathologist revealed that Moss had been very close to death, such that, if it had played any part at all, the morphine might only have shortened his life by one hour. The pathologist felt that death could not be attributed to the drug, 'otherwise we would have to include it for any people that died in a hospice' (BBC 2005e).

As the trial judge, Forbes J, reminded the jury, Martin was not subject to any lesser charge (such as manslaughter by gross negligence) so the question for them to consider was relatively straightforward: did Martin murder these patients? Answering in the negative, the jury was reportedly met with gasps and exclamations from the public gallery. The investigating Detective Superintendent, Harry Stephenson, dubbed this 'one of my most disappointing days' and argued that there had been 'a moral and legal obligation to investigate' (Wainwright 2005b: 8; Laurance 2005: 6). Martin's relief was nevertheless short-lived, as the GMC suspended him from practising. Martin claimed to be 'appalled', especially because he feared that doctors were being 'frighten[ed] away' from using morphine (Wainwright 2005c: 9). The reason for the suspension was, however, that further allegations against the GP were being investigated: by June 2006, the coroner was examining 16 deaths, while the police were re-considering eight of another 16 deaths they had already examined.[1]

Martin's case bears the hallmarks of every alleged case of euthanasia involving a doctor to date: seemingly considerable evidence of wrongdoing by a 'straight-talking' practitioner; doubts over whether the accused caused the patient's death; claims that the defendant intended only to relieve the patient's symptoms; a (virtually certain?) acquittal. 'Virtual certainty' is actually one of the key concepts here, and it is one that continues to confound the legal officials. Following the direction to the jury issued in the landmark case against Dr John Bodkin Adams, who spoke the words quoted at the beginning of this chapter, the law seems to have reached the point where a health professional may, with impunity, administer a course of treatment even where this appears virtually certain to cause death. Members of the public, however, may not: if they foresee death as a consequence of their actions, they might well be guilty of murder – although, as the two preceding chapters illustrated, it can be difficult to predict when this will be the outcome. Such inconsistency between health professionals and laypeople, which here rests on the legal version of the doctrine of double effect, is a recurring feature of those few cases where it is a doctor who, in the words of one such defendant, finds himself behind 'the iron spiked dock' (Moor 2001: 147).

The legal officials nevertheless insist that euthanasia is indistinguishable from murder and that, as Farquharson J said in relation to Dr Arthur, there

---

1   In February 2007, Durham police confirmed that it would be taking no further action, although some further inquests were still anticipated and the GMC and Dr Martin's Primary Care Trust had yet to conclude their investigations (Harry 2007: 20).

'is no special law in this country that places doctors in a separate category and gives them extra protection over the rest of us' ((1981) 12 BMLR 1, at 5; see also e.g. *Cox* (1992) 12 BMLR 38, *per* Ognall J, at 39; House of Lords Select Committee 1994b: 17). The two preceding chapters suggest that the rest of us are already afforded some degree of protection, and a trawl through the jurisprudence involving doctors sheds further light on the artifice of, and, indeed, the danger behind, the rhetoric of prohibition and equality before the law.

This chapter starts with the doctrine of double effect as it exists in English law, and will explain how there are problems with every attempt to explain its precise legal role and, often, with its application to doctors in the dock. Does the doctor not intend to kill? Does he not cause death? Is he afforded a defence? None of these questions is answered satisfactorily. Also unsatisfactory is the way that more straightforward allegations of euthanasia are dealt with in the courts: it becomes apparent towards the end of this chapter that the legal process sends some decidedly mixed messages, which once more suggests that the moral underpinnings of the law in this area need clarification.

I Double effect in English law

Four decades before the case against Harold Shipman (see Shipman Inquiry 2002), the trial of Dr Adams was the most (in)famous criminal case involving an English doctor ([1957] Crim LR 365). Dr John Bodkin Adams was a GP based in Eastbourne and, like Martin after him, he was allegedly implicated in more than one of his patients' deaths. The Attorney General, however, felt compelled to abandon a second trial, after the doctor was acquitted of the charge relating to 81-year-old patient Mrs Morrell (*The Times* 1957: 14).

At autopsy, high levels of barbiturates, morphine and diamorphine had been detected in the body of Mrs Morrell, who had experienced a stroke and suffered from cerebral arteriosclerosis. Adams' team argued that his sole intention had been to relieve the patient's pain. Summing-up, Devlin J (as he then was) noted that if 'life were cut short by weeks or months it was just as much murder as if it were cut short by years' (Palmer 1957: 375). Devlin emphasised that 'it remains the fact, and it remains the law, that no doctor, nor any man, no more in the case of the dying than of the healthy, has the right deliberately to cut the thread of life' (Williams 1958a: 289).

Adams' acquittal, however, no doubt hinged on a more famous statement:

If the first purpose of medicine, the restoration of health, can no longer be achieved there is still much for a doctor to do, and he is entitled to do all that is proper and necessary to relieve pain and suffering, even if the measures he takes may incidentally shorten life.

(Davies 1998: 347)

These words afforded the doctrine of double effect clear legal recognition,[2] and it is now accepted as an 'established rule' by the judges in the House of Lords and by the members of two Lords Select Committees, which reported in 1994 and 2005 (*Airedale NHS Trust v Bland* [1993] 2 WLR 316, *per* Lord Goff, at 370D). You will recall that the doctrine essentially forbids the intentional pursuit of 'bad' outcomes, although a result like death might be condoned where it is only incidental to the agent's 'good' purpose, such as striving to achieve pain relief for the terminally ill patient.

Of course, the moral doctrine is not restricted to the relief of pain, but in 1997 the High Court was asked to consider where the boundaries of the legal principle lay. Although previous judgments offered some comfort (e.g. *Arthur* (1981) 12 BMLR 1, *per* Farquharson J, at 4), Annie Lindsell, a patient with motor neurone disease, sought clear reassurance that her GP, Dr Simon Holmes, would be on safe legal ground if he sought to relieve her *distress* from the breathlessness she feared enduring at the end of her life (see Arlidge 2000). Holmes anticipated using opioid analgesics, but suspected that these might shorten his patient's life. In the event, not only was Ms Lindsell able to withdraw her application after a substantial body of medical opinion endorsed Holmes' proposal, but she was also to die peacefully soon after, reportedly without needing the relief sought (Murray 1997b: 9).[3]

2 Clarifying the clinical confusion

Commenting on Ms Lindsell's case, Dr Oliver, a hospice director, dismissed any 'supposed risk' because 'diamorphine is unlikely to cause death', provided it is 'used appropriately' (Oliver 1997). He confessed to being mystified by her application, because doctors engage in such practices 'daily without fear of prosecution' (ibid). However, this insight does not settle the question of whether doctors using such drugs *should* fear prosecution. In order to assess this issue properly, one needs to embark first on a closer examination of the reality of administering opioids.

2   Whether the doctrine existed in English law prior to this trial is a matter of some conjecture. The ruling in *Steane* [1947] KB 997 is particularly pertinent. The defendant gave broadcasts from Germany during the Second World War and was convicted of performing acts likely to assist the enemy with the intention of so assisting. The Court of Criminal Appeal quashed the conviction, as (*inter alia*) the jury was denied the opportunity to consider whether the defendant had acted with the innocent intention of saving his family from the concentration camps. This aspect of the ruling certainly has some of the flavour of double effect reasoning: the defendant may have issued broadcasts with the intention of saving his family, although this would incidentally mean assisting the enemy.

3   In 2007, Kelly Taylor, a patient with Eisenmenger syndrome who was expected to live no more than one year, approached the High Court for a declaration that it would be lawful for clinicians to sedate her and then, in accordance with her advance directive, withhold nutrition and hydration. She withdrew her application after deciding to explore alternative means of addressing her pain (Paris 2007).

2.1 Clarifying the clinical concepts

Clarity is important here, particularly as the judges have tended to employ words like 'morphine', 'diamorphine', 'heroin' and 'opioid' without explaining the meanings of, and relationships between, the terms (e.g. *Glass v UK* [2004] 1 FCR 553, at paras 25, 42, 61 and 78). Starting with morphine, this is an opiate analgesic (painkiller), that is, it is obtained from opium, the juice secreted by poppy seeds (see Huxtable and Forbes 2004). Opioid drugs act on the body's opioid receptors, and 'opioid' is an umbrella term that includes opiates and synthetic, or semi-synthetic, morphine-like drugs. Morphine itself is viewed as the most usefully versatile analgesic for addressing both moderate and severe pain. However, its side effects include nausea, vomiting and respiratory depression. Although the latter is less likely to occur in patients with chronic pain, since the pain opposes this potential to slow or stop breathing, morphine should nevertheless be used cautiously in patients suffering from chest disease.

In the clinical setting, addiction rarely results from the administration of morphine, although this may occur in *non*-patients when they abuse other opioids like heroin. 'Heroin' is actually another name for 'diamorphine', which is a more soluble and more potent opioid than morphine. Diamorphine has the same effects (and side effects) as morphine, and has great utility in caring for people with terminal illness, since effective dosages can be delivered in smaller volumes, thus providing more comfortable injections in the emaciated patient.

I noted in the first chapter how some words – on that occasion, 'euthanasia' – can carry very different meanings depending on the speaker and the context, and this is no less true in relation to opioids. 'Narcotic', for example, is also of Greek origin (*narke*, meaning 'numbness' or 'torpor'), and is avoided by British practitioners of palliative medicine (but not their American counterparts) – as is 'heroin', for perhaps understandable reasons.

2.2 When double effect matters

Although their use is not restricted to 'palliative medicine', itself a phrase with an interesting definitional history (see Woods 2007: 50–52), opioids evidently play an important role in end-of-life care. The problem, of course, is that these drugs might not only palliate symptoms: they might also shorten the life of the patient. Wilson has recently suggested that 'a quicker death was foreseen as a virtual certainty' in the case of Dr Adams (Wilson 1998: 130), and in the 1950s, Dr Havard conceded that normal (or even sub-normal) doses of morphine carried 'a very high degree of probability' of death (Williams 1958a: 290 n 1). This effect, however, was by no means certain. Indeed, contrary to Wilson's suggestion, a medical expert giving evidence in Adams' trial opined that a particular dose would kill, only to be informed that the patient had previously survived precisely such a dose (House of Lords Select Committee 1994a: 50).

More recently, Dr Doyle pointed out to the 1994 Select Committee that some 'overdoses' actually resulted in relief for the patient, rather than a premature demise (House of Lords Select Committee 1994a: 21). The committee thus concluded 'there can be no certainty that the secondary effect (shortening of life) will result' (1994a: 50).

Nowadays, specialists in palliative medicine, spurred by pioneers like Dame Cicely Saunders and with the backing of organisations like the World Health Organisation, are more emphatically certain that appropriate opioid use will *not* cause death:

> A dying patient receiving medication for pain and symptom control will eventually die after receiving a dosage of medication. It is a fallacy to conclude that the medication and not the last surge of the underlying disease caused the patient's death.... Legal and other lay colleagues may not fully appreciate the relative risks of opioids. Tolerance to respiratory depression readily occurs in patients on chronic opioid therapy. In such patients, increasing opioid use to ensure pain relief, and sometimes sedation in concert with other drugs, is rarely the direct cause of the patient's demise.
>
> (MacDonald and Roy 1998: 125)

Quite how rare this is was spelt out in a review of 17 clinical studies, published by Sykes and Thorns in 2003. They found that the risk of respiratory depression was 'more myth than fact', at least when the drugs are used appropriately (2003b: 313). Five studies were identified that examined the effect of opioid use on survival, and none of them reported that opioids had shortened life. This finding bears out the principle stated by renowned experts Hanks and Twycross: 'pain is the physiological antagonist of the respiratory effects of opioid analgesics' (1984: 1477).

The evidence therefore suggests that one does not often need the doctrine of double effect to justify the use of opioids in relieving pain. It might, however, assist the clinician faced with a patient in *distress*, who wishes to use sedative drugs other than opioids. Sykes and Thorns found that the majority of studies again suggested that life would not be shortened, although, in one of their own studies, they acknowledged that sedation might have shortened the lives of two of the 237 patients in their sample. In one case, 'the physician involved considered that sedation might shorten an already short prognosis', but that this was indicated by the patient's violent agitation and paranoia (Sykes and Thorns 2003a: 343). In the other case, 'sedation may have allowed development of pneumonia in the presence of [an underlying] lung disease'; again, the patient's delusions and otherwise unrelievable progressive agitation nevertheless necessitated sedation (ibid). Tellingly, only in these two cases did the authors see any need for recourse to the doctrine of double effect in order to justify the clinicians' actions.

Discussions with other clinicians confirm that the doctrine may indeed be helpful where the terminal patient's respiratory function is already severely compromised but they require relief from their constant and distressing breathlessness (Forbes 2006; Huxtable and Forbes 2004: 345). The overwhelming message, however, is that the double effect simply will not be present in cases where pain is managed using opioids, in accordance with accepted standards of practice. Only in the extremely rare case is the conscientious clinician advised to find moral comfort by carrying 'the doctrine of double effect in your back pocket' (Forbes 2006). However, it is also important to recognise that the less conscientious and less careful doctor should proceed cautiously, since the obvious implication is that opioids can certainly cause death when they are misused.

At this juncture it is worth noting that, while morphine can have a sedative effect, it is not itself indicated for use as a sedative agent; rather, it is best directed at the relief of pain. It warrants reiteration that it was *sedative* drugs that featured most prominently in the situations just described where the doctrine of double effect might have genuine utility. This is a hugely significant finding, and one that must be borne in mind when considering the ways in which the legal officials have approached the cases to date, which have gravitated around the use of morphine and diamorphine (see Williams 2001a). Unfortunately, some clinicians also appear overly concerned about the use of these drugs and seem to have difficulty in separating myth from fact: Wall has noted, for example, how some surgeons and obstetricians still believe that opioids should only be used for brief emergency periods (Wall 1997: 121).

2.3 Double effect or covert euthanasia

Against this backdrop there is ample reason to treat with caution those studies, often picked up by the national media (e.g. Boseley 2006), which are said to reveal the prevalence of opioid-induced covert euthanasia. Although Seale's study of 857 doctors appears to be one of the most rigorously crafted surveys to date, it included the following question:

> Did you or a colleague intensify the alleviation of pain and/or symptoms using morphine or a comparable drug taking into account the probability or certainty that this action would hasten the end of the patient's life or partly with the intention of hastening the end of life?
>
> (Seale 2006a: 4)

The inclusion of the clause 'partly with the intention of hastening the end of life' obviously complicates matters, but Seale separates out the 4.0 per cent of respondents who reported having had that intention. The first clause is still problematic, however, since such a question is based on the *assumption* that alleviation of symptoms is likely to hasten death and it is asked of doctors who *believe* this to be the case. A better view is that the 33.8 per cent who answered this particular question in the affirmative may have been concurring with one of two very different propositions and thereby occupying one of three very different groups (see further Forbes and Huxtable 2006).

First, the respondent might be claiming 'I used an opioid analgesic and invoked the doctrine of double effect; I did not kill the patient'. Where the doctor genuinely used the drug in order to palliate symptoms, and even in the rare event that the patient died as a secondary effect of that drug, this is an accurate application of the doctrine of double effect. Alternatively, the respondent might subscribe to the view 'I used an opioid analgesic and invoked the doctrine of double effect; I killed the patient'. However, this is a claim that permits of two very different interpretations. The respondent might be one of (probably very few) doctors who conceal covert euthanasia in the cloak of double effect – a theme to which I shall return. It seems more likely, however, that the respondent is unfamiliar with Sykes and Thorns' findings: this doctor intended to relieve pain, but believes, and reports, that his or her management of the patient's symptoms led to the patient's demise.

So equipped with more of the facts and fewer of the fictions about opioids, one should be in a good position to assess the lawyers' attempts to tangle with the doctrine of double effect. It becomes immediately apparent that the law in this area is incoherent, not least because it is hopelessly unclear how the principle arrived at in *Adams* was and can continue to be accommodated by English law. Does it rest on the idea that the doctor who uses potentially (but only very rarely) fatal drugs is absolved of liability provided he or she only *intended* to palliate? Or is it more reflective of the clinical reality, in that the use of such drugs will rarely *cause* death? Or, much more controversially, is it that the doctor using these drugs is a murderer, albeit a murderer who is afforded a *defence*? Not one of these explanations is satisfactory.

3 No intention

The first, and standard, reading of *Adams* concentrates on the doctor's *mens rea* (his intention in administering the drug): in Devlin's words, he 'is entitled to do all that is proper and necessary to relieve pain and suffering, even if the measures he takes may *incidentally* shorten life'. These words certainly capture the import of the ethical doctrine of double effect, in invoking a distinction between those outcomes that are directly sought and those that are incidental to the doctor's purpose. This distinction between 'direct' and so-called 'oblique' intention nevertheless presents numerous legal problems.

3.1 The guilty father and the innocent doctor

A first difficulty is that, when Devlin issued his direction, the offence of murder could be satisfied by 'mere' foresight of death as a certain consequence of the defendant's conduct (Williams 1958a: 286; Fletcher 1969: 73–74). If the unfortunate doctor in the dock could or did foresee death as a result of his management of the patient's symptoms, why was he – but not the layperson – exempted from the rigours of the criminal law?

Of course, the law in this area was not (and is not) static, especially during the 'foresight saga' of the 1980s and early 1990s, a period in which the courts kept having to consider the relevance of foreseeing death to the crime of murder (see Birch 1988). The extent to which the law differentiated between such foresight by a layperson and by a health professional will vary according to one's reading of the various rulings issued in that period (e.g. *Moloney* [1985] AC 905; *Hancock and Shankland* [1986] AC 455; *Nedrick* [1986] 1 WLR 1025; Price 1997, 327). What is clear, however, is that the disjunction has returned with the decision in *Woollin* [1998] 4 All ER 103, a case already encountered in Chapter 3, which concerned a father who had thrown his baby son against a hard surface. The Law Lords there decided that intention could generally be left to the common sense of the jury although, in the exceptional case, it could be directed that foresight of a virtually certain consequence either amounted to an intention to bring about that consequence or else at least provided evidence of such an intention, from which it could infer that the guilty intention was present.

The father in question actually had his conviction quashed on appeal but the principle was set: a layperson could be convicted of murder after foreseeing death. The *Adams* principle, however, emerged unscathed. Even the Court of Appeal has admitted that it 'may be difficult to reconcile' the two rulings (*Re A (Conjoined Twins: Medical Treatment)* [2001] 1 FLR 1, *per* Ward LJ, at 56C). Judges may be prone to pronounce that the law of murder applies equally to health professionals and laypersons but this seems just hollow rhetoric when a doctor can run the risk with immunity but a layperson cannot (Price 1997: 329). Either the doctrine of double effect is acceptable, and should apply across the board (contrast Skegg 1988: 137), or it is not, and we should expect to see more doctors both in the dock and in the cells.

Contemporary experts in palliative medicine will object that these arguments ignore the reality of administering opioids. According to them, death is rarely a virtual certainty, particularly if the drugs are used *appropriately*. The evidence base for and coverage provided by palliative medicine may not be complete, but it is growing, and the information is being disseminated (e.g. Woods 2007: 64). This suggests that the lawyers should take a particularly hard look at those cases in which there is reason to suspect that a powerful painkiller did contribute to the patient's death. However, the few prosecutions that have been mounted suggest that the legal gaze is far from penetrating, which in turn presents the additional hazard that *directly* intended deaths will be assumed innocent.

3.2 Double effect or covert euthanasia (revisited)

Before examining the cases involving health (usually, medical) professionals that have resulted in prosecution it is worth pausing to consider the many that have not, as revealed in a wealth of anecdotal evidence which suggests that covert euthanasia might be occurring under the guise of double effect. Nurses are positioned at the front line of care, at least in acute hospital settings, and it is perhaps telling that some of them expressed concern to the 1994 Select Committee over the use of the doctrine, even condemning it as hypocritical (House of Lords Select Committee 1994a: 20). Doctors too have their misgivings, with one junior doctor presenting the GMC with a dossier of alleged abuses, which included the claim that opioids were being administered *in order* to hasten patients' deaths (Macaskill and Ungoed-Thomas 2000: 1, 28). The media is replete with such stories: for example, Dr Davies has declared that many doctors of retirement age will have 'shortened a patient's life', usually as a 'result of increased dosages of pain-relieving drugs' (Davies 1992). Some openly confess to flouting the terms of the *Adams* protection. Witness, for example, Dr Colin Brewer's revelation to the police that he had administered what he had hoped would be a fatal overdose to a patient with cancer. The police declined to prosecute, citing insufficient evidence, but Brewer later contended that this would have been available had it been sought (Linacre Centre 1982: 24–25). Similarly, Jane Peugh, a retired nurse, admitted to having given a fatal overdose of morphine in the 1930s, under a doctor's instruction (*Today* 1986).

As was seen in the previous chapter, Michael Irwin, the former Vice Chairman of the VES, features particularly prominently in this debate, having approached the media in 1997 and 2003 to relate stories of assisting in his patients' demises. In 1997 he spoke not only of aiding numerous suicides but also of using morphine in performing euthanasia. He – in the event, accurately – dismissed the likelihood of prosecution, commenting 'In the eyes of the law, it was to relieve their pain' (Austin 1997: 1). Dr Mary Rayner expressed admiration for Irwin's compassion and candour and echoed his sentiment that morphine was being used surreptitiously as an agent of euthanasia (1997: 8). That same year, Baroness Warnock, the prominent medical ethicist, spoke of her husband Geoffrey's death being facilitated by GP Dr Nick Maurice (Bale 1997: 3). Maurice had allegedly increased the morphine with the consent of his patient and, despite also writing in his surgery newsletter of inducing two patients' deaths, neither the police nor the GMC mounted investigations. 1997 also saw the posthumous publication of Dr Hugh Walters' memoirs, in which he related similar experiences (Gibbs 1997: 16).

In the following year three more doctors informed *The Sunday Times* that they had brought about death at their patients' requests (Norton 1998: 14). One unnamed doctor claimed to have assisted in the deaths of five patients. Another GP, Dr Nigel Scott-Moncrieff, spoke of having his consultant commend him, 'You are learning', after his first experience of performing voluntary euthanasia. He had, he said, subsequently assisted two patients to die in addition to 'easing the passing' of others. The GP would inject a combination of diamorphine and barbiturates, such as phenobarbitone – 'the most delightful and delicious way to die' (ibid). Dr Christopher Hindley, again a GP, had, with their consent, assisted the deaths of ten patients, also using morphine. He berated the hypocrisy of the many GPs who deploy the *Adams* principle, because in reality in such cases he felt that 'the intention is to shorten life' (ibid).

Remarkably, that certainly appeared to be the intention of Lord Dawson of Penn, the physician who cared for King George V. In his diary entry for 20 January 1936, Dawson wrote of providing morphine and cocaine to the comatose and terminally ill monarch, in an effort to 'determine the end' (Ramsey 1994). The doctor saw this as 'a facet of euthanasia or so called mercy killing', although when the issue was debated in the Lords in December of that year, he spoke in opposition.

Beyond the anecdotes and confessions lie the surveys, and as many as 51 per cent of doctors reportedly believe that painkillers are being used 'with the intention of shortening life' (House of Lords Select Committee 2005a: 31). Of course, one would be wise to recall the earlier discussion of what such findings might really mean: all may not be what it seems, even to those who firmly assert that their attempts at achieving palliation come at the cost of the patient's life (see also House of Lords Select Committee 2005a: 81–82). However, that does not mean that we can dismiss the probably small – 4.0 per cent according to Seale (2006a: 8) – but nonetheless problematic group who talk of double effect but practice euthanasia.

What then is to be made of this evidence? Certainly, there may be many valid reasons why prosecutions are rarely mounted. Where the confessor is deceased, or the events happened many years before, or where bodies cannot be exhumed, the evidence is likely to be insufficient to warrant the CPS's attention. Moreover, where the prosecution is briefed by an expert in palliative medicine, they might rightly come to realise that drugs used appropriately have no effect on a patient's life expectancy. There might also be occasions where the CPS doubt that a jury will convict an apparently conscientious doctor, although that alone should not present an insurmountable barrier to prosecution, given that so serious a potential crime is in issue (see CPS 2004: 8).

However, this all assumes that any allegations have been referred on to the CPS – and it is notable that few cases appear even to have been investigated. Irwin may have been questioned on a number of occasions, but the investigations centred on allegations of assisting in suicide, rather than his alleged dealings with morphine. He hinted that there may be something amiss in the administration of the law when analgesics are implicated. It should be remembered that a robust application of the *Adams* principle will involve examination of the doctor's *intention* when using opioid analgesics: it does not straightforwardly confer innocence merely *because* an analgesic was employed. However, as Irwin put it, 'In the eyes of the law, it was to relieve their pain'. Equally, just because the drug might not in fact have *caused* death does not mean that the doctor's intention was benign: the prosecutors could always pursue a charge of *attempted* murder. This does not happen; indeed, prosecutions generally are rare. One begins to gain the impression that the legal officials will ease off in their investigations if analgesics have been used, an inference which the few trials to date tend to bear out (Brahams 1992: 2).

3.3 Double effect in the dock

The trial of Dr Thomas Lodwig, in 1990, is particularly indicative of the legal attitude to analgesics (see Gibb 1990: 3; Cole 1992: 37–38). Lodwig, a junior doctor, was charged with murdering Roy Spratley, who was in the terminal stages of cancer and 'no longer lucid' at the time of Lodwig's alleged actions (Brahams 1990: 587). Lodwig had been on duty for 80 hours, the last 18 without a break, when Mr Spratley's relatives urged him to do 'something, anything' to alleviate his pain, which was reportedly unresponsive to morphine (Wilkinson 1990:3). Lodwig administered a combination of potassium chloride and the anaesthetic lignocaine, 'an extremely dangerous combination,' according to the prosecution. Mr Spratley died minutes later. In court, however, the prosecution abandoned the case, citing uncertainties over whether Lodwig's actions had caused the patient's death and aware also that two experts were prepared to testify to the analgesic properties of the experimental drug combination. Recording a formal 'not guilty' verdict, Leonard J initially refused to grant costs to the defence, remarking that the doctor had brought the prosecution on himself. However, costs were eventually granted and Lodwig returned to clinical work, ultimately in general practice.[4]

The legal officials' willingness to stay this trial reinforces the suspicion that the mere use of a painkiller – even an experimental one – will point to innocence. Lodwig indeed maintained that his intention had been to relieve pain, but it is surely right to remind the court that he had allegedly remarked to a nurse, 'I'm going to send somebody up out there', and had then drawn a finger across his throat and pointed it in the air before he injected the drugs (Wilkinson 1990: 3). The nurse was sufficiently perturbed to contact her professional body, which notified the police, and she was rightly commended for this by the trial judge. For the legal officials to have concentrated on whether or not Lodwig's cocktail could be a therapeutic combination rather misses the point: the real issue is not *what* Lodwig was administering, but his

4   According to the GMC register, accessed 28 March 2007.

intention in doing so. Would it really have been wrong for his innocence or guilt to have been fully tested in court?

Of course, questions might still be asked of the legal process even where a full trial is undertaken. Consider the case of Dr David Moor, who was tried in 1999. In the wake of Irwin's revelations, Moor had allegedly informed a journalist that he had helped 300 patients to die. Also like Irwin, he claimed that he would be prepared to defend his actions in court. Unlike Irwin, his challenge was accepted: Moor was charged with the murder of George Liddell, a patient with cancer who was found to have excessive levels of diamorphine in his blood. The VES was a supportive presence throughout the hearing – indeed, Irwin himself was ejected from the courtroom for branding the trial 'disgraceful' – but Moor's lawyers, led by Arlidge QC, invoked the doctrine of double effect, in preference to any argument for the validity of euthanasia *per se* (Johnson and Bunyan 1999).

The jury took only 69 minutes to acquit, seemingly having been convinced that the intention had been purely to palliate. Although he chastised the GP for his 'very silly remarks', the tone of Hooper J's direction was otherwise extremely sympathetic. He noted that this was a doctor we might all wish to have overseeing our care, with his characteristic devotion to Mr Liddell – he had attended on his day off – ironically leading to the murder charge. Moor may have praised Hooper for his 'user friendly' summing-up (Moor 2001: 134), but the flimsiness of his direction on 'intention' has not escaped the notice of experts in criminal law. In *Woollin* [1998] 4 All ER 103, Lord Steyn appeared to hold that a jury *may* be directed that foresight of a result amounted to intending that result (at 112). Commenting on the decision, Wilson noted that the permissive, rather than imperative, tone could enable a trial judge not to so direct the jury, instead leaving the meaning of 'intention' to the jury's common sense (Wilson 1999: 458). He suspected that this might occur in a case like *Adams* and his prediction was then amply borne out in Moor's trial. Hooper told the jury that the GP intended to kill if he gave the injection 'for the purpose of killing that person' (Arlidge 2000: 39). JC Smith, the prominent criminal lawyer, approved of Hooper's only other statement on intention – that mere foresight of a high probability of death will not suffice for intention – but he understandably disputed the absence of the *Woollin* direction. According to Smith, that omission, which meant that intention was left to the jury to determine, 'may have saved [Moor] from a possible, but by no means certain, conviction' (Smith 2000: 44).

Its toxicological evidence dismissed as unreliable, the prosecution was left with Moor's public comments and the fact that he had lied to the police and health authority about the dose he had administered. Panic over the media furore prompted the deception, claimed Moor's team, and the comments were allegedly then misconstrued, since Moor meant only to enable pain-free deaths for the terminally ill. Following the acquittal, the CPS defended the decision to prosecute the doctor, who had retired early due to the stress of the case.

It may well be that neither Lodwig nor Moor breached the law of homicide, but, like Martin more recently, these appeared to be 'straight-talking' doctors and their incautious remarks undeniably necessitated the questioning they endured. It nevertheless looks as if further questions could be asked of such doctors and more particularly of the legal officials. The atrocities committed by Dr Harold Shipman, the Manchester GP convicted in 2000 of murdering 15 patients and suspected of killing many (perhaps hundreds) more, while extreme, should highlight the dangers of inadequate enforcement (see Shipman Inquiry 2002). Of course, Shipman is best described as a serial killer who happened to carry a stethoscope and many of his patients appear to have had no pain and been morphine-naïve, hence the rapidity with which they died. In sum, Shipman's actions could scarcely be accommodated by the doctrine of double effect, despite his employment of opioid analgesics.

Intriguingly, however, Shipman's name has been linked with two of the doctors already discussed in this chapter: Adams and Martin. The police officers investigating Martin may have expressly discounted the fact that he and Shipman had worked in the same health centre for 18 months during the 1970s (BBC 2005f), but the parallels between Adams and Shipman are less easily avoided. In addition to the fact that they had a colleague in common, there is the substantial allegation that the doctor who gave double effect a place in English law had far from 'pure' intentions; indeed, Kinnell (2000) suspects that Shipman found a role model in Adams.

The case against Adams hinged in part on his inheritance from the woman he stood accused of murdering, Mrs Morrell. Strictly speaking, motive forms (and formed) no part of the substantive criminal law in determining guilt, although Devlin J did allow that a defendant's motive might guide a jury in determining his intention (*The Times* 1957: 14). He nevertheless deemed the bequests, a Rolls Royce car and a chest of silver, too 'paltry' a reward for a respected doctor to risk a criminal penalty, which was, at that time, the ultimate penalty of death (ibid). The jury, of course, were quick to acquit, and the Attorney General refused to proceed with a second murder charge, fearful that a fair trial could not be ensured. However, following Adams' death in 1983, Hewitt, the Detective Chief Superintendent who had investigated the GP, presented a starkly different perspective (*The Times* 1983: 3). He noted that Adams had actually inherited under 132 wills and further implied that Adams also murdered a potentially vital prosecution witness, who could have disclosed where some of the doctors' (murdered?) patients were buried. Hewitt condemned the ensuing prosecution as hampered by 'blunders', and argued that a stronger case could have been mounted (ibid).

The interplay between motive – why a doctor has formed his aim – and intention – what the doctor's aim was – is bound to remain conceptually contested. It nevertheless seems reasonable to conclude with the warning to legal officials that to assume that a doctor using opioids has a purely palliative intention not only rests on a fallacious interpretation of the doctrine of double effect but may also be fraught with danger.

3.4 Killing by accident

The distinction drawn in *Adams* between 'direct' and 'oblique' intention was therefore legally problematic from the outset and remains so, insofar as it is out of step with the principles outlined in *Woollin*. Furthermore, failures to pursue seemingly serious allegations and at least one occasion on which an apparently guilty doctor, Adams himself, evaded penalty suggest that the law-in-action does not quite cohere with the stated terms of the principle Adams' trial introduced.

The problems stack up after remembering that the 'intention interpretation' of *Adams* is just that – an interpretation based on what the defendant doctor is believed to have *intended*. Merely because a jury is unconvinced that the doctor's intention was malign does not mean that the homicide law's arsenal is exhausted or that the doctor should be free from censure. As long ago as 1973, Glanville Williams suggested that only incompetence could explain fatal overdoses, given increased knowledge in the field of pain relief (Williams 1973: 15). Where there is evidence of a significant failure to observe accepted practice and it looks like the maladministration of the drug caused the patient's death, one might therefore expect to see an alternative charge or verdict of gross negligence manslaughter.

Such findings have, in fact, started to occur, albeit in cases where there was apparently no suggestion that the doctor intended to kill. Two GPs, Drs Raheem and Sinha, have been convicted for fatally miscalculating, by ten times, the magnitude of the doses required by their patients. Raheem received a one-year suspended sentence, while Sinha was sent to the cells for 15 months (*Guardian* 1999: 12; Katz 2004). The GMC has also found against Dr Gustaffson, another GP, and Dr Basnyat, an anaesthetist, for their parts in morphine fatalities, although both doctors were to continue in practice, albeit with some conditions imposed on the former (Cant 2002: 3; Crook 2003: 13). Other doctors, such as the three involved in allegedly administering 100 times the recommended opioid dose to a newborn baby, have been even more fortunate, in being cleared by the GMC (Boseley 1999, 9). It is notable that many of these cases, and the others under consideration here, involved GPs. Ognall J, presiding over the trial of Dr Nigel Cox to whom I shall turn shortly, asked the jury 'What did he know of the properties and potential of potassium chloride used in this way?' (*Cox* (1992) 12 BMLR 38, at 42). It seems a similar question might need to be asked of morphine of this group of doctors.

It may be too early to tell whether such findings represent a fresh challenge to the role played by double effect in English law. Any further developments will certainly have to be watched, especially as expertise in, and knowledge of, pain control expands. Particular attention will need to be directed to cases where the circumstances, and particularly the allegedly fatal dose, are more arguable. Some doctors might still evade conviction for murder, and maybe rightly so, given the presumption that the accused is innocent until they are proven guilty beyond reasonable doubt. They may indeed not have intended to kill. Neither might they have foreseen death as a virtually certain result of their actions. But whether they *should* have foreseen that outcome is a question that still deserves to be asked. The legal officials should ensure that a finding of manslaughter remains a real possibility for those doctors who 'are trained to kill only by accident' (see Tallis 1996: 3).

4 Not a cause of death

Doctors do seem to attract special protection, particularly given how unlikely it is that crimes other than murder will be charged (or substituted in court).[5] Perhaps some rationality can be restored, and some credibility conferred on this protection, if the *Adams* direction is recast as concerned with the *actus reus* of murder, that is, the question of *causation*.

Devlin J certainly allowed for this interpretation of the principle: 'the proper medical treatment that is administered and that has an incidental effect on determining the exact moment of death is not the cause of death in any sensible use of the term' (Devlin 1985: 171–172). Devlin was most explicit about this after the trial, when he stated that he was dealing with 'the commonsense cause' of death (Devlin 1962: 95).

4.1 The guilty layperson and the innocent doctor (revisited)

Nowadays we are told that Devlin's view is not as commonsensical as he avers, since the drugs used by Adams will seldom even have the 'incidental effect' of shortening life. Nevertheless, in those few cases where this is a possibility, the issue becomes whether Devlin's opinion on causation was right in law. Mitchell believes that it was, since at the time of the trial 'the accused could only be guilty of murder if his act was the substantial cause of the victim's death' (Mitchell 1990: 12).

That is not quite the case today. Despite this, in 1999, Hooper issued the simple direction to the jury in Moor's trial that the drug 'does not have to be

---

5   This is, of course, not the only context in which protectionism can be detected. Other prominent examples from the criminal law include the rulings that doctors will not be guilty of aiding unlawful intercourse when they issue contraceptive advice and treatment to underage minors (*Gillick v West Norfolk and Wisbech AHA* [1986] AC 112) and that doctors who withdraw life support will not be found to have caused the patient's death and thereby broken the chain of causation flowing from the (unlawful) act that led to the patient receiving treatment (*Jordan* (1956) 40 Cr App R 152; *Cheshire* [1991] 3 All ER 670).

the sole or principal cause' but it must have 'contributed significantly to the death' (Smith 2000: 42). This certainly conveys the basic tenor of the law governing causation but commentators are alert to the fact that such a direction neglects '[t]he orthodox proposition that shortening life involves causing death' (Ashworth 2003: 126). As JC Smith observed, Hooper's words could enable 'a conscientious jury to conclude that they were not sure that [Moor] caused [Liddell]'s death and so to acquit' (ibid). This (helpful?) failure to spell out the detailed principles governing causation echoes Hooper's resistance to explaining the intricacies of intention, and recalls the disparity between *Adams* and *Woollin*, which enables the doctor to plead double effect but leaves the layperson open to a possible murder conviction. From the outset, then, there is a bias in the way in which causation is handled by the legal officials in presumed cases of double effect.

4.2 Not a cause in fact

Does 'commonsense' dictate that the actions of a doctor like Adams will not *in fact* cause death? This initially looks like a plausible and defensible view, in light of the lessons learned from palliative medicine. Morphine will rarely cause death. But that must mean that the doctrine of double effect has no relevance in the majority of cases where morphine is used: the doctor who uses these drugs appropriately need seek no such justification. Justification in the form of the *Adams* principle of double effect is only really needed in those few situations outlined by Sykes and Thorns and colleagues – situations where *sedative*, rather than analgesic, drugs are being used.

Of course, Adams, like virtually all of the doctors who have followed him into the dock, was using opioids. This gives rise to a number of problems. First, even where a drug is used appropriately, it is simply wrong to maintain that it can have had no impact on the patient's life expectancy: Sykes and Thorns proved that it can have this (double) effect, albeit in the rare case. Moreover, Devlin's words should not be granted the power to free a doctor whose use of such drugs is *in*appropriate. Glanville Williams certainly found 'some difficulty' in Devlin apparently deeming causation absent in cases where respiratory failure or pneumonia ensued from the administration of analgesics. Williams did, however, concede a place for Devlin's approach in cases where death is caused jointly by the drug and the underlying disease (Williams 1958a: 290). Nevertheless, the fact that an injection of morphine (and the like) apparently precipitated an earlier death than had been anticipated should give the legal officials reason to pause. Critics condemn the courts' occasional tendency to 'manipulate the concept of causation' in this context (Skegg 1988: 137; Saini 1999: 108), and what should certainly be avoided is the blanket assumption that analgesics will not kill.

That such an assumption might be at work is nevertheless detectable in at least the trials of Moor and Lodwig. In both cases, the lawyers sought to argue not only that the GPs lacked any guilty intention, but also that their actions could not be proven to have caused death. The doctor has the right to mount a robust defence; what the courts need to remember, however, is that the concept of causation cannot unquestioningly be expected to bear the load of exculpating him or her.

4.3 Not a cause in law

Given the clinical data on opioids and the fact that clinicians should usually only be thinking about the incidental effects of administering sedatives, Devlin's direction starts to look less 'sensible' or at least at risk of misapplication by the courts. It cannot be denied that morphine can *in fact* play a role in causing death, and a substantial role at that in situations where it has been misused. Perhaps, then, Devlin's direction is better understood as signalling that morphine will not be recognised as a cause *in law*.

This is certainly the message that Andrew Grubb takes from the direction (1993: 234). Commentators have, however, been far from kind, condemning this recasting of the principle as 'simply legal sophistry' (Otlowski 1997: 182), borne of 'intellectual dishonesty' (Saini 1999: 108). It certainly looks like a legal fiction, designed to aid the doctor and notably, if perhaps understandably, unavailable to the layperson. Yet, even if this is a viable reading of Devlin's direction, the absence of causation does not equal innocence: the doctor could still be charged with *attempted* murder. However, this is highly unlikely, given the legal officials' apparent willingness to find the innocent intention.

5 Justified murder

Devlin's direction, both as stated and as applied, seems therefore to place the concepts of intention and causation under some strain. There is, however, one final interpretation of the *Adams* principle available, which is that it offers a substantive defence to a charge of murder.

5.1 Overstretching the judicial reach

The principle of necessity provides a fresh way of understanding Devlin's direction, and the moral doctrine has certainly been spoken of in this way by its supporters (Linacre Centre 1982: 48). In the legal realm, Mason has latched onto Devlin's reference to 'proper and *necessary*' pain-relief, which he infers offers the following defence: 'acting unlawfully is justified if the resulting good materially outweighs the consequences of adhering strictly to the law' (1988: 18, emphasis added). Glanville Williams similarly felt that there was little need to grapple with notions like intention and causation, 'when the legal doctrine of necessity lies ready to hand' (Williams 1958a: 290). According to the trial judge, however, 'Williams overestimates the length of the judicial reach' (Devlin 1962: 95). Devlin expressly denied that his direction was 'given on the basis that the relief of pain *justified* an act that would otherwise be murder in law' (ibid).

There is, however, another way in which Devlin might well have fashioned a defence. Although he was discussing legal causation at the time, the judge made reference to the notion of 'accepted medical practice' (ibid). This activates an alternative account of *Adams*: when an analgesic is implicated in a patient's death, the doctor has a defence to murder, so long as he acted within the boundaries of responsible practice. As implausible as it initially appears, there were glimmers of this approach in the Annie Lindsell case, where proceedings were stopped precisely because substantial medical opinion supported the use of opioids in relieving distress (Dyer 1997: 3). Even more support was to follow in Hooper's summing-up of the case against Moor. Writing after the trial, counsel for Moor noted that the judge 'was prepared to admit a substantive defence in certain very limited circumstances', expressed in terms of 'proper treatment', as (subjectively) understood by the defendant (Arlidge 2000: 38–39).[6]

This marks a new upturn in the fortunes of our unlucky doctor in the dock, for he or she appears able to appeal to one (or both?) of two defences. However, this take on *Adams* is imprecisely spelt out, and so leaves the nature and scope of the protection unclear. Some clarity might nevertheless be restored by acknowledging how proximate the two formulations just offered are. 'Accepted medical practice' summons the spectre of *Bolam*, the standard of care expected of doctors if they are to avoid clinical negligence (*Bolam v Friern Hospital Management Committee* [1957] 1 WLR 582). *Bolam* was subsequently called into service by the majority of the Law Lords in the *Bland* ruling, which was outlined in Chapter 1. In that ruling, the House of Lords decided that artificially administered nutrition and hydration could be withdrawn, in the patient's best interests, where a responsible body of doctors no longer felt that such treatment was warranted (*Airedale NHS Trust v Bland* [1993] 2 WLR 316). An assessment of the patient's best interests was therefore dependent, albeit controversially in that case,[7] on the view adopted within accepted medical practice. Notably, in the same ruling, Lord Goff explicitly characterised the *Adams* principle as concerned with serving the best interests of the patient (at 370D–F). An appeal to the patient's best interests brings us full circle, for it rests on the doctrine of necessity: a doctor's activities may be justified where they are necessary in order to save the life or limb of the

6   Initially, the jury were required *objectively* to judge whether the administration of the drug was 'proper treatment', on the basis of the evidence as a whole. However, as Moor's misdiagnosis of the patient's underlying condition might have raised the issue of mistake, the judge instead directed the jury on a *subjective* basis, according to what the defendant actually believed. The reference to the lawfulness of 'proper treatment' remained (see further Arlidge 2000: 38–39).

7   The controversy surrounding this aspect of the ruling will be discussed in the next chapter.

patient (*Re F (A Mental Patient: Sterilisation)* [1990] 2 AC 1; *Re A (Male Sterilisation)* [2000] 1 FLR 549). Looked at in this way, there are not two possible defences lurking in the *Adams* direction, but instead one, albeit rather amorphous, defence of necessity (see e.g. Lanham 1973: 201; Skegg 1988: 138–139; Mason 1995: 455–456).

5.2 The guilty layperson and the innocent doctor (re-revisited)

Devlin, of course, resisted this reading of his direction, although Hooper's subsequent statements show that such a view is not without foundation. Devlin was, however, right to be worried. For one thing, if the defence *is* purely one of 'accepted practice', then Hooper has achieved the rare feat of creating a hitherto unknown defence. More importantly, any court would have roundly dismissed a murderer's plea that his actions were in some sense necessary (at least until fairly recently) as it had long been established that necessity was not a defence to murder (*Dudley and Stephens* [1881–5] All ER 61). JC Smith pinpoints the problem with a direction like Hooper's:

> Notwithstanding the insistence of the courts that the law is the same for doctors as for everyone else, the effect must be to give the doctor a special defence. 'Proper treatment' must refer to accepted medical practice.
>
> (Smith 2000: 42)

Doctors, it would appear, can avoid a murder conviction by arguing that they understood their actions to be in line with the actions of other responsible doctors; laypeople, however, can raise no such defence. In order for the law to credibly avoid this particular charge of bias, it seems that *Adams* should be bundled, however uncomfortably, into one of the boxes marked 'intention' and 'causation'.

However, the prospect of *Adams* affording a substantive defence to murder (for doctors, at least) cannot be consigned to the history books. In 2000, the Court of Appeal ruled that it would be lawful for surgeons to separate the conjoined twins 'Jodie' and 'Mary', despite the certainty that this would result in the death of Mary, who was reliant on her sibling for her survival (*Re A (Conjoined Twins: Medical Treatment)* [2001] 1 FLR 1). Although there are many strands to the judges' reasoning (see Huxtable 2000b; 2002a; Burnet 2001), the majority of the Court of Appeal asserted that the operation could be justified by an appeal to necessity. The judges nevertheless sought to confine their reasoning to the immediate case, in an (optimistic?) attempt to override the principles and practices of judicial precedent (Huxtable 2001).

In addition to again favouring the medical over the lay defendant, this ruling gives credence to the possibility of a doctor pleading a special defence in the case of opioid use. It is also notable that the Law Commission, in its proposed revision of the law of homicide, felt that nothing in their recommendations would pose a risk to the doctor who invokes double effect. Although justifications like necessity fell outside the Commission's remit, its summary of the law is telling: 'It is now an accepted part of the common law that a doctor may lawfully prescribe such medication in such circumstances and, thereby, have a defence to a charge of murder' (2006: 117). Ironically, doctors themselves are unlikely to welcome this news, for now the message is substantially different: the doctor using opioids is a murderer, albeit a (legally) *justified* murderer.

5.3 Get out of jail free

As questionable as it might sometimes be, Hooper's belief that medical practice and its practitioners warrant special protection doubtless lies at the heart of the *Adams* direction. How else to explain the sheer variety of ways in which the principle is said to occupy English law? The very existence of these different interpretations, each as problematic as the last, suggests that the legal officials crave some means of freeing the doctor in the dock. It is certainly hard to disagree with the opinion expressed by Annie Lindsell's barrister that '[t]he law of murder as it applies to doctors and the unarticulated exception that seems to exist for doctors is permeated by anomaly, fiction and misnomer' (Saini 1999: 110). Otlowski picks up this theme, but sensibly issues the warning that 'manipulation or distortion of established legal principles tends to undermine the credibility of the law and bring it into disrepute' (1997: 182).

Doctors, for their part, do not necessarily see any problem with this, with one commenting that 'the law should remain as it is, unclear' (see Saini 1999: 112–114). However, assuming they share the opposition to euthanasia usually expressed by the professional medical bodies, the doctors might be less content if they realised that the confusion surrounding double effect might further the cause of those who are in favour of euthanasia. It was previously suggested that covert euthanasia might go unnoticed by the legal officials, given their apparent eagerness to brand death following the administration of morphine as a merely incidental effect of achieving pain relief. More controversially, the convoluted legal logic could be extended to overt instances of euthanasia. It may not necessarily be such a stretch for the judges to free a doctor who felt that the *necessary* response to the suffering of a patient *in extremis* was a lethal injection (cf. Ost 2005). Lest this be thought too fanciful, it should not escape notice that it was precisely the doctrine of necessity that was pressed into the service of (voluntary) euthanasia in the Netherlands, in a series of court decisions starting in the 1970s (Janssen 2002: 261).

Repeated attempts to openly accommodate voluntary euthanasia, or at least assisted suicide, in English law have nevertheless failed, as one can see in the Dianne Pretty litigation and more recently in the rejection of Lord Joffe's

Assisted Dying for the Terminally Bill. To date, the legal officials want only to afford an explicit justification to those doctors taking positive steps that might shorten life whose conduct can be reconciled, however shakily, with the doctrine of double effect. This does not mean that the doctor whose conduct exceeds the boundaries of the protection is destined for the cells. Instead, like the mercy killer, such a doctor is highly likely to escape the full rigours of the criminal law, as the next section shows.

6 Beyond the boundaries of double effect

We come finally to those health professionals who are alleged to have done more than just 'ease' a patient's passing. English lawyers tend only to think of Dr Nigel Cox in this regard and unsurprisingly so, since we apparently have to travel back some two centuries to find a comparable conviction of a health professional, on that occasion a midwife, who had helped a mother to drown her severely disabled newborn son ((1812) 54 *Annual Register*, Chronicle, 96–97).

Cox, a consultant rheumatologist, was charged over the death of Lillian Boyes, a patient said to have been so 'overwhelmed by her many and dreadful afflictions' that she was howling for relief ((1992) 12 BMLR 38, *per* Ognall J, at 38). Mrs Boyes died minutes after Cox had responded to her pleas by injecting her with undiluted potassium chloride. The injection had been given in the presence of a nurse, and was openly recorded in the notes by the consultant. After a nursing colleague alerted the police, Cox was called upon to defend a charge of attempted murder, because the prosecutors believed that they lacked the evidence to prove that Cox's action had caused Mrs Boyes' death.

Summing up the proceedings, Ognall J instructed the jury to concentrate on Cox's intention – not his motive – and referred to uncontested evidence that the drug used had no analgesic properties and could only have proven fatal (at 46).[8] Thus deprived of the double effect diversion, the jury had little option but to convict, which they did, albeit by an 11–1 majority. Cox was sentenced to serve one year in prison, although this was to be suspended for one year. Like Ognall J, the Professional Conduct Committee of the GMC felt that Cox had acted in good faith and so found that he could return to medical practice. However, his employer placed conditions on Cox's return to clinical work,

---

8   The defendant nevertheless argued (obviously unsuccessfully) that it was unproven that his primary purpose was to kill. In this respect, the jury were 'asked to consider why Dr Cox should mix a slow-acting tranquilliser with potassium chloride if his purpose was to kill quickly' (*per* Ognall J at 49). The defence alleged that Cox intended to alleviate the patient's pain and suffering. In his commentary, Grubb suggests that Cox could have (successfully?) argued that he intended to relieve pain by ending life, if the course adopted was the only one available. However, this was probably not the case, since sedation may have been a viable option (see Grubb 1993: 233).

including that he attend meetings to rebuild the trust of the team (particularly nursing colleagues), answer to a mentor and (significantly?) that he undergo further training, in palliative medicine (Jones 1992: 4).

Only one other doctor, a Dr Carr, seems to have come close to conviction in this sort of situation, when terminally ill Ronald Mawson died after an alleged overdose of phenobarbitone. Charged with attempted murder, Carr's team contended that the overdose was 'a ghastly mistake' (Hodgkinson 1986: 1). The prosecution, meanwhile, noted Carr's interest in euthanasia and urged the jury not to free 'a doctor minded to do this sort of thing because he has a bee in his bonnet' (Cole 1992: 45). In a summing up 'clearly hostile to the defence,' Mars-Jones J declared: 'A doctor is not entitled to play God and cut short life because he believes the time has come to end the pain and suffering and to enable his patient to "die with dignity".' (ibid) The trial judge emphasised that the patient did not wish to die, and that even if he did, killing him would have been illegal. After twice failing to reach a verdict, the jury were met with brief applause on deciding, by a majority, that Carr was innocent. Mars-Jones refused to grant costs to the defence. Dr Carr returned to his general practice.

If this was indeed a 'ghastly mistake', Carr might not be so fortunate today, given the apparent rise in findings of gross negligence manslaughter. However, conviction is by no means a certainty, even for the doctor whose overdose is far from mistaken. In this section I will argue that there is something amiss in the way that the law is being applied to those alleged mercy killers who happen to wear white coats. I will show that it is not just double effect that can aid these defendants. Although surveys suggest that some doctors do deliberately hasten death, the law is constructed and interpreted in ways that enable them to dodge the dock. Even if they do reach the dock, then it is possible that the jury will refuse to convict. However, the jury must rely on the judge's direction and the available reports imply that the judges are keen to help the jury reach a sympathetic result. These trends again suggest that the stated condemnation of euthanasia is unconvincing in (legal) practice.

6.1 Dodging the dock

It is immediately remarkable how few medical or health professionals have been brought before the courts. Quite how prevalent euthanasia is remains open to question and one needs to exercise caution over the data available, especially given the way that questions are asked, and data is generated, in relation to double effect. Nevertheless, various surveys imply that it is not only Dr Cox who has attempted euthanasia in recent years. The 2005 Select Committee helpfully summarised the findings, which suggest that 45 per cent of doctors think that their colleagues practice euthanasia, and between 4 per cent and 12 per cent actually admit to having assisted in or otherwise bringing about a patient's death (House of Lords Select Committee 2005a: 31, 136,

138, 143). More recently, Seale found that 0.16 per cent of doctors confess to having performed voluntary euthanasia, while, remarkably, 0.33 per cent report having practised euthanasia without an explicit request from the patient (2006a: 6). Where, then, are the prosecutions?

Many of the prosecutions that have occurred were spurred by the revelations of colleagues or other individuals (sometimes the doctor himself), as occurred in the cases of Cox, Martin, Moor, Lodwig, and Arthur, a paediatrician charged with the attempted murder of John Pearson, a boy with Down's Syndrome. In other instances, an arguably misplaced reluctance to 'blow the whistle' on a colleague and equally questionable adherence to observing patient confidentiality might serve to preclude proceedings from being brought. However, these cannot be complete explanations.[9]

Before the CPS even examines the strength of the evidence, both the prosecutors and the police must be satisfied that what they are dealing with could amount to a criminal offence. The law generated by *Adams* and similar subsequent trials appears to stay the officials' hands if opioids are involved. This may, for example, explain why the police were reluctant to proceed against Dr Maurice, Geoffrey Warnock's GP. An Inspector explained that Maurice's newsletter article did 'not suggest to us that there has been any infringement of legislation' and that the police would not wish to examine this 'medical and ethical issue' (Fletcher 1997). I have, nevertheless, noted already the risks inherent in taking too soft a look at cases that seem to fall into the double effect category.

However, further protection is available, as the allegation might be viewed – or constructed – as a mere 'omission', and therefore somehow exempt the doctor from the taint of criminality, following *Bland*. Fatal omissions are, nowadays, effectively settled in the civil realm but the prosecutors should still avoid assuming that a decision to withdraw or withhold life-sustaining treatment from a patient is compliant with the criminal law.[10] So far as criminal law scholars are aware, it is still possible to murder someone through neglect (e.g. *Gibbins and Proctor* (1918) 13 Cr App Rep 134). Despite this, some serious allegations have been denied scrutiny on the explicit basis that the doctors had committed no offence. The allegations against two paediatricians, Drs Jolly and Garrow, in 1981 are particularly noteworthy. These doctors had allegedly engaged in practices similar to those apparently undertaken by Dr Arthur, but the DPP abandoned proceedings before the trial of Dr Arthur had even concluded (Timmins 1981: 1). Arthur had prescribed an appetite suppressant (DF118 or dihydrocodeine) and ordered 'nursing care only' for John Pearson, a baby with Down's syndrome, whose parents had rejected him ((1981) 12 BMLR 1). John Pearson died 69 hours later. Arthur was ultimately tried for attempted murder, and was acquitted. However, the trial casts a

9   See further the arguments mounted in the previous chapter.
10   The issues surrounding *Bland* will be examined in more detail in the next chapter.

difficult shadow over the law in this area, one that I will examine more closely later in this chapter and in the next.

The legal tests, and the ways in which they are approached, can help filter out many allegations, but even where the investigation reaches the prosecutors, charges might still be dropped or reduced. Glanville Williams had some sympathy with this since he deemed a charge of murder 'inherently difficult to establish because of the nature of the evidence required', particularly where the patient was terminally ill and had been receiving large quantities of drugs (1958a: 291). Certainly, the CPS is constrained by the need for sufficient evidence, and rightly so. What is less defensible, at least in terms of the operation of the law, is the willingness with which rules are bent towards the accused doctor. Uncertainty over whether the doctor's alleged actions caused the patient's death has become an almost clichéd claim. As I suggested in Chapter 2, the same claim has been made in relation to laypeople, but it is much more common in cases involving doctors: it is one that was used in relation to Drs Arthur, Moor, Lodwig, Carr and Martin, and it is most vividly illustrated by the decision to charge Dr Cox with only *attempted* murder.

Mrs Boyes had died mere minutes after Cox administered the potassium injection but the prosecutors went to great pains to avoid a charge of murder, citing the fact that her body had been cremated, which meant they could not ignore the possibility that her death had been caused by her underlying condition. Even the trial judge conceded that this was a 'remote' possibility ((1992) 12 BMLR 38, *per* Ognall J, at 40). Lord Goff, writing extra-judicially, had the following to say:

> It cannot ... have been far from the minds of those responsible for the prosecution that conviction of murder would mean an inevitable sentence of life imprisonment, whereas the sentence for attempted murder would be in the discretion of the judge.
>
> (Goff 1995: 6; see also Grubb 1993: 233)

The Committee on the Penalty for Homicide (1993) agreed, making reference to Cox's case in its recommendation that the mandatory sentence be repealed.

6.2 Engaging the jury's sympathy

Cox was convicted of the lesser charge but he is the only recent example. The unlikelihood of conviction is, say some commentators, attributable to the juries who hear such cases (Meyers 1990: 282). Williams has observed how juries:

> may not only seize upon any defect in the evidence as a reason for acquitting, but may even acquit when the evidence and the judge's direction leave them with no legal reason for doing so.
>
> (Williams 1958a: 292)

Cox nevertheless bears out his proviso that 'a sentimental acquittal cannot be reckoned as a certainty' (Williams 1958a: 293). Cox's conviction was met with a cry of 'Oh no!' from the public gallery and three members of the jury were in tears on delivering the verdict (Chittenden 1992: 26). That jury's discomfort over its inability to avoid the finding of 'guilty' is further illustrated by the eight hours it took deliberating. Another accused doctor, Moor, recalled being told by a former patient that the less time the jury took, the more likely an acquittal was (Moor 2001: 83). Understandably, his 'spirits rose' when the jury returned after only 69 minutes, with the hoped-for result. Quick decisions are also a feature of some of the other trials, including those of Adams (43 minutes) and Arthur (two hours and four minutes), although the jury clearly had difficulty with the case against Carr. After twice failing to agree, the members retired overnight, returning to acquit the next day. One journalist concluded the panel was 'seemingly determined not to brand the doctor as a criminal' (Hodgkinson 1986: 1).

Such a determination is perhaps not unexpected when we learn that in the region of 69–82 per cent of British citizens support a change in the law to allow (voluntary) euthanasia (House of Lords Select Committee 2005a: 125–127) – although, once again, one needs to be careful about the data (Hagelin *et al* 2004; House of Lords Select Committee 2005a: 146). This might, nevertheless, give the prosecutors reason to abandon proceedings, as it may not be in the public interest to expend resources on a pointless prosecution. Discontinuance on this ground still presents a problem, however, since the gravity of the suspected crime would usually suggest that proceedings should be pursued: note, indeed, that there is much less resistance when the alleged mercy killer is a member of the public. But even when the trial goes ahead, the jury, however sympathetic, is bound to rely on the arguments and evidence presented, as then summarised by the judge. And there is good reason to question the extent to which the judges are directing the jury and the extent to which they are, in truth, directing the result.

6.3 Directing the jury and directing the result

Judges' directions are undeniably influential on the final outcome of a criminal trial, but they are surprisingly neglected in legal scholarship. It is therefore significant that Dr Arthur's case was one of 15 selected for inclusion in Robertshaw's study. Robertshaw scrutinised the truncated official report and the transcript, the latter of which he felt would have been particularly persuasive in guiding the jury towards an acquittal.

The jury's task, of course, is to determine the factual issues and appropriate finding, guided by the judge's summary of the law. From the outset, however, Farquharson J implied that the jury had a role in distinguishing between the legally permissible and legally impermissible, when he referred them to the 'grey areas' of law involved and mentioned their need to engage in 'line-drawing' (Robertshaw 1998: 78–79). In a further confusion of roles, he confessed that he would be likely to offer some opinions on the facts, but that these should be disregarded (Robertshaw 1998: 80–81). That, of course, is more easily said than done, and Farquharson's discussion of the evidence is very telling. Overtly at least, the damning prosecution evidence was cited while the defence evidence was described as 'lukewarm' ((1981) 12 BMLR 1, at 21), but Robertshaw argues that more subtle factors were at play (1998: 86–89). Forensic opinion may have favoured the prosecution, but 'the credibility/esteem factors weigh in favour of the defence' (Robertshaw 1998: 89). Thus, the use of dihydrocodeine and the order for 'nursing care only' was described as a 'holding operation', a misnomer according to Robertshaw: 'DF118 was never intended to maintain the status quo', as its known side-effects are the suppression of hunger and the impairment of the respiratory system (Robertshaw 1998: 86).

Even more remarkable are the terms used to describe the victim and the defendant. Of all the judge's references to John Pearson, 70 per cent were impersonal ('the child'), 7 per cent used his name, and, most shockingly, 23 per cent objectified the patient as 'it' (Robertshaw 1998: 77). 'The deceased is reduced and marginalized by euphemism and semantic slippage', as Robertshaw puts it (1998: 90). The defendant, however, was almost always referred to by name or profession, with frequent references made also to his good character – all 'highly positive labels for a defendant' on an attempted murder charge (Robertshaw 1998: 83; see e.g. (1981) 12 BMLR 1, at 4).

Farquharson is not alone in making these sorts of comments. *The Times* featured extensive coverage of Devlin's direction in the trial of Dr Adams, including his undoubtedly influential introduction of the doctrine of double effect. While he appeared otherwise even-handed in his words to the jury, Devlin nevertheless reportedly 'did not think he should hesitate in this case to tell them that here the case for the defence seemed to be manifestly strong' (*The Times* 1957: 14). With these words surely ringing in their ears – Devlin apparently spoke only three more sentences – the jury retired, returning to acquit within the hour.

Available accounts of Hooper's direction in the case against Dr Moor also reveal a far from hostile summation. Hooper fared better than Farquharson, in at least referring to the 'victim', Mr Liddell, by name, but the references to the good character and respected professional standing that Dr Moor enjoyed were, nevertheless, prominent. Moor himself recounts how Hooper made 'kindly points' and in his memoir he thanks the trial judge for his dismissal of medical evidence that could have proven vital to the prosecution (Moor 2001: 139). Hooper also left the jury with a precis of double effect and, on prompting from counsel for which he twice thanked him, a reminder that Mr Liddell was due to die shortly from natural causes (Moor 2001: 144). Clare Dyer, in *The Guardian*, felt his remarks to the panel 'nudged them towards an acquittal' (Dyer 1999a).

Such acquittals therefore cannot simply be attributed to sympathetic juries. That might reasonably be claimed in the case of Dr Carr, but even there one can arguably glimpse the influence the 'clearly hostile' trial judge had, given the members' difficulty in arriving at a decision. Of course, the jury also found it hard to decide against Dr Cox, and yet Ognall's direction contained elements that might have served the opposite result. Once again, there was talk of the defendant as a 'distinguished professional man of unblemished character and reputation', along with references to the strength of his bond with Mrs Boyes and the 'richly deserved' respect of his subordinates ((1992) 12 BMLR 38, *per* Ognall J, at 39, 40). Of course, Ognall could not and did not ignore the overwhelming evidence against Cox. However, with the seeming inevitability of the result, the judge still offered the jury some reassurance, in implying that Cox's beneficent motive would have some bearing on any sentence (at 39, 43).

6.4 Get out of jail free? (revisited)

The implication that Ognall would be merciful in sentencing was borne out in the suspended prison sentence that Cox received. Ognall saw the lethal injection as not only criminal but also a 'total betrayal' of the physician's 'unequivocal duty' towards a patient ((1992) 12 BMLR 38, at 47). He nevertheless indicated that 'humanity' and the public interest prevented immediate imprisonment, given the 'wholly exceptional, if not unique, circumstances' (Chittenden and Furbisher 1992: 1). Although some felt this to be a harsh disposal (e.g. Brahams 1992: 2), the result still stands in stark contrast to the rhetoric, which maintains that euthanasia is murder. Little wonder, then, that Cox appeared to be in jovial spirits when next he encountered Ognall, at a meeting of the *Medico-Legal Society* at which the judge was speaking. During questions, the consultant (erroneously) introduced himself as 'Cox, convicted murderer', which prompted laughter from the audience (Ognall 1994: 177).

The GMC too elected neither to strike Cox from the register nor to suspend him from practice, although conditions were placed thereon by his employer. Prior to the professional misconduct hearing, a member of the GMC predicted there was 'not a chance he'll be admonished' (Dyer 1992). As Lord Goff later remarked, he 'was simply admonished' (1995: 6).

7 Conclusion: compromise or confusion?

Despite countless allegations and revelations, Dr Cox is the only doctor to have been convicted for practising euthanasia in recent decades. His conviction serves as a reminder that, in order to plead double effect, the means used to kill (or try to kill) the patient must also be capable of delivering the primary effect i.e. the relief of pain, suffering or distress. Cox's case nevertheless shows that conviction need mean neither the end to one's clinical career nor the relinquishment of one's liberty. As with the mercy-killing relative or friend, the lawyers seem intent on affording a means of *excusing* the medical defendant from the full weight of the criminal law.

However, in stark contrast to the treatment of the lay defendant, the law as constructed for and applied to health professionals is more often premised on the notion of *justification*. According to the lawyers, it is entirely right to strive to palliate a patient's symptoms and thereby run the risk of shortening the patient's life. As this chapter developed the law looked increasingly partial, confused and even blatantly contradictory. But, despite disputes over its philosophical legitimacy, the principle on which Adams relied appeared also to have genuine value and utility in some, albeit very rare, treatment decisions. From the outset, however, the doctrine was out-of-step with prevailing legal principles and its precise status in law remains uncertain: is the doctor administering powerful opioids lacking a guilty intention, failing to cause death or a justified murderer? None of these explanations is satisfactory but the simple fact that there are so many interpretations available speaks volumes of the legal officials' own intention, which would appear to be to absolve the doctor. Sometimes the failure to pursue allegations will be appropriate (notice that none of the defendants encountered here claimed to be experts in palliative medicine); other times – as Adams so vividly demonstrates – it will not.

Once again, then, the legal process seems to have achieved an uneasy compromise of values. Adherents to the sanctity of life principle get recognition of the distinction between intended and foreseen outcomes, while critics who maintain there is no such distinction might at least believe that 'covert' euthanasia is afforded some place in law. Both sides have reason to be concerned, however, since there are fatal flaws in the ways in which the doctrine appears to be understood and employed in the legal domain. The risk of assuming a doctor's innocence is as real for proponents of euthanasia as it is for opponents: it cannot be forgotten that Adams seemed to have more in common with Shipman than with Cox. This should not, and in my concluding proposals will not, lead to the abandonment of the concept of double effect. Recalling Dr Martin's fears at the start of this chapter, the principle helps to ensure that patients are not denied appropriate care at the end of life. Seale's study found that the culture of medical decision-making in the UK is more informed by 'a palliative care philosophy' than many other jurisdictions, and there is good reason for ensuring that this culture continues to thrive (Seale 2006a: 8; Seale 2006b). At the same time, however, the principle requires careful monitoring, again for the sake of patient welfare, and also for the sake of legal coherence. It seems, therefore, that a more robust articulation (and application) of the doctrine is required, so that the innocent can continue to practice appropriate pain relief, but also so that the guilty are unable to hide behind legal confusion. Dr Adams declared 'it is impossible to accuse a doctor'. As this chapter has shown, an accusation is not impossible to countenance but a conviction is currently highly improbable.

Is this appropriate? If law is to perform its basic function, issuing clear and consistent rules for the guidance of its subjects, then there is reason to think that the current situation is not right (see Brownsword 1993; 1996). But I am not only dealing here with what is 'right' in purely legal terms: the ethical rights (and wrongs) of euthanasia obviously cannot be ignored. If the law is to achieve its primary aim, then what is needed is a fuller understanding of how the law pertaining to euthanasia, and end-of-life decisions more generally, has arrived in its current position. The next chapter will examine some of the sources of our current laws and will demonstrate how deeply the moral conflicts run in English law. Equipped with this knowledge, I hope then to discern a way forward that avoids the worst of the difficulties surveyed in these last three chapters.

Chapter 5

Beyond Bland

Hedging bets on the value of life?

This court is a court of law, not of morals

Re A (Children)(Conjoined Twins: Surgical
Separation) [2000] 4 All ER 961,
per Ward LJ, at 969d

We all believe in and assert the sanctity of human life

Re J (A Minor)(Wardship: Medical Treatment) [1990]
3 All ER 930, *per* Lord Donaldson MR,
at 938g–h

The principle of the sanctity of human life in this jurisdiction is seen to
yield to the principle of self-determination

Secretary of State for the Home Department v
Robb (1994) 22 BMLR 43, *per* Thorpe J, at 47

English law curtails a person's right to bodily autonomy in the interests of
protecting that person's life even against her own wishes. Thus deliberate
killing, even with consent and in the most pitiable of circumstances, is
murder: the mandatory penalty is life imprisonment.

R (on the application of Pretty) v DPP (Permission to
Move for Judicial Review) [2001] EWHC Admin 705
(unreported), *per* Tuckey LJ, at para 37

People have an amazing adaptability. But in the end there will be cases
in which the answer must be that it is not in the interests of the child to
subject it to treatment which will cause increased suffering and produce no
commensurate benefit, giving the fullest possible weight to the child's, and
mankind's, desire to survive.

Re J (A Minor) (Wardship: Medical Treatment) [1990]
3 All ER 930, *per* Lord Donaldson MR, at 938h–j

In 1976, the New Jersey Supreme Court was asked to adjudicate on the fate of Karen Ann Quinlan, and its decision spurred the world's lawyers, bioethicists, health professionals and, indeed, patients into carving the contours of the end-of-life debates that we continue to engage in today. Ms Quinlan had been diagnosed as being in what was then termed a persistent vegetative state (PVS). Her prognosis was not good: she would not recover higher brain function and so would never again participate in life in any meaningful way. Her brain stem was, however, functioning and her body could be sustained by medical means, including the use of a mechanical ventilator. The question for the court was: should this machine continue to help Ms Quinlan breathe or would it be lawful for the doctors to stop the respirator?

The court authorised the cessation of treatment (*In re Quinlan* (1976) NJ 355 A 2d 647). A plethora of ethical principles could have been called into service in this case. The idea that life is sacred could have required its maintenance but might also have permitted the discontinuation of treatment if this could be seen as 'futile'. Alternatively, the judges might have argued that Ms Quinlan's life was of too poor a quality to warrant further support. Or they might have fallen back on Ms Quinlan's own prior assessment of the value of life, thus giving prominence to the principle of respect for autonomy. In the event it was the latter principle which won out: neither the wishes of her parents nor the wishes of her clinicians carried sufficient weight to settle the matter. The court decided that 'there comes a point at which the individual's rights overcome the State interest' (at 664). But Ms Quinlan had not made her wishes known in advance of the accident that led to her hospitalisation as a permanently insensate and incompetent patient. The court avoided this difficulty by claiming that, had she been competent, Ms Quinlan would have had the right to seek the withdrawal of unwanted treatment. This right was not lost 'merely' because she was now incompetent (Burt 2005: s9). The ultimate decision was therefore passed to Ms Quinlan's father, who was empowered to decide on the basis of his daughter's assumed wishes, rather than his own judgement as to what would be in her interests. The ventilation was removed. Ms Quinlan, however, proved able to breath unaided and she survived for another 10 years (Biggs 2001: 162).

Many incompetent patients, amongst them Robert Wendland and Terri Schiavo, have followed Ms Quinlan into the American courtrooms and international media (see Lo, Dornbrand, Wolf and Groman 2002; Koch 2005), and it is unsurprising that English judges too have been asked difficult questions about when to let a patient live and when to let a patient die. In such cases, English judges tend to make the sorts of statements that opened this chapter, all of which appear, on purely legalistic grounds, to be good law. But whether the law in this area is 'good', on logical or moral grounds, is open to challenge.

We are told that the judges deal only with principles of law. The first statement was made in the ruling authorising the separation of the conjoined twins known as 'Jodie' and 'Mary', and similar sentiments were expressed in the ruling denying Dianne Pretty the right to be assisted in her suicide (*R (on the application of Pretty) v DPP* [2002] 1 FLR 268, *per* Lord Bingham, para 2). In both cases, however, the judges could not avoid devoting vast tracts of their judgments to distinctively moral concepts such as the sanctity of life, the right to respect for one's personal choices, and the relevance of suffering to end-of-life decision-making. The quotations further show that English lawmakers think that each of these concepts carries some moral force – but that the force ebbs and flows, depending on the particular issue before the court.

The three preceding chapters demonstrated how the law on euthanasia is confused and contradictory, and I began to suggest there that the problems derive, in a significant way, from a failure to work through the moral principles that are said to underpin the law. Only with a deeper understanding of the moral conflict will it be possible to work out an end-of-life ethic that can help law do its business, that is, guide people in their decisions about the end(ing) of life. In this chapter I will examine how deep the conflict is, before turning finally to consider where English law can go from here.

1 Quinlan's challenge: letting die and letting morality in

Karen Quinlan's case has been seen as providing the initial impetus for much of our modern theorising over the end of life (Burt 2005: s9). Her case certainly caught the attention of English legal scholars, who, in the absence of clear precedent, began to ask how our courts would respond to a similar request that life supporting treatment be discontinued. Various scholars argued that the doctor need not be found guilty of homicide and – although we now have clear precedent on the issue – a brief survey and critique of their arguments helps to show why the current law is problematic.

Writers like Ian Kennedy and Glanville Williams therefore predicted that the doctor who withdraws life support would be found innocent by the judges, a prediction which proved all too accurate. The problem with this prediction and the way the scholars justified it was that they claimed to be dealing with 'purely' legal arguments, but these were quickly contaminated by moral concerns. This intrusion, whilst understandable, unfortunately threatened to lead the law into inconsistency and confusion. Of course, the threat was made real, as the previous chapters show that the law is indeed in chaos. It is nevertheless instructive to return to Quinlan's challenge, in order to unearth the roots of these problems.

1.1 Quinlan's challenge

According to Kennedy, Ms Quinlan's case offered 'an invitation to explore the metaphysics of whether switching off is an act or an omission' because English law seemed to lack any clear answer as to whether or not the withdrawal of life-sustaining treatment could be authorised (1976b: 227). The law of homicide, in particular, had to be negotiated, since it was clear that a failure to rescue could amount to murder (*Gibbins and Proctor* (1918) 12 Cr App Rep 134). Kennedy later admitted that this had been a 'creative' exercise, albeit one that needed to occur within the twin constraints of existing legal principles and the conservatism of the judges (1997: 161).

In addition to Kennedy (1976a; 1977), the main contributors were Fletcher (1969; 1978), Williams (1973; 1977; 1983), Leng (1982b), Beynon (1982) and Skegg (1978; 1988), all of whom initially considered the Quinlan situation, that is, the withdrawal of treatment from an incompetent patient. Although Kennedy was sceptical (1977: 452 especially n 32) and Skegg merely conceded the possibility (1988: 141ff.), the majority of these writers felt that the withdrawal of treatment was (merely) an omission in law, such that the doctor's potential liability would turn on his or her duty to the patient. All six concluded that the doctor would not be liable, at least where the patient was enduring a poor quality existence. Leng put this in the boldest terms: 'sometimes *it lies within a doctor's duty to allow a patient to die*' (1982: 209, emphasis in original). Furthermore, it was generally agreed that it would be for doctors to determine whether or not they or their colleagues were liable. Again, Kennedy was more cautious than his co-contributors, but even Williams, who had initially resisted the idea that liability could turn on 'what doctors generally do', came round to the conclusion that reasonable medical opinion provided the key (1977: 635).

Williams (1958a: 291; 1973: 15, 27–31; 1983: 279) and Kennedy (1976b; 1977: 449–452; 1997: 162) were also joined by Skegg (1974: 523–528; 1988: 155–157) in considering the other case in which life support might be withdrawn: that is, when it is refused by the *competent* adult patient. Once more they argued that the doctor would not be liable for acceding to the patient's wish. Williams and Skegg again appeared to rest their conclusions on the fact that this would be a lawful omission of treatment, but Kennedy tried to resist that interpretation, preferring to analyse the issue in terms of the duty of the doctor.

Despite his efforts to avoid the 'unsatisfactory' distinction between acts and omissions intended to end life, Kennedy's analysis was not really so distinct from that of his co-contributors (1977: 449). His manoeuvre did not escape Williams' notice (1977: 635): Kennedy could only reach his conclusions by subtly re-casting withdrawing treatment as a more straightforward instance of withholding treatment (e.g. Kennedy 1977: 445–448, 452). As such, Kennedy was aligned with the majority view: withdrawing treatment, like withholding treatment, involves an omission, which may be lawfully performed where the doctor is duty-bound to honour the wishes of the patient or to acknowledge the patient's interest in being left to die, in accordance with principles accepted by the profession. In short, the theorists concluded that a doctor would not be guilty of homicide in these two situations.

1.2 Letting die as a moral matter

The doctor's acquittal in these two cases was not a foregone conclusion. Although they were rarely explicit about what they were doing, I believe that the theorists reached this conclusion because they felt that this was the morally right result, and they believed that the judges would share that view. Their job, then, was to ensure that the *morally* permissible translated into the *legally* permissible, all the while maintaining that the result was generated by purely legal principles.

Dunstan helps us see the truth in this. Some 20 years after the initial flurry of papers, Lowe (1997) revived the debate, by allying herself with a proposal discussed by Williams (1973: 21) and Skegg (1978: 435; 1988: 181). Here, we are asked to envisage a machine that automatically switches itself off at regular intervals. On Lowe's account, withdrawing treatment must be equivalent with withholding treatment, since failing to restart the machine is clearly an omission and clearly also analogous to a withdrawal of treatment. Of this argument, Dunstan asked: 'In whose interest is it to encourage doctors to employ mechanical devices to *excuse* themselves from that *moral* agency which their profession both entitles and obliges them to bear...?' (1997: 160, emphasis added).

Dunstan is right: these debates are undeniably concerned with moral agency, and will frequently rest on the belief that the doctor is morally entitled to stop the treatment. This was most apparent in the work of Williams, Skegg, Fletcher and Beynon, if only because they provided a *variety* of routes to securing the doctor's innocence. But even where only one solution was preferred, it is possible to find the underlying moral evaluation – and this is either one that is presumed to be present in the law somewhere (because the arguments were meant to predict the most likely legal response) or one that is favoured by the theorist him or herself.

Skegg's writing combines a mixture of prediction and personal preference. Note, for example, how he exchanges between discussing the approach the law 'will' or 'could' take and identifying the approach that he feels 'should' be taken (Skegg 1988). Kennedy, meanwhile, was more purely concerned with predicting how the law would express the moral judgement that the doctor is innocent, which for him meant observing existing precedents and doctrines, and the need to do justice in the individual case (1997: 161). Fletcher, by way of contrast, was more concerned with seeing his own moral evaluation given voice in law. 'The initial decision of classification determines the subsequent legal analysis of the case', claimed Fletcher (1969: 76), but his analysis soon transformed from the descriptive into the normative. He concluded that the withdrawal of treatment 'should' be seen as an omission, and the word 'should' recurs throughout his argument (e.g. Fletcher 1969: 74, 78). Why 'should' this classification be adopted? Because only by adopting this label could recourse be made to the relationship between doctor and patient, which would then enable 'the just evaluation of liability for permitting harm' (1969: 79; see also Fletcher 1969: 81). Where the doctor withdraws treatment because the patient has a poor quality of life, he is innocent; where, however, the doctor fails to act because he is playing bridge, he is guilty (1969: 75). Notice also the distinction Fletcher draws between the doctor in the first scenario (innocent) and the gunman who shoots the patient (guilty) (1969: 83). The layperson, we are told, must be convicted, because this captures 'a critical moral difference' (1978: 609–610). Fletcher's purpose – but also, I suggest, his pitfall – lies in fixing his analysis in order to capture that difference.

This manoeuvre is not Fletcher's alone, particularly when the theorists were in such close agreement on the key issues. Thus, Williams modified Fletcher's arguments, with Skegg ultimately agreeing to an extent, while Leng and Beynon reached similar conclusions, and Kennedy tried to resist but ultimately failed to offer a radically different rationale for the doctor's innocence. Despite what Fletcher claimed, the task did not begin with classification and end in (legal) evaluation. Instead, the 'omission' classification is chosen because this *should* help to engineer the (morally) right result.

1.3 Duties, doctors and intruders

Why is this moral contamination a problem? The first reason might be, simply, that a moral evaluation will be open to dispute and even to extension, for example on the consequentialist ground, considered in Chapter 1, that if we are willing to let someone die, we should also be willing to kill them. Furthermore, moral assumptions – rather than robust argumentation – can lead the law into incoherence and even injustice.

The problems are most apparent in a situation depicted by a number of the early theorists, in which a member of the public, rather than a doctor, withdraws the life support. This 'stranger' or 'intruder' is apparently guilty of some offence, while the doctor is not. Williams is the most explicit about this, in finding that the doctor 'omits' and is exonerated, while the intruder 'acts' and is guilty (1983: 282; 1977: 635; see also Fletcher 1978: 609–610; Skegg 1978: 432).

Williams appears to rest his distinction on either the relationship between the parties or the status of the doctor: the doctor 'has responsibility for' the patient (i.e. a duty towards and, in legal terms, apparently some duty to act in respect of the patient) (1983: 282), while the intruder does not. It should not be difficult to see the legal problems that this reasoning creates. For one thing, materially similar cases ought to be dealt with in the same way. Are these not materially similar cases, at least in terms of what the putative defendant was 'doing'? Williams thinks not, but Skegg understandably saw some difficulty with the issues being resolved by reference to 'who it was that switched off the ventilator' (1978: 432; 1988: 177–179). The status of the defendant, the lawyers tell us, should not matter, particularly when the charge is one of homicide.

Furthermore, the reasoning creates a paradoxical result. Let us momentarily assume that both the doctor and the intruder can be said to have omitted. In this situation, the intruder seemingly ought to be innocent: it is the doctor who, on usual legal principles, owes a duty of care to the patient, so it is him or her who ought to be convicted. There are only two ways a court could avoid this difficulty. First, it could deem both defendants to have 'acted' but it could afford the doctor a new defence. Or, second, the court could find that both omitted but declare that the intruder was under a duty not to interfere with the life support.

Of course, it might still be said that the cases are not materially similar, since, in the case constructed by Williams, the intruder has a very different motive from the doctor.[1] But that too is problematic, when the lawyers insist that motive forms no part of the substantive law of murder: simply put, the intruder's malign motive, and that alone, is not reason enough to convict. With the introduction of motive, however, comes another paradoxical result, again one which Williams would seek to avoid. If we postulate a case in which the 'intruder' merely *withholds* some life-supporting measure, then we once more confront the problem that the intruder could only be convicted if the court found him to be under a duty to provide that measure.

Consider also the situation where the layperson is not ill-motivated. In one of the cases in which the court was asked to determine the fate of a patient in a PVS, the patient was being cared for at home, including by her flatmate (see Hinchliffe 1996: 1580, 1585). What if the flatmate had opted to withdraw treatment because she sincerely felt that this was in the patient's interests? Given his permissive views on euthanasia and the like, Williams would probably have wished to acquit. It nevertheless looks unlikely that his arguments here would support that result: the flatmate looks like the intruder and only if Williams concedes the place that motive plays in his analysis will he be able to secure her acquittal. If he does that, however, he exposes the inconsistency in the law that his reasoning invites.

It could nevertheless be open to Williams to argue that the flatmate who withdraws treatment has 'omitted' and is innocent because she is no longer under a duty to preserve the patient's life. This is precisely what the theorists sought to achieve for the doctor. It is instructive to note how they here managed to invert the court's usual reasoning in relation to duties. 'It would not be correct to say that every moral obligation involves a legal duty; but every legal duty is founded on a moral obligation', was how Coleridge LCJ once put it

---

1   It should be noted that the intention of the doctor and the intention of the intruder may be the same. Although some doctors will not intend to end life when they withdraw life support, it is conceivable – in theory and in practice – that some doctors will have that intention. Williams' intruder also apparently intends death to occur. However, the intruder's reasons for intending this result may be very different – hence the focus here on the different agents' respective *motives*.

(*R v Instan* [1893] 1 QB 450, at 453; see also Ashworth 1989; 2003; Williams 1991; Norrie 1993). What Williams *et al* do is twist this framework to secure the opposite result: the doctor is *not* morally obliged to act. They can only get this answer by claiming, like Kennedy (1977: esp. 449–450), that the duty has dissolved or, like Leng (1982: 209), that it can be a doctor's duty to allow a patient to die, at least when the patient is enduring a poor quality of life. The difficulty with this is that the law of homicide purportedly pays no heed to the condition of the victim, or to the fact that the victim consented to his or her death (see Lowe 1997: 157).

This prompts another problem, which is that it falls to the doctor to determine the presence or scope of his duty to the patient. Beynon, for example, claims that the content of the doctor's duty rests on the contract by virtue of which he treats. That contract assumes the presence of clinical freedom, which in turn assumes that reference can be made to customary practice, in calculating what the doctor is obliged to do or not do (1982: 27–28).[2] The criminal law tends only to impose a duty to act in a relatively narrow range of cases (Norrie 1993: 126), which some claim to be premised on the basis of a contractual relationship (Norrie 1993: 127; contrast Williams 1983: 262–263) – even in the case of the parent and the child (Glazebrook 1960; contrast Ashworth 1989: 441). If that view is right, then the conclusion seems to be that any duty owed by the flatmate, intruder and doctor must have the same basis. Does it not follow that each of these potential defendants ought therefore to be able to claim that their duty can be determined by reference to what people in their respective positions would customarily do? But would the theorists allow the flatmate or the intruder to determine whether they are under a duty to prolong the patient's life? Are they all guilty or all innocent? Or does the question remain the one that Williams *et al* wanted to ask: *should* they all be deemed guilty or all deemed innocent?

At this point I will leave the six scholars to their somewhat tautologous and inherently questionable claims that the doctor *is* innocent because he *should* be innocent. This was a historical survey but an important one that, I think, helps to tease out the problems that exist with the law that we now have. Indeed, the arguments showed remarkable clairvoyance, as they are precisely the ones that the courts have adopted and developed. The problem, of course, is that the theoretical quibbles then transformed into very real difficulties for the law. Moore felt that all of the predicaments arose from the act/omission distinction, with the writers who took up Ms Quinlan's challenge revealing:

> how such a manipulable distinction can be used to smuggle notions of justification in under the guise of being 'omissions'. We think that medical

---

2   Notably, Beynon's claim that there is an underlying contractual relationship acquired some plausibility with the 1990 reforms of the NHS (see Hughes 1991).

personnel may disconnect respirators, whereas intruders may not, because we think the first but not the second is justified in (actively) causing death in this way.

(Moore 1993: 27)

One might still jib at Moore's conclusion that both the doctor and the intruder have 'acted' but Ashworth is nevertheless right to contend that the distinction 'should not be used as a cloak for avoiding the moral issues' (2003: 113). So how keen are the courts to peel back that cloak?

2 Beyond Bland: the problem of fatal omissions

If, in 1960, Glazebrook could describe the acts/omissions distinction as 'deeply embedded in the law' (1960: 387), then it is unsurprising that Williams and the rest of Ms Quinlan's respondents, and the judges after them, placed so much reliance upon it. Little wonder also that the law as expressed in landmark cases like *Airedale NHS Trust v Bland* [1993] 2 WLR 316 appears so haphazard when the judges explicitly referred to some of the arguments just surveyed. This section seeks to show how the problems of theory became problems in reality, and how much of the reason for this rests on the courts' resistance to peering behind the moral cloak.

2.1 Bland's challenge: letting the incompetent patient die

As we saw in the first chapter, the tragic case of Anthony Bland (who, like Ms Quinlan, was in a PVS) required English judges to consider some particularly difficult questions about when a patient should live and when a patient might die. They all agreed that Bland's doctors could stop providing him with food and fluid, which was being received through a nasogastric tube. Lord Browne-Wilkinson vividly described the central dilemma:

the conclusion I have reached will appear to some to be almost irrational. How can it be lawful to allow a patient to die slowly, though painlessly, over a period of weeks from lack of food but unlawful to produce his immediate death by a lethal injection...? I find it difficult to find a moral answer to that question. But it is undoubtedly the law and nothing I have said casts doubt on the proposition that the doing of a particular act with the intention of ending life is and remains murder.

(at 387D–F)

Proponents and opponents of euthanasia alike have united in attacking the 'misshapen' and 'illogical' law, which the Law Lords themselves recognised (e.g. Lord Mustill at 389A) but nevertheless affirmed. The ensuing difficulties are perhaps unsurprising, given the judges' (sometimes explicit) adoption of many of the early theorists' ideas. Removing the tube-feeding was indeed seen as an omission, even though some of the judges accepted that 'some positive step' was required (e.g. Lord Goff, at 369B-H). The issue then became whether or not the doctors were under a duty to continue the tube-feeding. The court concluded that they were not, and the majority of the Law Lords achieved this by adopting an approach from the law governing civil negligence, thereby resting their decision on the views of a responsible body of medical professionals (*Bolam v Friern Hospital Management Committee* [1957] 1 WLR 582; see *Re F (A Mental Patient: Sterilisation)* [1990] 2 AC 1; *Re A (Male Sterilisation)* [2000] 1 FLR 549). Since a responsible body of doctors felt that continued treatment was no longer in Mr Bland's best interests, the duty – or perhaps even the entitlement (see Lord Browne-Wilkinson, at 384–385; Lord Lowry, at 379B–D) – to treat had disappeared, and so the doctors would not be committing murder.

This remains one of the most important rulings in medical law and it has withstood numerous challenges, including that it violates human rights (*NHS Trust A v M; NHS Trust B v H* [2001] 2 WLR 942), but the reasoning is still surrounded by uncertainty and controversy. For one thing, the judges appeared to be exercising what was, at that time, 'a non-existent inherent jurisdiction' (Stone 1994: 206; cf. Bridgeman 1995; see now the Mental Capacity Act 2005). Furthermore, in contrast to the cautious approach more recently taken by Hedley J in the 'death tourism' ruling (*Re Z (Local Authority: Duty)* [2005] 1 WLR 959), the Law Lords used their civil jurisdiction to settle a question of criminality, despite the protests of at least one citizen (see *R v Bingley Magistrates' Court, ex p. Morrow* [1995] Med L Rev 86).

Most problematic, however, was the conflict with established precedent. Cases like *Stone and Dobinson* [1977] QB 354 and *Gibbins and Proctor* (1918) 12 Cr App Rep 134 demonstrate that a fatal failure to fulfil one's duty to act can be manslaughter or even murder, where the failure to act was intentional (see further Ashworth 1989). In those cases, laypeople were found culpable after essentially abandoning their dependents to die. The Law Lords felt that the doctors did indeed *intend* to bring about the end of Anthony Bland's life (e.g. Lord Browne-Wilkinson, at 383D–E). Some dispute this assumption (e.g. Finnis 1993: 331–332) but, once it was made, it should surely have entailed that Bland's doctors would therefore be guilty of murder. 'Of course', as Lord Mustill said, 'the cases are miles apart from an ethical standpoint, but where is the difference on the essential facts?' (at 395A).

The difference apparently rested on the duty that the doctors owed to Mr Bland: this had disappeared, so they were entitled, or perhaps even required, to stop the treatment. Indeed, to continue treating might have been a crime in itself, because the doctors could be deemed to be assaulting Mr Bland if they continued to do so (*per* Lord Lowry, at 379B–D). However, this reasoning only works if the judges had convincingly demonstrated that the doctors no longer owed a duty to Mr Bland. This rested on the controversial finding that nasogastric feeding was a 'medical treatment', or at least part of Mr Bland's 'care' (e.g. Lord Goff, at 372H). Keown is characteristically clear in his objection: what is being treated? (2002a: 219; see also Finnis 1993; McLean 1994; Jennett 1997: 181–182). Why, indeed, should criminality turn on *how* the nutrients are being provided? Although some judges objected (e.g. Lord Mustill, at 399H), the majority apparently had to characterise tube-feeding as a treatment so that – like Williams *et al* – they could resolve the matter through recourse to the views of the medical profession. This provided another of the moral cloaks to which Ashworth referred. Why should the answer rest on 'what some doctors actually do' (McLean 1994: 12)? Lord Browne-Wilkinson (at 386B–C) noted that doctors could justifiably disagree as to whether or not Bland's life should be prolonged. But, as Kennedy and Grubb pointed out, if the patient's best interests are to be determinative, then '[s]urely continuing *or* withdrawing is in the patient's best interests: not both!' (1993: 364).

Like Williams *et al* before them, the Law Lords shrouded the moral issues and left the law in disarray. This was not the first time this had occurred, as the problems can be traced back to Farquharson J's direction in the trial of Dr Leonard Arthur, the paediatrician accused of the attempted murder of John Pearson ((1981) 12 BMLR 1; see Mason and Laurie 2006: 539). It was allegedly Arthur who had (anonymously) written in *The Lancet* about offering parents 'some help in hastening the end of a life' (A Children's Physician 1979: 1123), and his trial came amidst a spate of stories that doctors were withholding life support from critically ill babies (see Linacre Centre 1982: 16–21). The preceding chapter revealed that Arthur was acquitted, following a summing-up that was remarkably sympathetic to the defendant.

Critics were particularly concerned about Farquharson's handling of the acts/omissions distinction, with his dubious references to 'holding operations' and the like, and his incomplete consideration of the duty owed to a disabled child (Gunn and Smith 1985: 707; Brahams and Brahams 1983: 13; Kennedy 1992a: 12; Kennedy and Grubb 1994: 1249; cf. *Miller* [1983] 2 AC 161). There were two main sources of conflict. The first, as in *Bland*, existed between the direction and the established authorities, which suggested that abandoning a child to die could amount to homicide (see Brahams and Brahams 1983: 14). The second oversight was perhaps more remarkable, since Farquharson made no reference to a Court of Appeal decision issued in the civil jurisdiction only months before Arthur's trial (Williams 1981; but contrast Beynon 1982: 17).

Like John Pearson, baby Alexandra had Down's syndrome, but the appeal court held that she *should* be treated for an intestinal obstruction since her life was 'still so imponderable that it would be wrong for her to be condemned to die' (*Re B (A Minor)(Wardship: Medical Treatment)* [1981] 1 WLR 1421, *per* Templeman LJ, at 1424). In one sense the cases convey the same message, since even the civil court accepted, as Templeman LJ put it, that it was not necessary to prolong 'demonstrably awful' lives (at 1424; see also Gunn and Smith 1985: 708). However, there was clearly disagreement and confusion over where the quality of life line should be drawn: Alexandra was judged to have been in a worse condition than John Pearson, but she was to live, while John Pearson was to die. And yet, argued Kennedy and a host of other commentators, it was wrong to even draw the line: the homicide law at that point held that a duty of care was owed to even the most compromised individual (Kennedy 1992b: 157, 170; see also Editorial 1981: 9; Brahams 1986: 389; Mason 1988: 64, 67).

Despite the tone of the judge's direction and the ensuing acquittal, the Attorney General insisted that the law governing homicide by omission remained unaltered (19 HC Official Report (6 Ser) Written Answers Cols 348–349, 8 March 1982). The DPP also announced that no similar prosecutions were being considered (Osman, Ferriman and Timmins 1981: 1). No wonder that, for Brazier, a 'confused picture emerged' from 1981 (2003: 345). Unfortunately, it is no less confused today. Dr Arthur's acquittal of the attempted murder of John Pearson cannot simply be dismissed as a historical curiosity (contrast Poole 1986: 384–386; Brahams 1986: 387; Mason and Laurie 2006: 547). The legal dilemmas that the trial and direction posed not only resurfaced in the Lords' ruling, but it is also apparent that there has since been little official action taken against doctors who are alleged to have withheld or withdrawn life-supporting treatment from incompetent patients.[3] This will reassure the clinicians, but what it does not do is explain *why* the lawyers believe that doctors may refrain from 'rescuing' their patients. The morality, and thus legality, of this behaviour is all too easily assumed and concealed (cf. *Attorney General v English* [1982] 2 All ER 903, *per* Watkins LJ, at 909e). In short, neither Farquharson J nor the Law Lords managed to navigate a way out of Williams' problem that, somehow, being a doctor matters to the question of (un)lawfulness.

2.2 Karapetian's challenge: duties, doctors and intruders (revisited)

So how should the lawyers respond to the 'intruder' who removes a life-supporting treatment? Although Williams, in particular, tied himself in knots with the theoretical dilemma, Lord Goff felt that he was on the right lines: the intruder has performed a positive act, and may be guilty of a homicide offence (but see Finnis 1993: 335; McLean 1994: 11).

It may not be (but should be) surprising to learn that this is exactly how the courts have dealt with individuals who have allegedly tampered

---

3   Allegations that either did not result or appear not to have resulted in official action are reported by, amongst others, Timmins (1981), Fenton (1995) and Dyer (2000; see also *Guardian* 2000: 6). I have previously outlined one case that did go before the GMC (Huxtable 1999). That case, against Dr Taylor, undoubtedly contained troubling aspects, but I am less comfortable now with my earlier decision to label it a case of 'non-voluntary euthanasia'.

with life-sustaining treatment (see also Menikoff, Sacks and Siegler 1992: 1166). In 1999, a Mr Karapetian was convicted of the attempted murder of his hospitalised grandmother and sentenced to an 18-month prison sentence, which was suspended for two years (Finn 1999: 9). Medical personnel had frustrated Karapetian's attempts to disconnect life-support machinery and tubes, but not before he had used scissors to cut a central line. He told police that he felt his grandmother was being 'tortured' and that he wanted 'to let her die a peaceful and natural death' (ibid). Passing sentence, the trial judge commented that Mr Karapetian was motivated 'to ease her passing, so this was in a sense a bizarre form of an attempt at a mercy killing' (ibid).

Obviously the medical staff in this case did not feel it was time to stop treating Mrs Karapetian. If, however, *they* had made that decision, it seems very unlikely that they would have been described as engaging in a mercy killing, and even less likely that they would have faced a homicide charge. This gives us a further reason for judging the law to be partial in its application. It cannot even be denied that the defendant had a motive alien to medical staff who might seek to withdraw life support: they too might want to 'ease the passing' of the patient. And in giving effect to this motive, the medical staff would need to perform many of the actions performed by this defendant: although lines would not be cut, they would have to be removed and machines would have to be switched off. So does this involve positive action or only an omission?

That the description will depend on the person becomes evident in the case against Mrs Watts ([1998] Crim LR 833). Her hospitalised young daughter, Abigail, had been severely brain damaged, and had died after a tracheotomy tube had been disconnected. Mrs Watts was charged with murder but convicted of involuntary manslaughter and, like Karapetian, sentenced to serve 18 months' imprisonment, again suspended for two years, and submit to a supervision order. Although there was no direct evidence that she had done so, the jury were apparently convinced that Mrs Watts had untied the binds holding a breathing tube in place (Shaw 1998). The trial judge stated that the sentence did not indicate approval of euthanasia, but was 'to mark disapproval of what you did' (Bunyan 1997).

On appeal, however, the conviction was quashed. The Court of Appeal found that the judge had failed to direct the jury adequately on the components of manslaughter, and in particular manslaughter by gross negligence. The appellate court felt, for example, that more needed to be said about the 'unlawful act' that Mrs Watts was alleged to have performed. The judges elaborated, in particular, on the meaning of 'unlawful' in this context. What they did not do, however, was criticise the idea that withdrawing the treatment, in this case, could amount to an 'act'.

Williams's prediction was right but with it comes all the problems of partiality and moral subjectivity previously considered. Evidently, the status of the defendant must matter. Mrs Watts was a psychiatric nurse but this had no bearing on her position here, which was as a mother, with all the duties that this should entail. Had she approached the High Court to ask that the doctors stop treating her daughter, then her wishes would have carried some weight (see Huxtable and Forbes 2004; Jackson and Huxtable 2005). In the criminal court, however, she becomes Williams's intruder – and, as Karapetian's case shows, this will be the case even where the motivation looks more benign.

These two cases also seem to bear out one of Gunn and Smith's more problematic conclusions on the import of *Arthur*: a bilateral decision to stop treatment, taken jointly by physician and relative, may be innocent, but a unilateral decision – at least one taken by a layperson – may be guilty (1985: 715). The disparity in the results of the cases against Dr Arthur and Mrs Watts is also remarkable. Abigail Watts had previously been deemed 'not for resuscitation' and yet an alleged attempt on her seriously compromised life was deemed criminal. John Pearson looked considerably more likely to thrive, but an alleged attempt on his life was deemed innocent. This at least suggests some confusion over the duty owed to what Gunn and Smith called an 'abnormal' child, and the threshold of 'abnormality' (see Kennedy 1992b: 170). What is the duty owed to such a patient? And how and why does it differ between health professionals and relatives?

2.3 Diverting doctors from the dock

Few would dispute that there is something distinctive about the healthcare endeavour, which – like the law – might be seen to have its own 'internal morality', and to entail the imposition of special responsibilities on those practising within it (Pellegrino 2001; Miller and Brody 2001; contrast Veatch 2001). It seems only just to accept that the imposition of these responsibilities in turn entails the acquisition of some special privileges. The differentiation between health professionals and laypersons might indeed reside in the relationship between the relevant parties: the person providing treatment and care is simultaneously bound and empowered by a special contract or covenant with the patient; the layperson is not (see e.g. Stirrat and Gill 2005). But how far the fact of being a doctor, nurse or other allied health professional ought then to skew our moral reactions to ending life is nevertheless open to question.

Like Williams *et al*, the judges do occasionally appear too keen to defer to the practises and opinions of doctors (in particular), and in doing this they assume, but do not explain why, there is something in these that is good and right, almost by definition. This tendency has come under attack, both publicly – in the wake of perceived scandals involving organ retention (see e.g. Rodgers 2003; Liddell and Hall 2005; Campbell and Willis 2005) – and in the legal realm itself – where efforts are being made to loosen the strangle-hold that the *Bolam* standard has had over much of medical law (*Bolam v Friern Hospital Management Committee* [1957] 1 WLR 582; see also *Bolitho v City and Hackney Health Authority* [1997] 4 All ER 771; Brazier and Miola 2000). On occasion it might make good sense to follow *Bolam* and let the doctors guide the judges on what the profession considers to be appropriate medical practice. On other occasions this looks less defensible, particularly where, as in Anthony Bland's case, the issues are more obviously ethical in nature, and so must hinge on more than just medical opinion (e.g. McLean 1994; 1996). Sometimes recourse to *Bolam* is particularly objectionable, because the standard 'embodies an empirical rather than a normative test of liability' (Harrington 1996: 352). This cannot be the whole story, however, since the test clearly does accommodate ethical values – albeit the values of the medical profession, rather than the values of society more generally.

And so it seems that, even if there are more issues lurking behind the cloak, the question of which moral position the law wishes to adopt cannot be avoided. Currently, however, that question is avoided, particularly in the context of discontinuing treatment. The judges' recourse to *Bolam* is not even something that the medical profession itself will always welcome. The doctors approach the judges for guidance on when they might let a patient die, but the judges in turn seek to resolve the issue by reference to what doctors do (Jackson and Huxtable 2005: 377). This does at least prompt the profession to issue its own guidance (e.g. RCPCH 1997; BMA 2001; GMC 2002). But, as Dyer (1999b) recognises, it is 'the current law, not the BMA, which puts the ball firmly in the doctors' court'. This even poses a new logical threat to the legal attitude to euthanasia. In the sphere of clinical negligence, it is established that the defendant can successfully defend a claim if he has complied with a body of opinion, even a small one, which supports his practice (see Khan and Robson 1995). In Chapter 4 I explained how *Bolam* has crept into the law as it applies to the use of painkillers in the terminally ill. The doctor might therefore successfully defend a murder charge, if he shows that his action was supported by medical opinion – even if there is reason to fear that some such opinions are misinformed about the realities of opioid use. However, some doctors also defend the practise of euthanasia, and some of them are even apparently willing to undertake this. If *Bolam* is our guide, then does this mean that a doctor who intentionally killed a patient could 'get out of jail free' simply by claiming that he was only doing what some of his peers would have done?

So far as the law is currently concerned, the answer to this question must be 'no'. This again suggests that the problems in the law relating to euthanasia and mercy killing are not wholly explicable in terms of the judges' deference to doctors. Indeed, once discovered, doctors like Harold Shipman, and nurses too like Beverley Allitt, who was also convicted of murdering her patients (see Goldring and Hunt 1997), will undoubtedly continue to face the full force of the criminal law – even if, by some remarkable occurrence, any of their peers felt willing to say that they too would have acted in the same way. Any deference shown to health professionals is clearly not limitless. This reinforces the impression that we will not get far if we continue to dodge the moral problems of ending life, and of euthanasia in particular.

2.4 Beyond Bland: letting die as a moral matter (revisited)

A fuller assessment of the ethical duty owed by the doctor is obviously needed – and, in working through this, it will quickly become apparent that the doctor cannot be considered in isolation. Certainly, the doctor does not resemble the intruder; but he or she might very well resemble the relative or flatmate. The proximity of their relationship with the patient at least suggests that they are not 'moral strangers' (cf. Engelhardt 1996). However, even the moral stranger, someone like the intruder, could be expected to owe some duty to the patient. In short, the central question on the value of life cannot be neglected. Only once we grasp the intricacies of this should we be in a position to identify exceptions and more particular rules which can be applied in particular situations and to particular moral agents. Unfortunately, like the theorists Williams, Kennedy and colleagues, the judges in the cases just discussed were content to *assume* a moral position on the value of life, without fully articulating and defending that position.

The moral distinction between doctors and laypersons is therefore assumed and it leads to the invocation of different descriptions and legal categories in order to facilitate the legal justification of doctors' behaviour (see Smith 1993: 879; Biggs 1996: 883; Ashworth 2003: 290). This prompts Magnusson to charge the judges who dealt with Anthony Bland with dishonesty:

> In their eagerness to distinguish euthanasia, the Law Lords camouflaged the central issue: whether withdrawing life-support and so ending a patient's life was justified in the circumstances. It is better to see the withdrawal of life-preserving treatment for what it is: *a form of non-voluntary euthanasia*, and to justify it on ethical or policy grounds, than to pretend that doctors are not, by withdrawing life-support from an incompetent patient dependent upon it, engaged in the killing business.
>
> (1996: 1118, emphasis in original)

While not quite as emphatically put, similar charges were levelled at Farquharson J's summing-up of the case against Dr Arthur. Kennedy, for example, condemned the 'linguistic or metaphysical sleight of hand' by which the trial judge let 'killing' become 'letting die' (1992b: 156). This, he argued, again diverted attention from whether the doctor's conduct was justified, although, as Davies suggests, the judge revealed where his moral sympathies lay when he sought 'to elevate a moral comment by the practitioners giving evidence into a statement of law' (1998: 323). However, the passive characterisation could not do all the moral work here, as there was still the doctor's duty to consider. Nevertheless, in both cases, the judges still managed to circumvent the conclusion that 'on normal principles both moral and legal responsibility would be established' (Ashworth 1989: 437). So, which set of principles is right – those that would convict the doctor or those that would free him?

3 Doctrinal difficulties: what is the value of life?

This chapter has sought to explain how the law pertaining to the cessation of treatment is as confused as that surrounding mercy killing, complicity in suicide and euthanasia as (allegedly) practised by doctors. Withdrawing treatment will involve similar questions to euthanasia but will also raise specific issues worthy of separate, more detailed analysis. The reason why I examine this topic is because the debates sparked by Ms Quinlan's case demonstrate how 'purely' legal analysis of difficult cases like this one can – indeed must – be infiltrated by moral concerns. The nature of the duty owed to a patient – whether by a health professional, a loved one or even society at large – needs serious contemplation, not least because, if the morality of the case is left in confusion and conflict, then so too is the law.

Although they are not always explicit, the lawmakers obviously do adopt some moral perspective when they address a situation like Ms Quinlan's. Which, if any, offers the best prism through which to view where the law currently is and where it could be? Three main claims are made in relation to ending a life of poor quality, which, as Chapter 1 explained, can be summarised as follows: that it is wrong because it contradicts the intrinsic value of life; that it may be right because life has only instrumental value, and so there is no need to preserve a life of suffering; and, finally, that it will be up to the individual to decide, because life has value only insofar as the person living that life judges this to be the case. More practical concerns, gravitating around slippery slope predictions and the like, will also be important, but it is the primary moral positions that are most significant here and it should come as no revelation to say that each of the three claims currently finds a place in English law.

3.1 The intrinsic value of life

According to one of its most ardent and articulate defenders, John Keown, the idea that life is intrinsically valuable has 'consistently been stated by the courts to be a governing principle of English law' (1997b: 481). Few would dispute that the principle has, or at least has had, a fundamental place in both law and medicine (e.g. Blom-Cooper and Drewry 1976: 187; Kuhse 1987: 5). It is true also that the principle known to English lawyers shares significant similarities with the doctrine known to Christian, and particularly Roman Catholic, thinkers. This remains the case even as society becomes increasingly pluralistic and we become more familiar with hearing the idea expressed in terms of a 'right to life', as protected in the Human Rights Act 1998. As Keown points out (2001: 56), the important thing to recognise is 'the principle of the inviolability of life, on which English law and Article 2 are historically based' – neither the precise words used nor the speaker's religious convictions (or lack of them) are necessarily important in themselves.

The courts nevertheless do not shy away from the theological underpinnings of the principle. In a suitable case, the judges will accept submissions from contributors drawn from particular religious perspectives (e.g. *Re A (Children) (Conjoined Twins: Surgical Separation)* [2000] 4 All ER 961; see Skene and Parker 2002; Gormally 2002), and they will occasionally use distinctively theistic terminology. One Law Lord, considering the prohibition on voluntary euthanasia, observed:

> that the arguments in support are transcendental, and I agree. Believer or atheist, the observer grants to the maintenance of human life an overriding imperative, so strong as to outweigh any consent to its termination.
>
> (*Brown et al* [1993] 2 WLR 556, at 588G)

Elsewhere, in the Crown courts, judges have opined 'that human life is sacred and that no one has the right to take it' (Ryan 1979: 3), and that 'our law exists to protect the sanctity of life, even if that life is of a person in a coma, on the verge of death' (*The Times* 1984: 3). The civil courts too have felt that the sanctity of life principle 'is the concern of the state, and the judiciary as one of the arms of the state, to maintain' (*Airedale NHS Trust v Bland* [1993] 2 WLR 316, at 362F–G).

So the basic prohibition on the intentional ending of life continues to exert considerable influence over the law surrounding euthanasia. Euthanasia, at least where this is achieved by some positive action, remains unlawful. A more general and perhaps even more obvious affirmation of the doctrine is the seriousness with which the law views murder: this is the only offence to attract a mandatory life sentence of imprisonment. The existence of other homicide offences further signifies the value attached to life in this jurisdiction (Blom-Cooper and Drewry 1976: 188).

There are also indications that the lawmakers find moral sense in the whole framework of principles associated with the theological doctrine. Chapter 4 showed the extent to which the ethical doctrine of double effect, which developed from the principle that life is intrinsically valuable, has been adopted by our courts. Equally, as this chapter has demonstrated, the judges have attempted to adopt the type of distinction between fatal acts and fatal omissions that is offered by theorists like Keown. It should be recalled that a belief in the sanctity of life does not require the provision of life support at all costs: it is not obligatory to administer 'extraordinary' treatments – those that are judged 'futile' or that involve more burdens than benefits for the patient. Notably, many of the rulings authorising the cessation of life-supporting treatment include explicit reference to such concepts as 'artificiality', 'burdensomeness' and 'futility' (e.g. *Re J (A Minor)(Wardship:Medical Treatment)* [1990] 3 All

ER 930, *per* Taylor LJ, at 945a–b, 945G–J; *Re R (Adult: Medical Treatment)* [1996] 2 FLR 99). Commentators like Raphael have therefore argued that the sanctity of life position finds a clear place in the law (1988: 8), including in such rulings as the one in which baby Alexandra's life-saving treatment was authorised, and those that deny 'wrongful life' claims (where the claimant argues that it would be better if they had not been born) a legal basis (e.g. *McKay v Essex Area Health Authority* [1982] QB 1166).

Keown is therefore pleased to see the sanctity of life principle given some place in law (e.g. Keown 2003). However, he is undoubtedly less satisfied with the ways in which other – competing – principles have also come to the fore. Further exploration of the law governing the end(ing) of life reveals 'a plethora of arbitrary definitions and dividing lines which do little to enhance the law's reputation for consistency and rationality' (Blom-Cooper and Drewry 1976: 188).

3.2 From intrinsic value to instrumental value

Contrary to what Raphael inferred, Alexandra's case actually planted the seeds of a judicial approach that is quite at odds with the sanctity of life ethic (Hornett 1991). The seeds sprouted in the case of *Re J (A Minor)(Wardship: Medical Treatment)* [1990] 3 All ER 930, which remains a leading authority on the non-treatment of seriously disabled infants.

Although he would and could experience pain, J had sustained severe brain damage at birth, which would result in spastic quadriplegia. He experienced fits and difficulty in breathing unaided, and the clinical opinion was that he would be unable to see, hold his head up or speak. Scott Baker J decided that artificial ventilation could be withheld from J, in his best interests, if this was deemed appropriate at the relevant time. The Official Solicitor appealed, instructing as counsel Munby QC – who was later to join the Bench and rule that a patient had a right to demand life-supporting treatment (*R (on the application of Burke) v General Medical Council* [2005] 2 WLR 431). That decision was overturned on appeal (*R (on the application of Burke) v General Medical Council* [2005] 3 WLR 1132), and Munby's arguments here were also rejected, as the Court of Appeal ushered in what looked like a new ethic, premised on *quality* of life considerations rather than the sanctity of life.

Munby's first, 'absolute' submission was that the judge's decision was contrary to the sanctity of life principle (Alldridge, Morgan and Wells 1990: 1544). Munby rested this argument on the courts' resistance to 'wrongful life' claims, which he felt demonstrated that the courts could not 'play God' in *J's* case (*per* Lord Donaldson MR, at 934c–d; see also Taylor LJ, at 944e). The appeal judges thought that these were 'wholly different' cases, seemingly because a wrongful life action involves a claim for financial compensation on the basis that the claimant would have been better off not being born (*per* Balcombe LJ, at 944h–j). The strong presumption in favour of life could, they ruled, be rebutted in 'exceptional circumstances' (*per* Lord Donaldson MR, at 938e–f; *per* Taylor LJ, at 943c). Lord Donaldson MR felt that there were 'few, if any, absolutes' (at 937a). However, he then dubbed 'thou shalt not kill' an 'absolute commandment' (at 938b–c), and remarked that, in any case, the sanctity of life was 'not in issue' (at 936b–c). It is difficult to see why it was not, but it is at least clear to see what sort of reasoning the court was willing to adopt.

That reasoning emerges particularly vividly in the judges' rejection of Munby's second submission. This 'qualified' submission took Alexandra's case as authority, which showed that J *should* be offered treatment. However, according to the appeal court, the reference in the earlier case to 'demonstrably awful' lives was not to be regarded as a 'quasi-statutory yardstick' for determining when a child could be allowed to die (*per* Lord Donaldson MR, at 938f–g; see also Balcombe LJ at 942g). The child's best interests held the key for the court, and they required an assessment of 'the pain and suffering and *quality of life* which the child will experience if life is prolonged' (*per* Lord Donaldson MR, at 938e–f, emphasis added; see also Balcombe LJ, at 942c–f; Taylor LJ, at 945g–h). Taylor LJ stated that an absolute insistence on upholding the sanctity of life was 'inconsistent at its extreme with the best interests of the child' (at 944d–e; but see Thornton 1991: 240). Ventilation could be withheld from J.

It was not long before this thinking was transferred to the case law involving incompetent adults. The decision that Anthony Bland's treatment could be stopped was said to mark 'a significant retreat from the sanctity of life ethic' (Magnusson 1996: 1115). Once again the judges claimed that the principle was 'not an absolute' (*Bland, per* Lord Keith, at 362F–G, and Lord Goff, at 367D–E). Although they could have argued that the doctors only foresaw death (along the lines of double effect) (see Singer 1994: 68–69), they instead held that the withdrawal of treatment was actually intended to cause death, but that this was permitted here (see Lord Lowry, at 379C–D, Lord Browne-Wilkinson, at 383D–E, and Lord Mustill, at 388G–H). This, of course, clearly conflicts with the central point of the principle, which is to prohibit intentional killings.

The principle rests on a holistic view of the person, who should, regardless of incompetence or inability, enjoy the same rights as more able individuals, including an equal claim on the right to life (Finnis 1993: 334; Keown 1997b: 493; Robertson 1996: 731). The reasoning of the Law Lords, however, was markedly different. Anthony Bland was not seen as a unified person: some judges explicitly adopted a Cartesian distinction between body and personality (e.g. Hoffmann LJ, at 355F–G; Lord Mustill, at 400B–C).[4] Attention could

---

4   Hoffmann relied on Dworkin (1993a). Keown criticises Dworkin for misrepresenting the doctrine and advocating a dualistic view of human life (Keown 2002a: 221).

then shift to the fact that Bland's personality was irretrievably lost. This, in turn, meant that his quality of life was poor, which enabled the judges to rule that continued treatment was not in his best interests. Mr Bland was said to be enduring a life of 'no affirmative benefit' (*per* Lord Browne-Wilkinson, at 386H); indeed, Lord Mustill suggested that he had 'no best interests of any kind' (at 398E). As one might expect, Keown (1997b: 494) strongly contested these arguments, for example claiming that it would certainly be contrary to Mr Bland's interests to use him as a sideboard.

Kennedy and Grubb appreciated that statements like the one from Lord Mustill could only avoid 'the *appearance* of pronouncing on who should live and who should die' (1993: 366, emphasis added). His Lordship still insisted (at 395E–F) that the state's interest in preserving life obtained regardless of the poor quality of a patient's existence. However, the true effect of the pronouncement must be that Mr Bland should die, since his existence lacked the qualities that make life worth living. Try as they might, the judges could not coherently deny that they were appealing to an ethic that judges the value of life as instrumental, rather than intrinsic, in nature (McLean 1994: 10; Kadish 1994: 307; Magnusson 1996: 1116; Fenwick 1998).

Critics of *Bland* believe that the adoption of the 'new' ethic is a moral mistake arising from a conceptual mistake (Keown and Keown 1995: 267). Vitalists hold that life is absolutely valuable, to the extent that every attempt must be made to prolong life (see Keown 1997b: 482). This, says Keown, is not what a belief in the sanctity of life entails, but it is how Munby QC, who represented both baby J and Anthony Bland, caricatured the principle. It is therefore unsurprising that the judges preferred an approach that would allow some patients to die (Keown 1997b: 499), and might also explain why, when the judges have attempted to apply the principle elsewhere, they seem to get it wrong.[5] Sometimes the judges err in claiming that the doctrine is on a par with other 'fundamental' doctrines: to its supporters, the sanctity of life doctrine is *the* fundamental consideration (Magnusson 1996: 730–731). Elsewhere, the judges have dismissed the doctrine as fundamentalist, since it apparently condemns any behaviour that might prove fatal (*Bland*, at 367D–E). However, according to its supporters, when properly understood, the doctrine does allow life to be ended in some situations, such as killing in self-defence (e.g. Keown 1997b: 495; Gormally 1997: 129).

Moreover, mistakes are still made even when the 'straw man' is given flesh (Magnusson 1996: 730–731). This was particularly apparent in the ruling authorising the separation of the conjoined twins 'Jodie' and 'Mary' (*Re A (Children)(Conjoined Twins: Surgical Separation)* [2000] 4 All ER 961). Ward LJ gave perhaps the most comprehensive judicial account of the

5   In *Re C (A Minor) (Medical Treatment)* [1998] 1 FLR 384, for e.g., the court apparently believed that Jewish parents were adhering to the sanctity of life ethic, when it looks more likely that they were supporting a stricter (vitalistic?) ethic.

sanctity of life to date, but the reasoning collapsed into the consequentialist conclusion that Jodie's interest in living a 'normal' life trumped the interests of her 'parasitical' and seriously compromised sister, Mary (see Huxtable 2000b; Huxtable 2001; Burnet 2001). The separation could occur, despite the fact that this would mean the inevitable death of – indeed, the murder of – Mary.

Peter Singer therefore thinks that we are witnessing a 'revolution in British law regarding the sanctity of human life' (1995: 337; cf. Finnis 1993). Quality of life reasoning is arguably here to stay. The Court of Appeal has confirmed that the Human Rights Act 1998 does not (re)impose any duty on the state to prolong the lives of patients like Mr Bland (*NHS Trust A v M; NHS Trust B v H* [2001] 2 WLR 942; see Keown 2001). Keown also continues to chastise the lawyers for further entrenching quality of life thinking, and he is particularly critical also of the medical associations for issuing guidance to doctors that further undermines the intrinsic value of life (2000; 2005; 2006; see also Gormally and Keown 1999).

Is the sanctity of life ethic really on the way out? This currently looks unlikely. The (formal) prohibition on active euthanasia remains. Murder is still considered to be the most serious crime, even despite calls for the abolition of the mandatory penalty (e.g. House of Lords Select Committee 1989). Foreseen, but not intended, deaths are allowed, but this again demonstrates the influence that sanctity of life thinking has over our current law. The acts/omissions distinction also looks unlikely to be abandoned. Indeed, so established is that distinction that Johnson J tried, in the High Court, to argue that the separation of Mary from Jodie amounted to the withdrawal of the life support that Jodie was supplying to her sister. The Court of Appeal may have rejected that reasoning, and with just cause, but even their decision that Mary's active murder was justified was narrowly confined to the facts of the case (but see Huxtable 2002a).

Having said all this, decisions that *are* based on a patient's poor quality of life represent a real challenge to the principle. The lawmakers nevertheless continue to resist extending that thinking into the realm of active euthanasia. Logically, one might think, once suffering or severe incompetence is accepted as a decisive criterion for the ending of life, then the door is opened to non-voluntary (and perhaps also involuntary) euthanasia that is effected by some undeniably positive act, like a lethal injection (e.g. Doyal 2006; see also Manninen 2006). As Browne-Wilkinson observed, the legal resistance to making this equation is 'almost irrational', but the resistance undoubtedly remains. We have, then, a legal framework in which two competing accounts of the value of life jostle to take up position as the superior standard.

3.3 From intrinsic value to self-determined value

To this, already confusing, framework is added a third contender for the title of primary principle. This next challenge to the idea that English law consistently recognises the intrinsic value of life is carried by the juggernaut that is the principle of respect for patient autonomy. The idea seems to crop up in virtually every area of contemporary medical law, leading some to see it as the central organising principle (e.g. Gunn 1994: 8). Very often it will be right to defer to the wishes of the patient, but sometimes the idea can be taken too far, as in Munby J's aforementioned ruling (overturned on appeal) which seemed to grant patients the right to demand – and get – medical treatment. On other occasions, according to its most staunch defenders, it is not taken far enough, such as when a patient like Dianne Pretty is denied the right to be helped to die (e.g. Biggs 2003; Freeman 2002).

As was seen in Chapter 3, Mrs Pretty's appeal to autonomy was judged insufficient to outweigh the state's interest in protecting life, including the lives of other, more vulnerable patients. The sanctity of life is alive and well, at least in this area. Elsewhere, however, it is clear that patient autonomy, at least as conceived by our judges, has made significant inroads into the idea that human life cannot intentionally be brought to an end. The first example of this must be the decriminalisation of suicide. In Parliament it was claimed 'that nothing in the Bill is intended to undermine the sanctity of human life' (HC Deb Vol 644 Col 838, 14 July 1961): compassion for, and protection of, the suicidal lay behind the reform (HC Deb Vol 644 Col 1423, 19 July 1961; HL Deb Vol 229 Col 258, 2 March 1961). It nevertheless remains difficult to disagree with the Lord Bishop of Carlisle's view that decriminalisation undermined the principle, which maintains that intentional killing, including self-killing, constitutes 'a dreadful offence against nature' (HL Deb Vol 229 Col 259, 2 March 1961).

At least two Law Lords have observed how the decriminalisation amounts to a triumph for autonomy over the sanctity of life (*Bland*, per Hoffmann LJ at 351H–352A; Lord Goff at 367G). However, this was nowhere stated in the Parliamentary debates, and Finnis (1993: 337) disputes the conclusion, citing the 1961 Act's penalties for assisting in suicide. To the extent that he detects no *right* to commit suicide, Finnis is correct, and the Law Lords confirmed this in Mrs Pretty's case (*R (on the application of Pretty) v DPP* [2002] 1 FLR 268, para 35–36, 105–106). At the very least, the decriminalisation signals that a suicidal person should not be punished by the criminal courts after failing in his or her purpose. However, the decriminalisation arguably also rested on an element of respect for autonomy, albeit probably in the weaker sense that the suicidal person has a (limited) *liberty* to end his or her life, as I suggested in Chapter 3.

Self-determination triumphs more obviously in cases where the competent adult patient seeks to have unwanted treatment withheld or withdrawn, even on unreasonable grounds (e.g. *Bland, per* Lord Mustill, at 393B–C). Sometimes, as I noted in Chapter 3, the patient will seek this precisely *in order* to die, that is, it is occasionally a wish one might fairly describe as suicidal. David Norman, a paralysed patient, made such a decision, but rather than request the disconnection of a ventilator, he chose to forego the insulin needed to treat his diabetes. Psychiatrists attested to the fact that Mr Norman had made 'a rational decision', and the doctors granted his wish, telling the coroner that they felt legally obliged to comply (see Jones 1995: 3; Jenkins 1995: 7).[6] So clear is the law in such situations that it does not need to be confirmed by a judge, although sometimes uncertainty about, or even opposition to, the request might prompt a court hearing (e.g. *Re AK (Medical Treatment: Consent)* [2000] 1 FLR 129; *Re B (Adult: Refusal of Medical Treatment)* [2002] 2 All ER 449).

The affront to the principle that life is inviolable has not gone unnoticed by its supporters (Keown 2002b: 238). To them, English law goes too far in respecting unreasonable and even suicidal decisions to reject life support, and it does so because it misconceives the principle of respect for autonomy. To writers like Keown, autonomy is subordinate to, and only explicable by reference to, the sanctity of life: freedom is gained, and appropriately constrained, by the proper promotion of human fulfilment (Linacre Centre 1993: 129, 132; Keown 1997b: 495).

The concept of autonomy enshrined in law is clearly not tethered to the particular notion of human flourishing offered in Keown's philosophy. Instead, rather like John Harris (1985; 2003), English law largely leaves it to the individual to determine the value of his or her life. This, however, poses a much-discussed problem: how can it be rational to allow the autonomous individual to be left to die but not to allow them to be helped to die? Lord Goff confirms that the latter will not be tolerated in law: 'So to act is to cross the Rubicon which runs between on the one hand care of the living patient and on the other hand euthanasia – actively causing death to avoid or to end his suffering.' (*Bland* at 368G-H) The claim that euthanasia is prohibited may not be wholly convincing, but adherents to autonomy reject the way that the acts/omissions distinction is, overtly at least, brought to bear on the law in this area. The courts, they argue, 'have chosen to improvise lines of distinction ... at the cost of some coherence' (Kadish 1994: 297), thereby producing an 'apparently irrational result' (Dworkin 1993a: 184).

The critics have a reasonable enough case: the sanctity of life ethic is apparently being dismantled, and the intrinsically subjective version of autonomy that is adopted by our judges can be employed to justify voluntary euthanasia. Inconsistent regard for the principle of respect for autonomy can be found elsewhere in the case law, for example around the competent minor's right to decide about undergoing medical treatment (Huxtable 2000a: 84–87), but it is in the euthanasia debate that the point is most poignantly made. According to some supporters of the principle, the onus has now shifted to

---

6 Of course, the law does not insist that the decision must be 'rational' before it must be respected.

opponents of voluntary euthanasia to show why, on some other grounds, it should not be embraced by the lawyers (e.g. Battin 2005: 97). And, they continue, the case against cannot rest merely on the opposition of some doctors to performing euthanasia. The autonomy of doctors can also be respected by ensuring that they have a right not to be involved, as is already the case with terminating pregnancy and conducting embryo research (Abortion Act 1967, s 4; Human Fertilisation and Embryology Act 1990, s 38). Indeed, this right to conscientiously object was affirmed in Ms B's case and Lord Joffe also included a clause to this effect in his proposed Bill.

Some advocates of autonomy also think that the principle should be accorded greater priority in decisions made to withdraw treatment from patients who are no longer autonomous. One option would be to adopt a 'substituted judgment' approach to ascertaining the incompetent patient's best interests. On this approach, which can be glimpsed in the opening case of Ms Quinlan, a surrogate decision-maker places themselves in the position of the patient and seeks to give effect to the decision that the patient would have made. There will, of course, be occasions when that approach will be wholly artificial and therefore wholly inappropriate: we can never place ourselves in the position of the critically ill baby who has never been able to form, let alone express, the values by which they might live and die. Nevertheless, the approach might have some utility – although its precise place in English law is uncertain (see Lewis 2006: 228).

The more obvious option, honouring an advance directive that the patient made while competent, is also said to have been mishandled by the judges (McLean 1996: 55–56). McLean, for example, has criticised the courts for sometimes being too keen to ensure that the directive reflects the patient's most recent views. She sees this as inconsistent, when the judges are much less wary about 'permitting death' where the patient has never been competent or, like Ms Quinlan, has never made their views known (ibid). McLean finds it equally paradoxical that the judges have appealed to patient autonomy in a case Anthony Bland's, when genuinely autonomous requests to die are simultaneously ignored (1996: 52; see also Morgan 1992: 1652).

In short, a major moral problem with the principle of respect for autonomy – that of its extent (Kadish 1994: 293) – has become a significant legal problem. Autonomy shares this shortcoming with the two other, competing principles, which respectively assert that human life has an intrinsic value and that life is only instrumentally valuable. None of these positions, at least as they are conceived in English law, seems to have been taken to its logical conclusion. Instead, there is conflict and confusion at the level of ethical principle, as they all vie for a position in the law.

4 Conclusion: hedging bets on the value of life

Cloaking the moral conflict that underlies the areas of law under consideration here does not look tenable, particularly when it results in contradictory rules that simply cannot guide the citizens who must be bound by them. The judges, however, refuse to peer too closely at the moral conflicts shrouded by the cloak. Three philosophies – respectively premised on the intrinsic value of life, the instrumental value of life, and the right of the patient to choose the value that should be accorded to his or her life – find some place in the law, but none of them is taken to its seemingly logical limit. Where should law go from here? According to Ashworth:

> The proper solution is not to warp the concepts of omission, duty, knowledge and causation, but to provide for ... cases to be determined on new principles of justification. This would require the courts to be explicit about the grounds for exonerating doctors or nurses, rather than concealing the reasons behind the act/omission distinction.
>
> (1989: 437)

No amount of theorising is likely to do away with the main claims that follow from each of the three competing philosophies surveyed here, so Ashworth's search for new principles looks likely to be a long one. He is nevertheless right to insist that we pull back the cloak, and seek a more honest appraisal of the rights and wrongs of ending life in English law. This was precisely what the Law Lords sought, after the difficulty they had endured in working out Anthony Bland's fate (see Lord Browne-Wilkinson, at 387C–D; Lord Mustill, at 392D–F). The ensuing Select Committee (1994a), however, recommended few cures to the ailments that continue to impinge on the law in this area. That may not be surprising, since working through, and working out, the moral commitments underlying the law is indeed a considerable undertaking. It is, however, one that must now be embarked upon.

Chapter 6

Euthanasia and the middle ground

From conflict to compromise

Moral debates of the sort surrounding euthanasia involve the engagement
of frequently very different visions of human goods. How the common
law approaches such issues provides a glimpse of how a solution is often a
patch-up of various elements, a feeling towards a sustainable moral position
... Of course the euthanasia debate will rumble on ... but the defence of
the middle ground, currently occupied by English law, is a worthwhile
enterprise.

(McCall Smith 1999: 207)

Rather than reaching a more finely honed consensus about the values and
practices that undergird end of life care, conflict has come to dominate the
discussion. The consequences are serious for patients, health care providers,
family members, and society.

(Dubler 2005: s19)

Perhaps real resolution is not possible and consensus a silly dream. But
perhaps resolution and consensus are possible; it is the moment at which
the current discussion ought to begin in earnest to try to seek them ... After
all, these are not trivial social issues, and the circumstances in which these
dilemmas arise – where, as a result of the epidemiological transition in
the causes of mortality, death at the conclusion of a long, terminal illness
awaits an ever-increasing proportion of the population of the developed
world – are what the future increasingly brings.

(Battin 2005: 38)

Should Dianne Pretty have been granted her plea for assistance in dying?
Should life support have been removed from patients like Anthony Bland and
Karen Quinlan? Should Bernard Heginbotham have been convicted for the

mercy killing of his wife Ida? Which, if any, of the various methods of assisting in suicide that Michael Irwin allegedly offered ought to have been subject to censure? And should Dr Howard Martin, and indeed any other doctor, be able to rely on the doctrine of double effect?

The legal answers to these questions are, I have argued, muddled, and the muddle poses not only a theoretical but also a significant practical problem to anyone seeking to know the boundaries of the legally permissible in end-of-life situations. We should all be able to agree that inconsistent law cannot serve to guide anyone; and yet, if it is about anything at all, law is concerned with what Lon Fuller described as 'subjecting human conduct to the governance of rules' (1969: 96). To achieve this most basic purpose, the rules should not conflict and they should do what they claim they will do. I have suggested, however, that our existing laws are in constant tension and sometimes outright contradiction, and that the official, prohibitive line on euthanasia is not all that it appears.

The solution, according to many of those with an interest in the regulation of euthanasia, lies in identifying an appropriate ethical prism through which to view the various practices that might or will lead to the ending of life, and ensuring that this viewpoint is uniformly adopted in the law. There is no shortage of perspectives, the most prominent of which were surveyed in the first chapter and the final section of the preceding chapter. Thus, Keown (2002a) will argue that the law ought to ensure that all lives are protected as equally and intrinsically valuable, and he will also condemn any moves towards accommodating euthanasia as unsafe and unworkable; Doyal (2006) will emphasise the quality of mercy and will urge for the humane eradication of suffering through legalised euthanasia; Brock (1993), meanwhile, will prioritise the principle of respect for autonomy and turn the decision to end life (or continue living) over to the patient.

All of these viewpoints have been adopted, in one way or another, into English law. However, it is not clear which, if any, of these rival accounts of the value of life offers the best way forward. The arguments on all sides have some plausibility and moral pull, but I argued in the first chapter that they also all appear to leave out some important feature of the morality of ending life and to be beset by difficulty and controversy.

In this concluding chapter, I seek to move this debate on from the current conflicts, which are couched in 'noisy rhetoric' and populated by 'hostile sides entrenched over an issue constructed as "choice" versus "killing"' (Battin 2005: 35). Against this moral backdrop, McCall Smith has a good case for arguing the merits of the middle ground. I will suggest, however, that he is a little too complacent about the state of our current laws. Dubler and Battin are also right to insist that we should find areas of agreement between the competing claimants, but they appear overly optimistic about the prospect of engineering complete consensus. Yet, constructing a compromise looks both possible and desirable and so I propose that the time has come to split the difference between the various answers given to the 'ancient question' of euthanasia (*R (on the application of Pretty) v DPP* [2002] 1 FLR 268, *per* Lord Bingham at para 54).

Although this can only be the beginning of this new debate, I will explore why a compromise is worthwhile and the form it might take. I will suggest, perhaps controversially, that a compromise position will mean that the legal answers that should be given to the questions posed by Dianne Pretty *et al* are essentially those already offered by our courts. This might seem surprising but adjustments will be required in order to restore a much-needed measure of coherence to the law. The task will be difficult since the contours of the compromise, indeed the very attempt to move to the middle ground, might be attacked from all sides. Nevertheless, serious thought must now be given to moving beyond 'the present impasse', in which 'we heatedly debate "right-to-die" legislation' (Fraser and Walters 2000: 122).

I From conflict to creativity and consensus

As Chapter 5 drew to a close it became apparent that English law occupies an ethical junction: one road leads to respect for autonomy, another fork points us in the direction of the intrinsic value of life, while a third takes us into judging the quality of life. In Chapter 1 I suggested that there is promise, but also peril, in taking the law too far in any one of these directions. If the primary ethical injunctions do not appear to point the way forward, then where should the law go from here?

In this section I will consider three answers that, whilst undeniably worthwhile, do not yet offer a sufficient solution. The first, offered by McCall Smith, is simple and has some intuitive appeal: the law should remain where it is. Alternatively, as Battin has recently proposed, we could find a wholly new direction to go in. She too is right to insist that we need to find new ways of thinking about these issues. And yet another alternative, hinted at by Moreno, is that we should make the best of where we are, and only travel to destinations on which everybody can agree. Engineering such consensus also looks like a reasonable solution.

Yet, none of these options provides a wholly suitable roadmap. McCall Smith seems to come closest, in favouring compromise over conflict, but he appears too eager to condone the current situation, in which the various competing official pronouncements and other legal authorities frequently fail to delineate the permissible and the impermissible. Battin and Moreno, meanwhile, are too optimistic about the prospects for innovation and agreement. All of these ideas are nevertheless worth exploring, since they can each help in granting Brock's plea, raised in Chapter 1, for the euthanasia debate to be illuminated by more light and less heat (1993: 203).

1.1 Condoning conflict and confusion

The first option is to settle for what we already have, which is precisely what Alexander McCall Smith has argued. Mindful that he will be charged with complacency and conservatism, he nevertheless commends the existing 'morally sensitive compromise which should be left undisturbed' (McCall Smith 1999: 194). So, he says, the law reflects the intrinsic value of life in prohibiting euthanasia, the autonomy principle in permitting the refusal of treatment, and elsewhere offers a 'zone of indeterminate application' for the humane disposal of the mercy killer (1999: 197). Others have reached the same conclusion, including Kalven who, four decades previously, favoured 'leaving things as they are and trusting for awhile yet to the imperfect but elastic equity in the administration of the law as written' (Kalven 1956: 1237; see also Ramsey 1956: 1201; House of Lords Select Committee 1989: 547, 549, 568). Mercy killers can therefore seek solace in diminished responsibility and complicity in suicide, while the doctrine of double effect and the acts/omissions distinction are said to afford 'the medical profession a considerable amount of elbowroom, in which its members may take a variety of actions to shorten life' (McCall Smith 1999: 205).

McCall Smith's argument deserves to be taken seriously: there are, as he says, 'worse places to be' than the middle ground (1999: 207). Preserving the *status quo* does at least mean that the various worthwhile insights offered by the competing ethical viewpoints on the value of life can continue to exert influence on the lawmakers and the resulting law. The problem is that all of the hypocrisy and inconsistency unearthed in Chapters 2, 3 and 4 will also remain. These present serious difficulties not only for the conceptual rigour and defensibility of the law, but also for anyone seeking to know when they might, and when they might not, fall foul of the rules.

Such uncertainty means that the rules are not fulfilling a basic function of law: guiding the activities of those to whom they apply. Working from Fuller's concept of law, Roger Brownsword has developed a framework for assessing any area of the law, which echoes discussions occurring in jurisprudence and on the 'rule of law' (Brownsword 1993; 1996; see also Beale 1935; Rawls 1972: 235–243; Raz 1977; Finnis 1986: 266–274; Radin 1989; Craig 1997). In summary, Brownsword argues that law ought to be rational in three senses: *formally*, such that the rules should not contradict, *instrumentally*, such that, in particular, the administration of the rules should be congruent with their stated terms, and *substantively*, which means that the rules should conform to some justifying end or principle. The first two of these criteria appear uncontroversial but, I have argued, English law governing the end(ing) of life all too frequently fails to meet the relevant standards. As the preceding chapter drew to a close I nevertheless suggested a reason for this, which Brownsword would describe as a crisis of 'substantive rationality': the rules do not rest on a coherent moral framework.

Whether law ought to be substantively rational, and what substance it ought to have, are of course much more controversial matters. McCall Smith evidently believes – albeit without offering any robust philosophical defence – that the law is in the right place ethically, so for him the problems of formal and instrumental irrationality assume less importance. He has a point, but he wrongly downplays the confusion wrought by such irrationality. Perhaps, then, better legal answers can be found by working through the ethics of ending life.

Here, however, conflict inevitably returns. Brownsword, for his part, supports a deontological ethic, which would embrace voluntary euthanasia and assisted suicide, and so grant Mrs Pretty her request and enable doctors like Irwin (and, indeed, Cox) to undertake practices deliberately designed to end life (see Beyleveld and Brownsword 2001).[1] Of course, with this proposal we are forced to re-enter familiar debates about whether our legal system ought to gravitate towards the view that life has an individually determined value, an intrinsic value or an instrumental value. The 'practical' arguments around allowing euthanasia will also resurface but, contrary to what some writers suggest (e.g. Battin 2005), we are not quite at the point where these should take priority. Indeed, it is particularly important for the principled arguments to remain centre stage when, as I observed in Chapter 1, new proposals for permitting euthanasia, particularly of a non-voluntary form, are being advanced. As I averred in the first chapter, the difficulty then becomes one of selecting from a pool of three rival accounts, all of which have their merits, but none of which is flawless.

1.2 Creativity at the end of life

There may be a different way forward. Margaret Battin, a leading authority on end-of-life ethics, thinks that the 'for-and-against' format has run its course: echoing Ashworth's point in the previous chapter, she believes that we need to find new ways of thinking about euthanasia. Battin is surely right to argue that the debate needs to move on, and she helpfully suggests that we should be reconsidering notions like the 'right' and the 'good' and re-engaging with the question of what respect for autonomy should mean. This work is already well under way (e.g. Donchin 2000; O'Neill 2002; Gaylin and Jennings 2003) and the scholarship occasionally bears out Battin's suspicion that such re-engagement will not mean 'that the debate will be resolved in favour of the "pro" side, but means only that the debate must focus more directly on the deeper issues at hand' (2005: 36). Indeed, another of these issues must be justice, and particularly the relevance of economic constraints on end-of-life care. Patients are already playing what Harris dubs 'the survival

---

1   I have previously mounted a similar argument (Huxtable 2005a).

lottery' (Harris 1980; cf. Ravenscroft and Bell 2000: 437), but letting money dictate the (non-)provision of care raises the spectre of eugenicist policies that disfavour the elderly, disabled and disadvantaged. Yet, even here advances are being made in clarifying the role played by scarce resources (e.g. Callahan 1995; Burt 2005: s13; Epstein 2007).

This is important work, which should enhance the debate, but ultimately Battin is a little too optimistic, since no amount of fresh theorising looks likely to provide a complete or radically new answer. The arguments I have surveyed certainly do not exhaust the moral lexicon, but whatever language is used – whether old or new – it is difficult to conceive of an ethical framework that will have no place for the principal claims I examined in Chapter 1. Van Zyl (2000), for example, has considered euthanasia from the perspective of virtue ethics. Here, one sees an old ethical template being applied in a relatively new way (but see e.g. Foot 1977). This is undoubtedly a vital corrective to the dominance of principled, deontological and consequentialist thinking. However, van Zyl's work only re-clothes the familiar discussions: respect for autonomy becomes the virtue of respectfulness; the beneficent duty to remove suffering becomes the virtues of benevolence and compassion; and so on. Virtue ethicists may yet provide a different way of thinking about euthanasia (see Solum 1998) but van Zyl, at least, does not take us in a wholly new direction.

In short, no discussion of euthanasia is going to get far if it does not incorporate and take a position on whether life is intrinsically valuable, instrumentally valuable or subjectively valuable, and whether the practice can be undertaken in a way that avoids the slippery slope(s) and other practical objections. And yet, as I sought to demonstrate in Chapter 1, 'moral mayhem' clouds these key arguments (see Doyal 1990: 7). Where can the debate go from here?

1.3 Consensus and convergence at the end of life

According to Jonathan Moreno the answer could lie in locating the issues on which proponents and opponents of euthanasia can both agree. He suspects that consensus is achievable because the contributors are not completely:

> wedded to one or another all-or-nothing viewpoint. As the population ages, and as the dying process is continually modified, further accommodations will surely be needed concerning end-of-life treatment. True respect for competently expressed wishes to abate treatment would go far to alleviate public concerns about dying tethered to machines, and the development of training programs in palliative care would greatly reduce, if not eliminate, the basis for fears about suffering at the end of life. This is not to dismiss the issue but only to indicate some elements that may provide the basis for consensus.
>
> (1995: 34)

Solum, also commenting on the American context, broadly agrees that it is possible to 'search for common ground':

> Our common public reason and our shared political values may yet allow us to reach a measure of agreement. We may yet resolve the debates over euthanasia, morality, and law in a way that each of us can affirm as legitimate, even though many of us would choose otherwise if the choice were ours alone.
>
> (1998: 1122)

Indeed, Dubler has also recognised how, in America at least, 'it seemed as if a tentative consensus had been reached that death is not always the worst outcome', following the ruling that Ms Quinlan's life support ought to be discontinued (2005: s19). In the UK too there are various points of harmony. Every contributor believes that human life has some value, and also that suffering should be avoided. A good death, everyone agrees, is something to strive for. The potential for abuse, meanwhile, must be minimised or ideally avoided; at the very least, this seems to leave everyone opposed to the practice of involuntary euthanasia.

From such general areas of agreement, concrete ethical and legal guidance can then be generated, which can help take the sting out of some of the more abstract battles being waged (Wong 1992: 778). Everyone, it seems, wants to support practitioners of, and practices in, palliative medicine; everyone also agrees that it can be appropriate to discontinue life support; and no one, it seems, supports involuntary euthanasia. The rationales offered and terminology employed may differ, with Keown talking of 'futile' treatments and 'double effect', and Singer describing 'quality of life' assessments, but the end point – in terms of the decision reached – may not be so different in these three cases. As such, it then falls to the lawmakers to ensure that the law appropriately reflects these areas of agreement. This would, for example, require an adjustment in the approach to involuntary mercy killing, so that it is not quietly condoned, as I suggested in Chapter 2, but instead openly condemned. Similarly, the inconsistent approaches to fatal omissions would need to be brought in line with the common viewpoint.

Unfortunately, like Battin, Moreno and the other supporters of consensus are rather too optimistic. For one thing, it is not necessarily the case that a consensus position can claim moral validity. On a more practical level, even if some consensus can be reached, it seems unlikely that conflict will be completely eradicated. As Dubler points out, 'consensus is hard to achieve, and even harder to maintain, in a dichotomized society' (2005: s19). Interpretive battles will surely reignite amongst the moral philosophers over the value of life, how far autonomy ought to be respected, how suffering should be ended or otherwise dealt with, what a 'good' death really is, and what can be seen as an 'abuse'. Indeed, people who arguably have an even greater stake in the decision at hand – patients, their families, and healthcare professionals – will have their own, divergent interpretations.

Sometimes the conflict is all too apparent in practice (e.g. *Glass v UK* [2004] 1 FLR 1019; *Re Wyatt* [2006] Fam Law 359; *Re L (A Child) (Medical Treatment: Benefit)* [2005] 1 FLR 491), although here at least consensus might still be achieved by refocusing attention on practical methods of minimising and ending disputes. Mediation and recourse to clinical ethics committees offer a glimmer of hope (Huxtable and Forbes 2004; Jackson and Huxtable 2005; Dubler 2005; Burt 2005), particularly when the latter have proven so effective in resolving dilemmas involving, for example, the withdrawal of treatment (e.g. *Re G* [1996] NZFLR 362; see also McCall Smith 1990; Doyal 2001; Hendrick 2001). If, as Doyal has observed, moral indeterminacy can be a real problem in modern medicine, then reference to a committee can help to air the differing views and work towards a practical consensus (Doyal 1990; Doyal 2001: i45–i46).

But no matter how valuable these proposals are, they still do not settle the primary question: should euthanasia be tolerated? On this issue, at least, consensus looks unlikely. Does it really lie in the provision of palliation, such that, as some authors imply, a practice like terminal sedation (along with the voluntary refusal of nutrition and hydration) provides an answer to the euthanasia debate (e.g. Quill and Byock 2000)? Not really, says Battin, and with good reason. For one thing, such a practice itself raises difficult ethical questions (Jansen and Sulmasy 2002). Battin herself does of course commend the victories of palliative medicine, which manage to elide some of the difficulties associated with the acts/omissions distinction and also, on her account, to encompass 'actions that are functionally equivalent to euthanasia' (2005: 37). What they do not offer, however, is what the proponents really want: the provision of euthanasia itself, least of all in those cases where palliative care cannot deal adequately with a patient's symptoms and wishes. Instead, the palliative care argument really only represents a victory for one side: it might settle some of the debates around tackling suffering, but it does so under a broad sanctity of life umbrella, which still prevents people from being 'the architects of the ends of their lives' (ibid).

Battin therefore finds it:

> difficult to find a writer with a foot firmly planted on each side of the fence, or, better still, for whom there is no longer any fence at all. I do not yet see the kind of genial, comprehensive summation of the issue that is sensitive to the concerns of both sides, one that manages synthesis without ignoring or trivializing the principal concerns on both sides, one that could be called a real resolution of the issues, one that could elicit consensus and agreement at both policy and practical levels.
>
> (2005: 38)

Battin is undoubtedly right to call for this sort of development. Unfortunately, the answer she sketches again looks more like it awards a win to one side, rather than articulating a truly centrist position – although this time the victory is achieved by those in favour of euthanasia.

Battin suggests that the sort of answer we need might rest on formulating a default position for end-of-life decision-making, which will necessarily include a range of liberal and conservative options for selection by the individual patient, who will themselves have been asked to provide a 'personal end-of-life policy' that conveys the values to which they subscribe (2005: 40). I can see why a default position can be helpful, rather than waiting to address disputes at a time of crisis, when emotions will run high and more rational reflection might not be feasible. However, what Battin does here appears ultimately to side with the autonomy lobby, when she introduces the notion of personal policy-making, as she implies that *any* personal decision – apparently including a decision for euthanasia – ought to be respected. This then looks unlikely to furnish a true consensus position, since people committed to the sanctity of life principle will scarcely be willing to concede so much.

2 The case for compromise

Although Battin is right to seek a fuller 'resolution of the issues between the "for" and "against" sides of the debate' (2005: 37), complete consensus looks improbable. So too it appears unlikely that new thinking will eradicate the familiar convictions that many of us hold on the value of life. What I think we need is a policy that manages these conflicting perspectives and does so through a set of rules by which we can all be clearly guided. Of course, all of the contestants who have staked a claim on the value of life in English law might well attack any suggested solution; nevertheless, I maintain that it is time to look beyond conflict, and even beyond consensus, towards compromise.

2.1 The conditions of compromise

Few theorists have given thought to what a compromise on euthanasia might look like. I, nevertheless, believe that various features of our current debates about euthanasia – and the confused state of English law – combine to suggest that we are at the point at which we should invest our energies in this enterprise.

Notice, first, the dearth of factual certainty relating to the end of life. Medicine is not as exact a science as it is sometimes depicted: it is not always obvious how an intervention will affect a patient's life or quality of life, nor is it clear how the science will progress. Can and should the potential for scientific development render the case for euthanasia moribund? Other factual predictions, like the slippery slope arguments, also remain contestable. Evidence from different societies can be manipulated to suit a theorist's cause, and, in any case, need not indicate what should happen in our *own* particular jurisdiction (Battin 2005: 47–68).

There is also significant philosophical uncertainty. Some philosophers believe that the problems are more pronounced in the realm of abortion (e.g. Battin 2005: 35) but, in my opinion, the uncertainty is no less significant in the present context. Here too the ontological and moral status of the subject (of euthanasia) is disputed, with Harris and Singer denying that patients like Anthony Bland are 'persons'. As I have argued throughout this book, opinions are also split on the value of life as it is conceived in the euthanasia debate and related discussions, which prompts tangible dilemmas about, for example, when (not) to provide life support. We cannot even agree on how to define and categorise the types of conduct usually in issue. Is withdrawing life support a form of euthanasia, and if so is it active or passive in nature? What is assisted suicide and (how) does it differ from euthanasia?

Such uncertainty can only impact adversely upon any attempts to discuss the rights and wrongs of ending life. Indeed, the moral complexity of the issues bolsters the case for compromise, since each of the opposing arguments possesses some merit. We want to allow people to make important personal decisions for themselves; we want to deal humanely with suffering; we want to protect life in many situations. Nevertheless, we differ in our understandings of these ideas and no matter what our view, we are all locked in an ongoing social relationship: we are probably all, at some point, going to be patients; we are also all going to die. 'All of us', says Martin Benjamin, 'whether extreme conservatives, extreme liberals, or some type of moderate, are members of a single nation requiring uniform policy on matters of life and death.' (1990a: 164) Everyone has a stake in crafting this policy, even if it must always remain open to revision (Wong 1992).

Furthermore, a clear policy is obviously needed. I suggest that we have a legitimate interest in knowing how life – including our own – should, and should not, come to an end. The current legal answers are thoroughly confused and the law is simply not achieving its basic aim, since contradictory rules can guide nobody. The rules conflict, medical science continues to progress, the situations and settings in which we die alter, and the arguments for and against euthanasia constantly ebb and flow. Metaphysical or moral closure nevertheless appears a will-o'-the-wisp. In sum, this issue – where lives are at stake – is scarcely one on which we should lack a clear policy, informed by the multitude of moral claims made on all sides.

Although he himself says little about euthanasia, it is remarkable how readily these features of our current discussions about the issue mirror the conditions for compromise identified by Benjamin (1990a), since our discussions are beset by uncertainty and moral complexity, the various stake-holders are locked in an ongoing relationship, and we desperately need to reach a defensible decision. Benjamin's endeavour, which resembles the codification of compromise in controversial bioethical matters, is itself not uncontroversial

– indeed, one might even suspect that, for Benjamin, any and every bioethical controversy must end in compromise since, by definition, their existence rests on ethical conflict. Whether or not that is a fair accusation, I believe that on this specific issue, at least, we appear to be at the point at which Benjamin would say we need to find ways of splitting the difference between the competing viewpoints.

2.2 Condoning compromise

As necessary as it appears, the move from conflict to compromise nevertheless poses its own risks, of spelling an end to moral theorising (why seek new answers if we are only going to be told to make the best of a bad situation?) and individual integrity (what will happen to my sense of myself if I am compelled to abandon my convictions?). However, neither of these concerns need amount to conclusive arguments against adopting a compromise, providing that we take the existence of moral pluralism seriously and are willing to concede something to the conceptual framework offered by moral pluralists.

It is an unavoidable matter of fact that moral values (duties, principles and the like) will clash. Sometimes an appeal to another value can resolve the particular dilemma; sometimes it cannot, but a decision will still be needed. Consider a case in which a doctor has respected the patient's autonomous wishes in all possible ways, including by withdrawing (seemingly) life-sustaining treatment at her request (see Huxtable 2007). The patient, however, has survived and is now in a pitiful state. She asks that the doctor take positive steps to end her life.

The doctor is likely to feel the pull exerted by autonomy and the suffering of the patient, but simultaneously feel constrained by the duty to preserve life. As I argued in the first chapter, supporters of each of the different values being brought to bear on the ending of life will seek to accord priority to their chosen value, but there is insufficient reason for letting any one come to dominate. Sometimes the nature of the value in question will itself be contested. Respect for autonomy, for example, commands widespread support but Doyal has shown how efforts to apply this one idea can produce moral indeterminacy and 'inconsistent moral practices' (Doyal 1990: 11).

Similar problems exist even if we move back from the level of applied ethics and look to the underlying comprehensive ethical theories from which such norms are derived. Proponents of various theories of these sorts will claim that a solution can be found. Kant, for example, would say that 'perfect' duties cannot conflict: the doctor's dilemma is more apparent than real, since appropriate reflection on the meaning of such duties should provide the answer (e.g. Kant 1991: 84–85). Modern deontologists mount similar arguments (e.g. Beyleveld and Brownsword 2001). However, the deontologists do not (yet) appear to have provided a sufficient account of the diverse duties that one might feel compelled to honour (see Benjamin 1994: 263–266).

Even attempts to spell out the *various* principles that can guide the good life do not completely avoid this problem. Beauchamp, who – with Childress – devised the four principles approach mentioned in Chapter 1, has argued that it is possible to apply a (Rawlsian) method of 'reflective equilibrium' in order 'to match, prune, and develop considered judgements and principles in an attempt to make them coherent' (1994: 11). He nevertheless concedes that 'principlism' only offers 'the point at which the real work begins' (1994: 12). In short, appeals to a monistic principle or even to a set of principles will not eradicate moral conflict and the need for further interpretation, and they will also fail to capture the subtleties of lived moral experience (see Wong 1992: 768–769; Solum 1998: 1118–1119).

The same can be said of various other comprehensive ethical theories, such as utilitarianism. Utilitarians like Mill (1962b) and, nowadays, Singer (1993) will direct our doctor back to some version of the principle of utility, which would require him to act in a manner that promotes the greatest good for the greatest number. This also does not automatically and self-evidently dissolve the dispute, when utilitarian arguments can be employed to reach different conclusions on the suitability of allowing euthanasia (e.g. Velleman 2004). It might, for example, be best to adopt a policy of preserving life – but it might also be preferable to support a rule valuing autonomous choice over all other considerations.

Of course, battles will also be waged between exponents of the different ethical theories. Had Kant and Mill sat on the same ethics committee, one can only wonder how the committee would have reached agreement on myriad issues. Sometimes they would agree; on other occasions, as the euthanasia debate itself demonstrates, they would not, and the source of the dispute could well be the underlying ethical framework. I think it worth repeating that no single moral theory can (yet?) claim to have the monopoly on moral truth, or at least perhaps not a sufficiently robust one on which to rest our entire legal response to euthanasia. There is undoubtedly something important in these sorts of attempts to map the moral life but the theories cannot hope unambiguously and decisively to solve moral dilemmas.

These contests between rival values and between rival accounts of what is valuable are not mere theoretical quibbles – they can have a significant practical impact. I described in Chapter 1 how two central figures in the case for allowing voluntary euthanasia have been subjected to very real attacks: the philosopher Peter Singer has reportedly been assaulted while lecturing on the topic, while the clinician Dr Cox was issued with death threats following his trial. The conflict will obviously not always be so pronounced – but it will probably always be present in some form.

People will, in other words, have different 'world views' and different ways of conducting their lives in accordance with the values they hold dear (see Benjamin 1990a: 169; 1994: 267–269; Battin 2005: 39). The values will vary between cultures and societies; they will also vary between people who live in the same society and even people who share the same basic set of principled commitments, such as those offered by Roman Catholic or more broadly Christian teaching. Thus, Catholic parents of conjoined twins may reach different decisions about the appropriateness of surgical separation (Huxtable 2002a). Furthermore, in contrast to the orthodox view, RM Hare believes that a Christian can consistently support euthanasia, through an application of the Golden Rule – 'do unto others as you would have them do unto you' (Hare 1975).

Some Christians who decide to perform euthanasia might nevertheless feel that their consciences are torn. Sometimes their conscience might be salved by adjusting their world view towards a better understanding of their guiding values; on other occasions, they might allow other, perhaps new, values to come to the fore. Clashes will nevertheless still occur: one might, for example, feel bound to one's loved ones but recognise also some duties towards strangers, such as those who are starving in the developing world. Essentially, as Benjamin puts it, 'our identity is constituted in part by a complex constellation of occasionally conflicting values and principles' (Benjamin 1990b: 385).

This complex constellation is not static, since an individual's values may not only evolve but may also accommodate conflict. One can see this in the euthanasia literature, when the same person finds their attitude to the practice changing, as occurred with Alison Davis and also the prominent doctor and bioethicist Raanan Gillon (e.g. Gillon 1969; contrast Gillon 1999: 1432). Battin, an advocate of euthanasia, similarly admits that her views have changed and that she nowadays has no 'official recipe' for resolution (Battin 2005: 13). Notably, like Gillon, she is generally a firm supporter of patient autonomy, but she feels the pull of other norms in relation to euthanasia.

In short, lived moral experience tells us that values are plural and that they will remain in tension and sometimes outright competition. Moral pluralists accept this fact and, moreover, believe that there may be no 'one-size-fits-all' framework for resolving moral disputes. Pluralists therefore concede the existence of genuine moral dilemmas, to which compromise can be the best solution. As David Wong has argued, it is possible to accept, with the pluralist, the case for moral accommodation without surrendering to a sceptical or relativistic view about the existence of moral truth (Wong 1992: 773). WF May takes up a similar argument. For him, relativists and absolutists only *appear* opposed, when absolutists think that some principle is exceptionless but relativists identify exceptions and therefore reject the principle. The absolutist might, of course, seek to avoid the difficulty of possible exceptions by appealing to some other overriding principle. However, this does not completely remove the problem: they must, implicitly, be inclined to the view that some principle or other can still be considered a sort of moral 'trump card'.

According to May, absolutists and relativists alike must believe that principles are universal: 'The value of a good, the heft of a principle, depends upon its supremacy, its overridingness in all circumstances' (May 2003). The pluralist, meanwhile, finds that principles are only:

> true for the most part in the sense that they reach their territorial limit in those cases where they must yield to another principle or good ... Such is the rough landscape of policy-making in which one may need to compromise, not in the sense of defecting from duty but honoring duties which are multiple.
>
> (ibid)

In my opinion, the euthanasia debate can seem dominated by absolutists. I suspect that Keown, Singer and Doyal, for example, offer norms that they see as universally applicable, and they would probably complain that compromise undermines their integrity. However, there is reason to believe that we should acknowledge moral conflict as part of living a truly integrated or 'whole' life. Sometimes consistency and wholeness will conflict, and on these occasions a compromise can provide the best answer – for now, at least.

> One will, in walking such a tightrope, be responding to both sets of duties while fully doing justice to neither. The resulting ambivalence is part of the price we must pay to avoid the dehumanization of simple consistency in an unavoidably complex situation.
>
> (Benjamin 1994: 277)

Theory should nevertheless continue to flourish. Indeed, Wong has observed that a decision about what we actually *do* about an issue marred by moral conflict 'need not require a determinate answer to the moral rights and wrongs of the issue' (1992: 775). Supporters of various principles might occasionally be required to compromise, especially in practice where decisions must be made and policies formulated, but this need not mean that they surrender their commitments (see Benjamin 1990a: 172; 1990b: 385; cf. Tännsjö 2007: 342). Indeed, if we are truly to arrive at decisions and policies that do not skirt over important moral complexities, then we need the competing positions to be defended as clearly and powerfully as possible. T V Smith has argued to similar effect in his discussion of compromise in politics. The politician would not be able to achieve a compromise if contributors to the debate pulled their punches:

> It is their business to find a middle course between two sincere and tangible positions. To locate the middle ground they must reckon from stationary banks. If you do not insist upon your cause, they will have to deal with shifting banks as well as the whirling currents of conflict in their efforts to locate the middle of the stream.
>
> (Smith 1942: 13)

3 The contours of compromise

Where is the middle of the stream down which the euthanasia debate flows? It is not to be found down the tributary in which the 'whirling currents of conflict' have transformed into smoother waters. Synthesis and consensus have their value, as do attempts to break down moral problems into more manageable components, and any other initiatives that prevent either side from demonising the other. Compromise, however, is a different matter, since it should 'require concessions by both sides and be able to be seen by the opposing parties as somehow splitting the difference between them' (Benjamin 1990a: 166).

3.1 Compromise by committee

One method of securing the type of compromise I think we need involves devising a suitable *procedural* mechanism or forum for airing diverse viewpoints with a view to engineering a resolution. Various ideas have been advanced (e.g. Rawls 1972; Habermas 1990; Capps 2006), but perhaps the most obvious – not least given its familiarity in bioethical and clinical circles – involves recourse to a committee. Provided that its members reflect a diversity of moral world views and can agree that they must formulate a policy or – if we think of clinical ethics committees – must issue advice on the care of an individual patient, then a committee can clearly help to split the difference on fraught moral matters (cf. Wong 1992: 772, 783; Solum 1998: 1120–1121; Benjamin 2001: 29).

This is precisely the mechanism that Martin Benjamin favours, and in his writing he concentrates on a particularly fractious moral issue: the status of the embryo. Benjamin specifically cites the *Committee of Inquiry into Human Fertilisation and Embryology*, chaired by Baroness Mary Warnock (Department of Health and Social Security 1984), which considered how the moral status of the embryo should influence the law governing embryo research and related decisions at the start of life.

The Warnock committee confronted 'pro-life' and 'pro-choice' positions on the worth of the embryo, familiar from the abortion debate. The latter position, argues Benjamin, 'is by its very nature pluralistic' (1990a: 169): pro-choice advocates concede that their values hinge on time and place and that, in different circumstances, they might have held different views – perhaps even those of the pro-life advocates (see also Wong 1992: 770). The latter group, however:

> do not see their world view and way of life as contingent, as only one among many. Theirs is not a world view and way of life; it is, rather, *the* (only true) view of the world and the way to live.
>
> (Benjamin 1990a: 169)

To them, compromise is an illegitimate affront to their integrity. I do not mean here to charge this group with fanaticism; rather, I mean merely to point out that, for its members, there are no good reasons for believing that any other world view can be defended. Benjamin, however, believes that the Warnock committee was right to place both views on a par and split the difference between them, by allowing research only up to the fourteenth day after the creation of the embryo, at which point the embryo develops the primitive streak and so the central nervous system begins to develop. This 'pragmatic' position was then adopted in law (Montgomery 1991; see Human Fertilisation and Embryology Act 1990).

I think that Benjamin has a good case for arguing that this committee achieved a compromise. If we return to some of the perspectives on the value of life that I have surveyed, one can see how the Warnock committee managed to take elements from each of the moral positions, without wholly endorsing any one of them. However, it might initially appear that this committee tacitly favoured the 'pro-choice' autonomy viewpoint, at the expense of the sanctity of life position. Finnis has taken issue with a similar manoeuvre by Jurgen Habermas, which allegedly occurs in the latter's influential work on resolving disputes through the processes of rational discourse that he constructs (Finnis 1999: 367–370). However, I do not think that the same can be said about Warnock's conclusions: it certainly did not take respect for autonomy or, for that matter, quality of life thinking to the places where ethicists like Harris and Singer want them to go. Certainly, Keown might feel that his position is diminished by Warnock's decision; but, as he should recognise, Singer also lost out, as he could complain that the 14-day limit is arbitrary and does not capture a true point of differentiation between 'no moral worth' and 'moral worth'. This is not only (or simplistically) a numerical quantification. It involves an important conceptual compromise: Keown's stance on inviolability certainly loses out, but one does not find in its place a Singerian world view, in which not only foetuses but also young babies are denied full moral status (cf. Wong 1992: 782).[2]

Despite having respect for a plurality of autonomous decisions as its basic premise, the Warnock committee genuinely appears to have split the difference between Singer and Keown. Can the same be achieved in the euthanasia debate? Advice from the professional medical bodies on discontinuing life

2   Chris Cowley has suggested to me that this is no compromise: the solution proffered by Warnock amounts to a brute overruling of Keown, which seems to signal a victory for Singer's utilitarian stance. Forrester makes a similar point in his review of Benjamin's book. He suggests that, in condoning compromise, Benjamin's pluralists are 'emphasizing their utilitarian side' (1993: 87). Whilst I can see the basis for this criticism, I still maintain – for the reasons just given in the main text – that the substance of the compromise wrought by Warnock does not mean an outright win for Singer. I will leave it to others to assess whether the quest for accommodation is necessarily utilitarian in nature and, indeed, to consider what the substance of the compromise I defend owes to that school of thought.

support starts to suggest to me that it can, since these combine insights from the sanctity of life tradition and more consequentialist quality of life thinking (e.g. BMA 2001: 4; GMC 2002: 8; contrast Keown 2000). This is perhaps unsurprising, given the problems I explored in Chapter 1 with interpreting the claim that a treatment is 'extraordinary' or 'futile'. But even more pertinent are the two House of Lords Select Committees that examined euthanasia itself. The first, reporting in 1994, did not compromise on the central issue: euthanasia was firmly opposed. The second, reporting a decade later, was more circumspect.

In keeping with its remit, the 2005 committee basically advised that the issues raised by Lord Joffe's Bill could still be examined by a future Parliament. There were 'differences of opinion among members of the committee on the relative importance of issues and on the interpretation of the evidence' and so the committee sought only to provide a summary of the arguments 'in as balanced a manner as possible' (House of Lords Select Committee 2005a: 90–91). This might reflect the diversity of the views of the members, who included Lord Joffe himself, clearly an advocate of euthanasia, and Baroness Finlay, a consultant in palliative medicine, who is not (see Finlay 2005).[3]

Parliamentary time ran out, so the Bill failed, but rather than 'ruling on the acceptability or otherwise of this particular Bill' (House of Lords Select Committee 2005a: 6), the committee identified various concerns arising from the evidence that any future Bill would need to address. On one view, the opponents of euthanasia succeeded: the Bill failed. But it also needs to be borne in mind that, in recommending closer attention to various aspects of the case for change, the committee was implicitly conceding that the proponents' position might ultimately be made strong enough to succeed.

This seemingly 'practical' focus did not necessarily mean that the case for allowing euthanasia *had* succeeded in principle. Instead, I think the committee can be judged to have laid the groundwork for a thorough debate on the principled issues: notice, for example, its reservations about the data indicating public support for voluntary euthanasia and assisted suicide. The Select Committee indicated that the argument – typically mounted by organisations like Dignity in Dying – that most people want the law to be changed cannot yet be accepted, because the surveys conducted tend to be 'one-dimensional' (House of Lords Select Committee 2005a: 75). Whether majority support is sufficient to justify change is, of course, itself open to debate. However, one can still read the committee's report as signalling that better evidence might indeed become available – but that, at least until then, the conditions for compromise remain. As such, although the 2005 Committee

3   As such, Martin Benjamin would surely support the composition of this committee, and arguably also the balance it achieved.

stalled the debate, the stage was set for a more informed discussion, in which both sides could – as T V Smith advised – mount their cases from 'stationary banks'.

3.2 Moral discomfort, justification and excuse

I have suggested throughout this book that the principles occupying the banks of the euthanasia debate are already pretty stable. What, then, should a committee decide? Benjamin admits that the task will be difficult and that his main aim was only to show that compromise is conceivable, rather than achievable (1990a: 171). I think that in the present context it is time to be bolder, such that we need not stop with a plea for *procedural* resolution – instead, it is possible to describe the *substance* of a compromise policy on euthanasia.[4]

The endeavour is not without difficulty. One problem, which T V Smith identified, is that 'To be a claimant and a compromiser at the same time is to injure conscience and to weaken the claim.' (1942: 13) Indeed, how can I coherently and conscientiously defend a compromise, particularly when I have occasionally detected strengths in the arguments on one or other side of the debate (e.g. Huxtable 2005a)? This, in turn, suggests a second problem with this attempt, which is that it might appear arrogant or at least optimistic for one individual to believe that they can stipulate a solution that, in locating the middle ground, can, if not quell, then at least reduce the battles being waged over the value of life.

The answers to these possible charges are three-fold. First, as I argued earlier, any individual can recognise the merits of competing claims on the value of life, as, indeed, Battin has done. It must therefore be conceivable that an individual can, in good conscience, seek to locate the area between them.[5] Second, I maintain that the contours of the middle ground can coherently be defended provided that the key claims on all sides are each given a fair airing and appropriate accommodation. Indeed, I submit that the compromise outlined here is one that Martin Benjamin's hypothetical pluralistic committee could – indeed, should – reach. As to the third charge, I think that we are at a point where we arguably do not need to make that committee real in order to see how the difference might be split between the various views on offer. If I am candid, aspects of the following proposal cause me some disquiet; what

---

4   It follows that I am not about to defend the use of committees to decide on the (un)suitability of euthanasia in individual cases, in a manner akin to the Dutch policy (see Janssen 2002). I will, however, argue that committee deliberations can have a place, specifically in the realm of withdrawing treatment.

5   A related point is that not every individual will adopt one of the 'hard-and-fast opposing positions', as Wong describes them (1992: 771). In short, there will be people whose convictions already occupy the middle ground.

I am not doing, however, is suggesting that this is the final answer. The ideas outlined here seek primarily to take up Battin's call for new ways of resolving these long-standing differences; they themselves remain subject to further discussion, amplification and revision. Indeed, this is essential in a democratic society (see Wong 1992: 779–780; Benjamin 2001: 28).

However, my aim is not entirely modest: I do believe that if we step back from the current to-and-fro of these debates we will begin to see, with the compromiser, that the conflicting values can operate as vital checks and balances against any one perspective being taken too far. As Robert Burt explains, there are some powerful, but occasionally overlooked, forces at work in the euthanasia debate. Benjamin referred earlier to the uncertainty and hesitation that comes with compromise and Burt certainly detects ambivalence at the heart of these discussions: ambivalence about death and its rights and wrongs. This 'visceral discomfort' as Woods describes it (2007: 28) explains why we have not yet abandoned notions like the acts/omissions distinction, despite its alleged demolition by Rachels. Our policies cling to the sanctity of life ethic and resist embracing death because of 'some lurking, ineradicable sense of its wrongfulness, juxtaposed against all rational arguments for its inevitability and even preferability' (Burt 2005: s11). So, says Burt, the alleged logical tenuousness of the rules that permit life support to be withdrawn or withheld but forbid the more obviously active ending of life 'promotes conscious acknowledgement of ambivalence – that is, of the close proximity of these actions to wrongful conduct' (ibid). So too the doctrine of double effect performs a 'psychological protective function, serving simultaneously as permission and a warning sign about dealing with death' (Burt 2005: s11–s12).

Advocates of euthanasia, like Rachels, think that the logical problems support their case for reform. Burt disagrees: 'far from justifying this "next step" toward purposeful killing, the plausibility of their logical claims about existing practices should raise concerns that these practices have themselves lost their function as protective expressions of our ambivalence toward death.' (2005: s12) If we keep the lines we can at least preserve a 'conscious awareness of moral discomfort' (ibid). To my mind, splitting the difference must involve acknowledging this moral discomfort and ambivalence; it must, in other words, convey something of what Gillett described as the 'moral pause' (Gillett 1988). And in order to do this, both sides must gain victories and incur losses.

The moral language capable of describing this ambivalence already exists, although it has fallen from favour in discussions of euthanasia. What the main contributors tend to do is argue about what is (not) *justified* and in doing so they overlook the concept of *excuse*. As classically described by Austin, people who plead a justification for a particular action 'accept responsibility but deny that it was bad', while those who plead an excuse 'admit that it was bad but don't accept full, or even any responsibility' (1956). It has been pointed out that there is a two-fold assumption of priority underlying this sort of distinction: that, logically, an excuse exists where a justification does not; and that, normatively, excuses are inferior to justifications (Husak 2005). Whilst I am mindful that there may be problems with both of these assumptions, I nevertheless think that the latter assumption has its merits, even if one would prefer to describe the basic idea of an excuse as one of 'partial defence' (cf. Husak 2005: 580). The basic idea to which I am referring is essentially that it is possible to reach a 'refined moral judgment' on the practice of euthanasia: as Ramsey said in 1956, a notion like excuse or partial defence communicates 'a sense of the accused's tragic involvement in some unspecifiable degree of guilt' but also, as Kalven commented in the same journal, expresses 'compassion for the actor' and 'compassion for the suffering of the subject' (Ramsey 1956: 1201; Kalven 1956: 1235).

Equipped with such concepts, the compromiser will be inclined to shape a legal framework, which is sensitive to the 'refined moral judgements' that attend intentional killing. The compromiser specifically tasked with appraising and improving the framework that exists in English law will, I suggest, need to focus on three areas: the denial or removal of life support; the use of opioids and sedatives in terminal care; and instances of euthanasia and mercy killing. I will examine each of these in turn in the following sections.

3.3 Clarifying the compromise on fatal omissions

First, a compromiser would surely wish to preserve and protect the practices of withholding and withdrawing life support. The acts/omissions distinction, on which the permission relies, is borrowed from the sanctity of life tradition. Although it sometimes appears illogical, the distinction must be allowed to linger, since it provides a clear point at which it is possible to split the difference between writers like Keown and Rachels. Rachels is still denied 'active' euthanasia; Keown, however, is forced to lose some ground to quality of life and autonomy-based arguments.

As I explained in the previous chapter, the prospect of refraining from saving life raises some difficult questions about when a duty is owed to the subject of that life and what the duty requires. The answers apparently hinge on whichever account of the value of life is preferred but, in terms of their content, the answers need not be so very different in practice: Keown and Rachels can sometimes agree that it is best not to treat a particular patient. This shows that consensus is achievable. However, a compromise requires Keown to concede both that treatment can be stopped at the patient's request, even when the request appears to be suicidal, and that a life of poor quality need not always be prolonged. Indeed, as I suggested in the first chapter, Keown might even be *required* to recognise a place for quality of life thinking, in order to give meaning to his claims that treatment can sometimes be 'extraordinary', that is, 'futile' or 'burdensome' (Price 2001: 643).

Keown, of course, firmly resists Price's point, instead claiming that the sanctity of life position itself offers the most appropriate compromise (2000: 71). He has a point, but it is one that is most clearly conveyed by Burt: there is a need to refocus on the 'moral discomfort' that comes with withholding or withdrawing treatment. This could require us to scale back on what has already been allowed in law and clinical practice: certainly, a diagnosis of Down's syndrome looks insufficient to justify withholding life support. However, the circumstances in which non-treatment will be allowed, and how any such decision might be described, will undoubtedly remain disputed, not only amongst supporters of diverse moral theories, but also amongst those patients, families and healthcare professionals who must deal with these dilemmas in practice. As I noted earlier, conflict is an unavoidable reality. What now needs to occur is for the debate to move to means of addressing these disputes, in which different understandings of 'futility', 'quality of life' and the like can be aired with a view to securing consensus and compromise. As Reiter-Theil observes, 'the language of ethics can serve as a common language in which conflicting viewpoints can be discussed' (2001: i22). And one should certainly recall that ethics committees and mediators can play an important role here.

As McCall Smith implied, the resulting policy will not be so very different from that which we already have. There will, however, be a more urgent need to resolve disputes and to adjust the (mixed) messages that are currently sent. First, the compromiser must be willing to countenance some fatal omissions but, particularly in so fraught an area, must have a method for hearing from all interested parties and securing agreement or compromise in a particular case. In order for this to occur, some degree of state involvement looks unavoidable and this seems to require the compromiser to accept the doctor's elevated position as the individual empowered to provide and to omit treatment. However, the doctor – no more than Williams's intruder or the more benignly motivated flatmate considered in chapter five – should not be entitled to embark on 'a frolic of his own' (*Joel v Morrison* (1834) 6 C & P 510, *per* Parke B, at 503). Instead, any individual seeking to refrain from saving life must be required to go through the appropriate justificatory channels, in which their views will still be given due weight, albeit alongside other pertinent perspectives. Unilateral decisions must be avoided and, on occasion, condemned.

This reminder should in turn help to resolve one of the major areas of confusion illustrated in Chapter 3: how to respond to the suicidal individual and, in particular, whether or not efforts ought to be made to save his or her life. Respect for autonomy should entitle someone like Sara Johnson to commit suicide. However, in keeping with Keown's belief that life should not be taken lightly, the state should be empowered to ensure that she clearly and autonomously wished to die. Someone in her position is therefore advised to make their wishes clear, such as through a suitable advance directive declining medical intervention. There will, of course, remain difficulties of interpretation with these; what this requirement should nevertheless achieve is a compromise in which there is a presumption in favour of saving life, albeit one that can be rebutted when it is clear that the life is no longer wanted (cf. Gewirth 1978: 263–264; Huxtable 2005a). Where an appropriate direction exists, people like Sara Johnson's parents ought to be free from censure; where it does not, the prospect of a homicide conviction (even a conviction for complicity in suicide) should remain.

These clarifications should restore some coherence to the law. Not every inconsistency will be eradicated: the fact that complicity in suicide could still be 'committed' by omission continues to look out-of-step with Parliament's intention. However, that problem no longer appears so pressing when viewed from the contours of the middle ground. Other problematic inconsistencies, such as the clash with established precedent that seemingly forbids the cessation of life-support (*Gibbins and Proctor* (1918) 12 Cr App Rep 134), arguably lose their urgency altogether: one should be able to see why it can be acceptable for doctors to take treatment- (and life-) limiting decisions.

This can only be the start of this particular discussion. Nevertheless, it is time to rethink when we are willing to refrain from rescuing some patients and the procedures we have in place for making such a decision. For now, though, a compromiser should acknowledge that it can be acceptable to withhold or withdraw life support because this preserves an essential component of the sanctity of life position and, despite falling short of allowing 'active' euthanasia, accords some weight to the arguments offered by its supporters.

3.4 Clarifying the double effect

The compromiser should also be inclined to support a policy that sanctions the use of opioids and their like in terminal care, even when the drugs look likely to hasten death. The permission again operates from within the sanctity of life framework, in which the doctrine of double effect plays a central role. However, even critics of the traditional ethic can support the practices condoned by this doctrine, although they would dub them instances of 'covert euthanasia' and would additionally wish to embrace more overt practices. This suggests that the law has rightly proceeded along the middle course: Chapter 4 shows that it apparently permits rather more than the original moral doctrine, but it still resists calls for more open accommodation of euthanasia. Indeed, it was previously suggested that there is also consensus on this issue, since no one contributing to these debates wants to see patients dying in pain, or distressed and suffering: for this reason, if no other, practitioners of palliative medicine must be granted legal protection.

There is, however, every reason to think that the present protection needs both clarification and better enforcement and that it should actually be returned to the boundaries provided by the moral doctrine of double effect. This initially looks like a considerable victory for the sanctity of life perspective. Yet, even critics should concede the need for re-thinking this area of the law. Their case for euthanasia rests on two pillars: the suffering of the patient and, with voluntary euthanasia and assisted suicide at least, the patient's autonomous choice to die. It is the moral imperative to relieve suffering that is particularly pertinent here.

The current law, both as stated and as applied, seems to stretch the mantle of double effect too far. Dr Adams looked more like Dr Shipman, but he successfully invoked the doctrine. Other doctors, meanwhile, might overlook the lessons of palliative medicine, but the lawyers appear not as willing as they should be to ask whether the doctors' actions would be supported by experts in this field. Instead, the lawyers concentrate on the subjective intention of the doctor and appear all too eager to enable the defendant to 'get out of jail free'. In sum, the ill-motivated murderer and the incompetent practitioner can apparently both plead double effect.

Even a supporter of euthanasia, like Singer, should agree that this is too permissive. Leaving aside the question of what the patient wants, Singer's case for euthanasia recognises a moral necessity premised on the patient's suffering.[6] The current law, however, can work to exonerate doctors even when that necessity is absent. As Battin recognised, palliative medicine cannot provide a complete response to the case for euthanasia: some patients will still suffer; some will still want assistance in dying. However, it *can* successfully respond to the suffering of many patients, and thereby obviate the moral imperative to provide those patients with euthanasia. Singer would surely not want euthanasia to be practised *unnecessarily*. He too should therefore oppose condoning the doctor who was either more concerned with securing an inheritance or who did not know about those techniques for relieving suffering, which would satisfy the moral imperative but fall shy of ending the patient's life.

In short, euthanasia – or, following Singer *et al*, 'overt' euthanasia – warrants separate consideration, after the policy issues pertaining to the relief of symptoms in the terminally ill have been resolved. Where symptoms can be controlled, doctors ought to do so – and they ought to do so in accordance with expert opinion, and secure in the knowledge that they are not breaking the law. As Annie Lindsell's barrister said, 'one would like to see – for the safeguarding of patients *and* doctors – some clear guidelines as to when they should be doing this' (Saini 1998). This necessitates reconsideration of the ways in which the lawyers currently conceive and apply the existing protection.

I once thought, like others, that we needed legislation in this area, but this now seems an unnecessarily excessive response (Huxtable 2004; cf. Ramsey 1956: 1201–1202; HC Deb Vol 302 Col 1025ff, 10 December 1997). Instead,

---

6   It should be noted that this is precisely the rationale underpinning the permissive Dutch policy.

attention should be focused on the legal officials: better guidance must therefore be formulated, which clarifies when the doctrine is of genuine clinical utility and when it might merely operate as a cloak for concealing incompetence or killing. The lawyers need to be reminded that the clinical evidence can help to clarify the doctor's intention: if, on autopsy, the dose appears excessive, then questions must be asked. Equally, they need to understand when particular drugs might cause death: as I explored in Chapter 4, morphine will rarely kill if it is used appropriately, and the doctrine has more clinical relevance in the realm of sedation. The question must therefore become whether the doctor's actions were appropriate, when judged against expert opinion on managing symptoms. In accordance with established legal principles, the doctor will be entitled to argue that his or her *subjective* intention was to relieve suffering; their plea of double effect must nevertheless fail if it can be shown that their action was not *objectively* supportable.[7]

In asking these sorts of questions we return to the original parameters of the doctrine, without making any significant break with past precedent. In doing so an important area of agreement is preserved and the middle ground is better organised. As with preserving the acts/omissions distinction, the existing legal irrationality is not completely eliminated. Many of the more legalistic problems of Chapter 4 persevere. We could, however, still opt to remove one of these: *Woollin* [1998] 4 All ER 103 could be overturned, so that foresight of a consequence does *not* equate with intending it. By doing this, efforts to accommodate the sanctity of life position in the law would be reinvigorated and a major source of disparity in the expression and administration of the law as it pertains to doctors and non-doctors would be removed. No doubt such a bold move could cause difficulties in the broader criminal law;[8] nevertheless, as the mercy killing cases involving laypersons demonstrate, justice might require the *Woollin* principle to be revised or removed in the particular context I am examining. I will consider this issue again in the context of complicity in suicide. In any event, a key point is that the other sources of inconsistency must then be relegated as having less importance than the concern to ensure that the law occupies the middle ground.

Occupants of the middle ground should therefore accept that if a doctor's actions were out-of-step with prevailing clinical wisdom, then the most appropriate finding must be gross negligence manslaughter, despite the criticisms

---

7   Hooper J's approach to Dr Moor's case, analysed in Chapter 4, therefore fell short, since he ultimately asked the jury only to consider the doctor's *subjective* understanding of 'accepted practice' on controlling symptoms. It is better, I think, for the legal officials to also ask whether *objectively* (on the basis of such practice) the doctor's understanding was defensible.

8   An oft-cited example is the terrorist bomber, who might argue that he or she only intends to further some political or allegedly principled cause, albeit in the virtually certain knowledge that the bomb they plant will kill or cause serious harm. Should this bomber not be deemed to have intended harm and thus (only?) be convicted of a lesser crime than murder (see e.g. Ashworth 2003, 265)?

levelled at that offence (e.g. Quick 2006). If, instead, the doctor's intention was to kill for some malevolent reason, then the most appropriate finding must be murder. But what about a doctor like Cox, whose intention was to perform euthanasia? And what about other doctors who unilaterally or malevolently seek to withhold or withdraw life support? Equally, how should the compromiser respond to the layperson who is either Williams's intruder, or the flatmate from Chapter 5, or even the straightforward mercy killer encountered in Chapters 2 and 3? How, in these various situations, is it possible to satisfy Battin's plea for a policy 'that is sensitive to the concerns of both sides' of the euthanasia debate (2005: 38)?

3.5 Clarifying the 'shadowy area' of mercy killing

Just like the 2005 Select Committee, the compromiser would unquestionably encounter impassioned arguments both for permitting and for prohibiting a policy of euthanasia. They would appear to be left with a simple choice: the practice must either be justified (albeit subject to certain conditions being satisfied) or it must not. However, the Warnock Committee, which examined the status of the embryo, demonstrated that it is possible to split the difference, and I believe that this can be achieved here by eschewing talk of justification and replacing it with the language of excuse. As Meyers once commented, such a development 'offers a reasonable alternative or middle ground to what many see as either continuing the present approach and trusting to the flexibility of the law as administered, or changing the law and affirmatively sponsoring such mercy-killings' (Meyers 1970: 155).

In short, the compromiser should recognise euthanasia as a particular type of killing, which can be governed by a distinct offence of 'mercy killing' (or some other suitable synonym like 'compassionate killing') that will also operate as a partial defence to other homicide charges. As was noted in Chapter 2, the Law Commission revived this idea in its 2006 report and recommended that it be the subject of further consultation. The idea is not new (e.g. Royal Commission 1953: 63–64; Criminal Law Revision Committee 1976: 31–34; House of Lords Select Committee 1989), and it already exists in, for example, the laws of Switzerland and Germany (e.g. Vickers 1997; Otlowski 1997: 460–461). However, the Law Commission's original, provisional proposal rested on shaky foundations, since it perpetuated the myth, exposed in Chapter 2, that mercy killers will typically have acted under 'diminished responsibility'. What is required is a more sincere method of dealing with such killings. Fair labelling and proper scrutiny of the issues are, as Ashworth argues, important goals (2003: 89–92). For this reason, other commendable reforms, like abolishing the mandatory life sentence for murder (House of Lords Select Committee 1989), do not go far enough towards occupying the middle ground on the specific problem of euthanasia.

To an extent, there already exists a law that achieves this: the offence of complicity in suicide enshrined in s 2 of the Suicide Act 1961, which is substantially the preserve of the mercy killer. In keeping with the sanctity of life, complicity in suicide has remained a crime; in keeping with the arguments from autonomy and suffering, suicide itself is not unlawful and the maximum penalty for infringement of the s 2 offence (14 years' imprisonment) is much less than that for murder. Indeed, the expectation – at least in paradigm cases – is that the merciful assistant in suicide will be humanely dealt with. However, as I explained in Chapters 2 and 3, the operation of the law is notoriously uneven, with a variety of crimes being charged, convictions secured and disposals passed down to mercy killers whose actions appear to differ little from one another. Uniformity and a more honest articulation of the compromise must now be sought.

The compromiser can certainly defend the existence of the offence of complicity in suicide, but he or she should also agree that a new legal category of mercy killing is warranted. The moral compromise that exists in relation to assistance in suicide must similarly obtain for other mercy killings that do not involve the participation of the patient and so cannot be categorised as such. The Suicide Act is actually a helpful model for this sort of reform, since – unlike the manslaughter model – it enables an attempt to be charged. Someone like Mr Bouldstridge, who failed in his efforts to asphyxiate himself and his chronically ill wife, will therefore still be called to account, but the crime will now be one of attempted mercy killing. Like the 1961 offence and, indeed, manslaughter, the offence should be chargeable in its own right and should also exist as a partial defence and alternative verdict to other homicide charges (see also Grubb 2001: 91). However, unlike the 1961 offence but just like manslaughter, the new crime should be subject to a maximum term of life imprisonment. This should preserve a measure of the condemnation sought by sanctity of life theorists and go some way to reflecting the belief, advanced by some proponents of assisted suicide, that voluntary euthanasia is less acceptable.

Adding this new crime of 'mercy killing' to the criminal arsenal should not automatically mean the repeal of s 2 of the Suicide Act. Certainly, this could be considered, particularly if the existence of the new crime meant that the 1961 offence fell into virtual disuse or otherwise appeared otiose.[9] If it did appear redundant and were to be removed, the criminal law would still be equipped to condemn the behaviour of unmerciful assistants in suicide like McGranaghan, as indeed other prosecutions for alternative offences already demonstrate (e.g. *Glenn Paul Wright* [2000] Crim LR 928, discussed in Chapter 3). However, proponents of assisted suicide want to mark this out as preferable to voluntary euthanasia, apparently because it involves a more robust expression of patient autonomy, in requiring the patient to take the final, fatal step. Although the

9   Similar discussions have occurred around the offence (and partial defence) of infanticide, which predated the creation of diminished responsibility and is nowadays seldom prosecuted (see Law Commission 2005: 222).

logic of the two practices is not really distinct, the difference they seek can be preserved by retaining the 1961 offence; indeed, this will also mean that there is not too much legal upheaval (see Fuller 1969). However, it will also be important to guarantee that the boundaries of this offence and the new offence are properly demarcated and policed.

For a start, Mrs Lyons and Mr Robey should no longer face a legal lottery. The evolution of prosecuting and sentencing guidelines should ensure that cases in which knives (and the like) are held in place are uniformly dealt with. If the patient took the final step, the crime is one of complicity in suicide. If the assistant did so, the crime is the new crime of mercy killing.[10] In either case, however, the sentences must be consistent. The judges already seem to have a suitable response to a typical case of compassionate killing: probation or a similar community order, usually with some form of counselling or psychological support, looks like a suitable disposal.

Keown and colleagues are likely to complain that this is far too light but it must be remembered that the aim is to occupy the middle ground. Keeping euthanasia in the criminal context can be punishment – and discouragement – enough. As Sanders commented in 1969, 'perhaps the anxiety and discomfort of going through a criminal trial is both a sufficient deterrent to others and an adequate display of public censure' (1969: 358–359; see also House of Lords Select Committee 1989: 569). Indeed, it is notable that the public themselves appear comfortable with this sort of compromise. The Law Commission has summarised two studies conducted by Mitchell in 2003 and 2005, in which the majority of respondents were particularly sympathetic to cases of mercy killing. Most of these respondents nevertheless felt that an official inquiry (including prosecution or police investigation) was warranted and 'that a community-based disposal, with the emphasis on counselling for the killer, would be appropriate' (Law Commission 2006: 149).

Elsewhere too the boundaries between the permissible, impermissible and excusable must be clarified. I have already outlined some of the (in)activities that the compromiser can defend and to this one more situation can be usefully added: the modern phenomenon known as 'death tourism'. Euthanasia is tolerated in some jurisdictions and it seems paternalistic of the compromiser to deny the option of receiving this to citizens who happen to be living in this jurisdiction. Instead, as Hedley J suggested, the compromiser can strive to ensure that life is not lightly taken by insisting that the state is empowered to check that the patient in question is autonomous (*Re Z (Local Authority: Duty)* [2005] 1 WLR 959). Where this is the case, the patient must be free to travel and, in contrast to Hedley J, the lawyers should clearly signal that such a person can be advised or helped to travel, and that their assistants will not be prosecuted.

10 There might remain problems in delineating the two in practice but efforts should, at least, be devoted to ensuring that the approaches taken are consistent.

Granting permission to travel does not mean that autonomy wholly wins out: Diane Pretty, for example, will still be denied her request for obtaining assistance in suicide in this jurisdiction. Indeed, the message that suicide assistance will not be tolerated here can be more boldly issued, by resolving the difficulty posed by Mr Chard's release in favour of conviction. As I explained in Chapter 3, Mr Chard himself might not have intended to assist a suicide by purchasing pills for his friend. If *Woollin* [1998] 4 All ER 103 is indeed abandoned, then someone who only foresees suicide as a consequence of their actions or advice will be acquitted. Alternatively, it seems the very least we can ask here is that the judges refrain from giving the *Woollin* direction in these sorts of cases, and that they instead leave intention to the jury's common sense. However, someone who does have the direct intention to assist must remain subject to the 1961 crime.

This still leaves one area of possible ambiguity: the provision of advice on committing suicide, particularly where the advice is directly intended to assist someone to die. Battin herself mounts the plausible argument that allowing people access to information on committing suicide represents a compromise: 'proponents would give up the right to assistance in bringing about one's own death by a physician one trusts; and opponents have to live with the fact that terminally ill patients were committing suicide with impunity.' (2005: 310–311) She refers specifically to advice (in 'suicide manuals' and the like) that can enable patients to create and administer their own suicide pills. Battin seems to assume, but does not entirely justify, a distinction between, on the one hand, *advising* and, on the other, *assisting* the patient in some more positive way. I endorse Battin's view that the permission accorded to suicide must remain, as this represents a compromise of values. However, I am not yet convinced that the boundary between advice and more overt assistance can be easily defended and so, in an attempt to remain on the middle ground, I suggest that the intentional provision of both must remain subject to the criminal law. As such, rather unlike the current position as described in Chapter 4, the prospect must remain that the deliberate issuance of advice could lead to prosecution.[11]

In permitting 'death tourism' but leaving other forms of assistance in suicide criminal, I think the policy reflects the ambivalence about death and commitment to preserving life to which Burt referred. As such, if someone like Brian Pretty was willing to help their loved one to die, then he must know that he is liable to prosecution, either under the 1961 Act or, if the loved one proved unable to participate, under the new offence. This should be the case

---

11 I nevertheless anticipate that I might be charged with incoherence, since I am simultaneously willing to permit advice and assistance to be given in the specific instance of 'death tourism'. The least I can say in this regard is that, as Benjamin pointed out, 'simple consistency' must occasionally lose out in the effort to compromise.

even where, as in Sue Rodriguez's case noted in Chapter 3, the mercy killer is a doctor. The legal officials must be reminded of the need to apply the law impartially. Irrespective of their professional standing, the defendant should be required to prove that his or her conduct fitted the new crime.

So what should the mercy killer be required to prove? Qualifying criteria will need to be specified and some existing proposals, including by the VES as it then was, provide helpful starting points (e.g. House of Lords Select Committee 1989: 669–671). At a minimum, the defendant will have (directly) intended to kill, and (leaving attempts aside) will have caused death, from the motive that they wished to bring an end to the patient's pain, suffering and/or distress. They will not have been ill-motivated: guidance should insist that the courts are alert to the presence of malign or even mixed motives, such as Mrs McShane's desire to inherit ((1977) 66 Cr App Rep 97). Malign motives should disqualify the defendant and should render them susceptible to a different charge; mixed motives need not, but should, require the courts to pass down a more punitive disposal, as occurred in Mrs McShane's case, as we saw in Chapter 3. However, it should not necessarily be the case that the prospect of inheritance destroys the plea: it was a recurring feature of Chapter 2 that many mercy killers are close relations or friends of the deceased, and so precisely the people likely to be offered some bequest.[12]

Of course, all of these requirements will need careful thought and amplification. Most urgent amongst these are the condition of the victim and the categories of euthanasia that ought to be covered. First, it seems appropriate to insist that the defendant ought to have a reasonable belief, formed in good faith, that the victim – the patient – is suffering unbearably. Further work needs to be done on this criterion, particularly if the possibly dangerous scope of quality of life considerations is to be kept in check. Explanatory notes or even a code of practice can help here and some form of monitoring or auditing will also be essential.[13] Once the basic criteria are defined then we will need to watch how the judges and juries approach the new offence. However, in theory, the judges should not find too much difficulty in applying the new concepts: as I suggested in Chapter 2, their current interpretations do at least approximate

12 There is another way in which the disquiet over killing might be conveyed: the mercy killer could be denied any inheritance they might otherwise have been bequeathed. I suspect that this need not occur, since the criminalisation itself serves that function. It is nevertheless an idea worthy of further exploration.

13 It might be necessary, for example, to create a professional monitoring committee. The Dutch system similarly requires doctors to report instances of euthanasia but under-reporting has been a persistent problem: only 54 per cent of cases were reported in the most recent study of Dutch practice (see Jackson 2006: 965). That system obviously relies on doctors revealing their private practices; one hopes that under-reporting would be less of a problem in the system I propose, since it would involve monitoring the judges' public practices in relation to the new crime of mercy killing.

to a paradigm of mercy killing that parallels many of the discussions in the bioethical domain.

I argued, however, that the judges have appeared content to treat involuntary euthanasia as on a par with other types of compassionate killing. This raises a general problem: which of the various categories discussed in Chapter 1 ought to be included and which excluded? This is a particularly thorny predicament, but one on which some conclusions can be drawn. Voluntary euthanasia must be included, in order to split the difference between the arguments for and against that practice. Arguments are also being made for and against non-voluntary euthanasia. Although it might appear controversial, it is clear from Chapter 5 what the law already appears to allow in some situations where life support is discontinued, so it seems sensible also to include cases of active non-voluntary euthanasia in the new offence.

What should also be accepted is that the new crime could be satisfied by an act or by an omission. This does not mean that Anthony Bland's doctors suddenly become mercy killers by omission – if, that is, one is even sympathetic to the belief that those doctors only 'omitted' to treat. Instead, as I previously contended, a compromise means accepting that some omissions are justified – provided that appropriate efforts have been made to air and resolve disagreements. No one should be entitled to make these decisions unilaterally. Where that has occurred, then the new crime of omission can be employed to deal with the problem provoked by Williams *et al*: distinguishing between the benign doctor, the malign intruder and the benign flatmate. The flatmate or family member like Mr Karapetian who makes a well-motivated but unilateral decision can be charged with the new crime; but so too can the doctor, if he or she has taken the decision without appropriate consultation. Although the courts will still need to work on how the conduct of these various agents should be described, the compromiser should also agree that the intruder ought to be prosecuted. However, if their motivation is indeed not compassionate, it will not be the new crime, but rather some existing homicide offence, that should be charged in that case.

What, then, of involuntary euthanasia? I noted in Chapter 1 that nobody appears willing to suggest that this can be justified, since it represents an affront both to the sanctity of life and to the autonomy principle. The judges' behaviour to date nevertheless implies that they would want this to be covered in the new crime. Indeed, if one concentrates on the compassionate motivation of the defendant, then the logic of quality of life claims seems also to imply that it is still not as heinous as straightforwardly ill-motivated killings. There is also Ashworth's point about fair labelling to consider. Is there really so striking a contrast between the actions of Mr Fox and Mr Killick, who acted without the consent of their (autonomous) loved ones, and Mr Heginbotham, who also did not have his wife's permission to end her life, but whose dementia may have prevented her from providing it?

The centrist should conclude that, if there is going to be an attempt to excuse any such mercy killings, then one needs to recognise them all or else face new charges of hypocrisy and arbitrariness. Indeed, what data there is seems to suggest that the public do not necessarily draw a sharp distinction between Mr Killick and Mr Heginbotham. Mitchell's research for the Law Commission found that cases of non-consensual euthanasia 'would be more serious' than those that were consensual, 'though not necessarily amongst the most serious' (Law Commission 2006: 149). Some respondents explicitly said that they would be just as sympathetic to a case of euthanasia in which there was no request to be killed (Law Commission 2006: 148). The data nevertheless demonstrates that there also remains distinct moral unease around involuntary killing. The challenge therefore lies in crafting a legal response that captures this unease, without ignoring the current legal reality or the demands of fair labelling. The answer, albeit one that requires much more discussion, is that the compromiser should include these killings in the new offence but should insist on a suitable *minimum* penalty of imprisonment, to send the appropriate message of condemnation. Quite what that penalty should be is deliberately left open, but a minimum of one year's incarceration is a good place for this particular debate to begin.

There is undoubtedly more to be said about this central reform to our current policies on euthanasia. However, a move in this direction should at least minimise many of the problems of inconsistent law that I have examined and should do so in a manner that more honestly and coherently conveys a compromise. In so viewing euthanasia as an excusable, but not a justifiable, class of killing it is possible also to satisfy Mitchell's desire for 'a clear indication of the status and categorisation of mercy killings; the current situation which consists of *ad hoc* decisions by individual courts is highly unsatisfactory' (House of Lords Select Committee 1989: 577). The desire to excuse is already present in the legal framework (see House of Lords Select Committee 1989: 541, 547). As Mitchell implies, the lawyers cannot plausibly complain that the proposal does not fit with existing legal thinking: motive is already being taken into account, especially in the cases I have examined (Norrie 1993: 45–46; Wells 1994: 72–73).

The ethicists, however, might have more grounds for complaint. Whenever this sort of reform is advocated, opponents raise many of the practical objections described in Chapter 1 and additionally say either that this undermines the protection of human life or otherwise that it does not go far enough towards recognising the case for euthanasia. Yet, these very complaints substantiate the belief that the proposal splits the difference: both sides simultaneously lose and win. Revised in this way, the law better conveys the moral intuitions of the Detective Inspector who dealt with Mr Heginbotham, and whose case I discussed in Chapter 2: like him, the new law sees such killings as 'tragic' but it also admits that prosecution can be appropriate, because 'at the end of the day he's killed his wife' (Bunyan 2004).

4 Conclusion: from conflict to compromise

This is only the beginning of a new debate, in which attention shifts from conflict and contradiction to compromise. The precise legal form that this compromise should take remains open to discussion and revision. The set of rules we need is one that treats like cases alike and is not so easily manipulated by those who administer the law or, indeed, administer medicines. Open acceptance that euthanasia is a particular type of killing, subject to particular moral norms which are themselves the source of much conscientious competition, must be a move in the right direction.

There are, in summary, three areas of the law that are amenable to reconfiguration along the lines of compromise. None of them involves major legal upheaval although, contrary to McCall Smith's argument, they all require some revision to the *status quo*. The first, central reform is that the law ought explicitly to recognise mercy killing as an offence, which is also available as a partial defence to other homicide charges. In keeping this a crime, we can remain focused on the moral pause that should precede any attempt to kill; in making it a lesser crime, it is possible to admit that some deaths are not so bad, at least when the deceased was suffering and, in some cases, desperately wanted the escape that death can afford. The crime, which should be rigorously enforced against laypersons and health professionals alike, should be subject to a maximum term of life imprisonment, although community disposals should be anticipated in typical qualifying cases. Which cases do qualify requires careful thought, so that we can reach a workable understanding of what it means for two cases to be 'alike' and thus amenable to similar disposals. In this manner, I have suggested that even involuntary euthanasia must be covered – although, here at least, a more punitive penalty should be expected.

This new category of killing will then have to be made to work alongside existing offences, particularly complicity in suicide. The compromiser must certainly strive to clear up many of the ambiguities surrounding the latter crime. The legality of 'death tourism', for example, should be clearly signalled; but so too should the illegality of assisting a suicide in this jurisdiction. This might not leave us with a fully coherent law; however, when considered in a compromising spirit, proponents of euthanasia gain something here, albeit something which ought not to pose too great a threat to its opponents' viewpoints.

The same can be said of the two other areas of the law that are due for some revision, the omission of life-sustaining treatment and the double effect defence. As is currently the case, fatal omissions should be allowed, but efforts must again be directed towards clarifying the qualifying criteria and ensuring that disputes can be resolved effectively in practice. Given the (ethical and practical) disputes that can arise in such cases, recourse to ethics committees and mediators should help to air diverse viewpoints and identify a way forward. No single viewpoint should automatically take priority here and unilateral decisions must be avoided. This should even be the case where the patient refuses treatment in order to die: he or she will only be entitled to have that decision respected if it is clear that they have satisfied the relevant criteria for autonomous decision-making. Once again, that position broadly mirrors the existing rules, but it does at least clarify when and why the state has an entitlement to intervene in suicide attempts, at least until the patient's autonomy is confirmed.

Finally, the doctor's defence of double effect will also remain, but it must be subjected to greater scrutiny and more rigorous policing. Advice from the experts, specifically in palliative medicine, must be brought to the attention of the legal officials, who should in turn ensure that the defence is not used as a cloak for killing or negligent malpractice. Related changes, such as the possible abandonment of *Woollin* [1998] 4 All ER 103, could also help to restore coherence to the law in this area. Complete coherence may not be attainable but, for the compromiser at least, that will not be the goal as such: instead, the aim is to meld the conflicting contributions into a set of legal rules that are as rational as possible, in the sense that they can guide the various agents whose conduct will, or might, shorten patients' lives.

What would be the answers generated by this new framework to the questions asked at the outset of this chapter? Dianne Pretty would still be denied the legal right to be assisted in her suicide. Someone like her could, however, refuse any unwanted treatment; or, commit suicide before she lost her ability to act; or, even after losing that ability, travel to another jurisdiction (even with assistance) where her request could be acted upon. If someone was willing to help her to die in this jurisdiction, then – whether they are a doctor like Michael Irwin, some other health professional, or a loved one – they must know that they will be subject to investigation, prosecution and conviction – at least if the legal officials are interpreting and enforcing the law appropriately. The crime will either be complicity in suicide or mercy killing, depending on the extent to which the defendant in question assisted the death. Even if the patient did not consent to death, the latter crime will still be charged and so someone like Mr Heginbotham will still face criminal proceedings. However, few of these defendants should expect a prison sentence: that disposal will be reserved for less obviously excusable killings, where the motive is not, or not completely, benevolent or where the victim manifestly did not want to die or was not asked.

Patients like Anthony Bland, meanwhile, might still have life support withdrawn, albeit under a policy that more explicitly accounts for the views of all genuinely interested parties. His doctors should not expect to be called to account unless they have failed to give due weight to competing views of the value of the patient's life. Similarly, a doctor like Dr Martin should remain able to claim that his aim was only to relieve suffering but he should now be aware that his actions will be even more closely scrutinised, as the legal officials will be educated in when double effect is a reality and when it is a convenient fiction.

In making these various suggestions and asking for a renewed focus on numerous issues, I am seeking to move English law – candidly and, so far as possible, coherently – onto the middle ground. All of the various positions on the value of life gain something in this endeavour, but all of them also lose out to some extent. That is precisely what compromising is all about, and, as scholars like Margaret Battin are coming to argue, the time has come to seek an end to the constant to-and-fro.

This should not and, in any case, cannot spell an end to theorising about the end(ing) of life. The need remains for us to devise new ways of thinking about patient autonomy, the relevance of resource constraints at the end of life, and the scope and content of a doctor's duty, and how this might differ from the duty that the rest of us owe to other moral agents. Equally, the piecemeal legal revisions I have considered need to be situated in broader debates about what a good death really is (and here we need more informed data); when a killing is excusable;[14] the weight to be accorded to expert medical evidence in both civil and criminal trials; and how improvements in the certification and reporting of death might better enable us to assess how people really are dying in this jurisdiction.

This is but the start of a discourse and process, in which we all have a stake. Allowing everybody's voices to be heard is an essential pre-condition to locating the middle ground, on which democratic and liberal premise we should still not find ourselves wholly committed to honouring personal autonomy, with the result that we end up embracing voluntary euthanasia. Instead, I have argued that we need to find the point between seeing the value of life as determined by the individual, as dependent on the happiness or suffering of the individual, and as inviolable in recognition of its intrinsic worth. In moving from justification to excuse, by marking out euthanasia as a distinct (but reduced) crime, I believe that we begin to get there.

We already have, and have long had, an 'unofficial defence of euthanasia' (Lanham 1973: 202); it now needs to be made official. Nothing else seems to work; or, remaining mindful of the fact that theory will (necessarily) evolve and expand, it does not work yet. In short, the time has come to compromise.

14 How, for example, should the law deal with the killer who was a victim of domestic violence?

Bibliography

A Children's Physician (1979) 'Non-treatment of defective newborn babies', *The Lancet*, 2: 1123–1124.

Alexander, L (1949) 'Medical science under dictatorship', *New England Journal of Medicine*, 241: 39–47.

Alldridge, P, Morgan, D and Wells, C (1990) 'An unsuitable case for treatment', *New Law Journal*, 140: 1544–1545.

Amarasekara, K and Mirko B (2004) 'Moving from voluntary euthanasia to non-voluntary euthanasia: Equality and compassion', *Ratio Juris*, 17(3): 398–423.

Anonymous (1997) 'Letter: Why my mother killed herself', *The Guardian*, 5 July.

Appel, J M (2005) 'Defining death: When physicians and families differ', *Journal of Medical Ethics*, 31: 641–642.

Ardagh, M (2000) 'Futility has no utility in resuscitation medicine', *Journal of Medical Ethics*, 26: 396–399.

Arlidge, A (2000) 'The trial of Dr David Moor', *Criminal Law Review*, 31–40.

Ash, C (1982) 'Complicity in suicide: Publishers at risk?' *New Law Journal*, 132: 178–181.

Ashcroft, R E (2005) 'Making sense of dignity', *Journal of Medical Ethics*, 31: 679–682.

Ashworth, A (1989) 'The scope of liability for omissions', *Law Quarterly Review*, 105: 424–459.

—— (2003) *Principles of Criminal Law*, 4th edn, Oxford: Oxford University Press.

—— and Fionda, J (1994) 'The new Code for Crown Prosecutors: (1) Prosecution, accountability and the public interest', *Criminal Law Review*, 894–903.

Atkins, K (2000) 'Autonomy and the subjective character of experience', *Journal of Applied Philosophy*, 17(1): 71–79.

Austin, J L (1956) 'A plea for excuses', *Proceedings of the Aristotelian Society* (1956–57), 57: 1–30.

Austin, M (1997) 'Doctor admits killing 50 people', *The Sunday Times*, 20 July.

—— (1998) 'Suicide pill to be sold on the internet', *The Sunday Times*, 7 June.

Avery, D (2003) 'Assisted suicide seekers turn to Switzerland', *Bulletin of the World Health Organisation*, 81(4): 310.

Bachelard, S (2002) 'On euthanasia: Blindspots in the argument from mercy', *Journal of Applied Philosophy*, 19: 131–140.

Bale, J (1997) 'GP helped Lady Warnock's husband die', *The Times*, 19 September.

Battin, M P (2005) *Ending Life: Ethics and the Way We Die*, Oxford: Oxford University Press.

Bayertz, K (ed) (1996) *Sanctity of Life and Human Dignity* (52 Philosophy and Medicine), Dordrecht: Kluwer Academic Publishers.

BBC (2003) 'Son walks free over "mercy killing"', *BBC News Online*, 16 May. HTTP: <http://news.bbc.co.uk/1/hi/england/london/3033857.stm> (accessed 28 March 2007).

—— (2004) 'Carer detained for "mercy kill"', *BBC News Online*, 28 October. HTTP: <http://news.bbc.co.uk/1/hi/england/northamptonshire/3963541.stm> (accessed 10 April 2007).

—— (2005a) 'Suicide brother has "no regrets"', *BBC News Online*, 21 January. HTTP: <http://news.bbc.co.uk/1/hi/england/4196811.stm> (accessed 28 March 2007).

—— (2005b) 'GP "killed three with overdoses"', *BBC News Online*, 26 October. HTTP: <http://news.bbc.co.uk/1/hi/england/4379084.stm> (accessed 25 April 2007).

—— (2005c) 'Family shocked by accused doctor', *BBC News Online*, 2 November. HTTP: <http://news.bbc.co.uk/1/hi/england/4400860.stm> (accessed 25 April 2007).

—— (2005d) 'Praise for murder accused doctor', *BBC News Online*, 25 November. HTTP: <http://news.bbc.co.uk/1/hi/england/4470090.stm> (accessed 25 April 2007).

—— (2005e) 'Doctor backed by expert witness', *BBC News Online*, 14 December. HTTP: <http://news.bbc.co.uk/1/hi/england/4491858.stm> (accessed 25 April 2007).

—— (2005f) 'Probe following GP murder trial', *BBC News Online*, 15 December. HTTP: <http://news.bbc.co.uk/1/hi/england/4530842.stm> (accessed 28 March 2007).

Beale, J H (1935) 'The nature of law', in Fuller, L L (ed) *The Problems of Jurisprudence: A Selection of Readings Supplemented by Comments Prepared by the Editor*, pp 346–355, Brooklyn: The Foundation Press.

Beauchamp, T L (1993) 'Suicide', in Regan, T (ed) *Matters of Life and Death: New Introductory Essays in Moral Philosophy*, pp 69–120, New York: McGraw Hill.

—— (1994) 'The "four principles" approach', in Gillon, R and Lloyd, A (eds) *Principles of Health Care Ethics*, pp 3–12, Chichester: John Wiley & Sons.

—— and Childress, J F (2001) *Principles of Biomedical Ethics*, 5th edn, Oxford: Oxford University Press.

—— and Davidson, A (1979) 'The definition of euthanasia', *Journal of Medicine and Philosophy*, 4: 294–312.

Behan, M W H, Veasey, R, Higson, M and Sulke, A N (2005) 'Second thoughts', *British Medical Journal*, 331: 1552.

Benjamin, M (1990a) *Splitting the Difference: Compromise and Integrity in Ethics and Politics*, Lawrence, Kansas: University Press of Kansas.

—— (1990b) 'Philosophical integrity and policy development in bioethics', *Journal of Medicine and Philosophy*, 15(4): 375–389.

—— (1994) 'Conflict, compromise, and moral integrity', in Campbell, C S and Lustig, B A (eds) *Duties to Others*, pp 261–278, Dordrecht: Kluwer Academic Publishers.

—— (2001) 'Between subway and spaceship: Practical ethics at the outset of the twenty-first century', *The Hastings Center Report*, 31(4): 24–31.

Beyleveld D and Brownsword, R (2001) *Human Dignity in Bioethics and Biolaw*, Oxford: Oxford University Press.

Beynon, H (1982) 'Doctors as murderers', *Criminal Law Review*, 17–28.

Biggar, N (1998) 'Response', in Gill, R (ed) *Euthanasia and the Churches*, pp 109–113, London: Cassell.

Biggs, H (1996) 'Euthanasia and death with dignity: Still poised on the fulcrum of homicide', *Criminal Law Review*, 878–888.

—— (1998) 'I don't want to be a burden! A feminist reflects on women's experiences of death and dying', in Sheldon, S and Thomson, M (eds) *Feminist Perspectives on Health Care Law*, pp 279–295, London: Cavendish.

—— (2001) *Euthanasia, Death with Dignity and the Law*, Oxford: Hart Publishing.

—— (2003) 'A pretty fine line: Life, death, autonomy and letting it B', *Feminist Legal Studies*, 11(3): 291–301.

Birch, D J (1988) 'The foresight saga: The biggest mistake of all', *Criminal Law Review*, 4–18.

Birmingham Evening Mail (1981) 'Judge frees mercy killer', *Birmingham Evening Mail*, 1 May.

Bliss, M R (1990) 'Resources, the family and voluntary euthanasia', *British Journal of General Practice*, 40: 117–122.

Blom-Cooper, L and Drewry, G (1976) *Law and Morality*, London: Duckworth.

—— and Morris, T (1964) *A Calendar of Murder: Criminal Homicide in England Since 1957*, London: Michael Joseph.

Board for Social Responsibility of the Church of England (2000) *On Dying Well: An Anglican Contribution to the Debate on Euthanasia*, London: Church House Publishing.

Boseley, S (1999) 'Doctors cleared of cover-up', *The Guardian*, 24 April.

—— (2006) 'Euthanasia: doctors aid 3,000 deaths', *The Guardian*, 18 January.

—— and Dyer, C (2006) '"I believe I must end my life while I am still able"', *The Guardian*, 25 January.

Bosshard, G, Ulrich, E and Bär, W (2003) '748 cases of suicide assisted by a Swiss right-to-die organisation', *Swiss Medical Weekly*, 133: 310–317.

Blugrass, R (1980) *Psychiatry, the Law and the Offender – Present Dilemmas and Future Prospects*, London: Institute for the Study and Treatment of Delinquency.

Brahams, D (1986) 'Arthur's case: (2) Putting Arthur's case in perspective', *Criminal Law Review*, 387–389.

—— (1990) 'The reluctant survivor', *New Law Journal*, 140: 586–587, 639–640.

—— (1992) 'Criminality and compassion', *The Law Society's Gazette*, 30 September: 2.

—— and Brahams, M (1983) 'Symposium 1: The Arthur case – A proposal for legislation', *Journal of Medical Ethics*, 9: 12–15.

Brazier, M (2003) *Medicine, Patients and the Law*, 3rd edn, London: Penguin Books.

—— (1996) 'Euthanasia and the law', *British Medical Bulletin*, 52(2): 317–325.

—— and Miola, J (2000) 'Bye-Bye Bolam: A medical litigation revolution?' *Medical Law Review*, 8: 85–114.

Bridgeman, J (1995) 'Declared innocent?' *Medical Law Review*, 3: 117–141.

BMA (British Medical Association) (2001) *Withholding and Withdrawing Life-Prolonging Treatment: Guidance for Decision Making*, 2nd edn, London: British Medical Association.

Brock, D W (1993) *Life and Death: Philosophical Essays in Biomedical Essays* Cambridge: Cambridge University Press.

Browne, A (1989) 'Assisted suicide and active voluntary euthanasia', *Canadian Journal of Jurisprudence*, 2: 35–56.

Brownsword, R (1993) 'Towards a rational law of contract', in Wilhelmsson, T (ed) *Perspectives of Critical Contract Law*, pp 241–272, Aldershot: Dartmouth.

—— (1996) '"Good faith in contracts" revisited', *Current Legal Problems*, 49: 111–157.

Bunyan, N (1997) 'Judge frees mother in baby killing case', *The Electronic Telegraph*, 26 September. HTTP: <http://www.telegraph.co.uk/htmlContent.jhtml? html=/archive/1997/09/26/nbab26.html> (accessed 28 March 2007).

—— (2004) '100-year-old cut his ailing wife's throat in "act of love"', *The Daily Telegraph*, 9 July.

Burgess, J A (1993a) 'The great slippery-slope argument', *Journal of Medical Ethics*, 19: 169–174.

Burgess, M M (1993b) 'The medicalization of dying', *Journal of Medicine and Philosophy*, 18: 269–279.

Burnet, D (2001) '*Re A (Conjoined Twins: Medical Treatment)*: Conjoined twins, sanctity and quality of life, and invention the mother of necessity', *Child and Family Law Quarterly*, 13(1): 91–99.

Burns, B (1998) 'Heyse and Storm on the slippery slope: Two differing approaches to euthanasia', *German Life and Letters*, 51(1): 28–42.

Burt, R A (2005) 'The end of autonomy', *Improving End of Life Care: Why Has It Been So Difficult? Hastings Center Report Special Report*, 35(6): s9–s13.

Calabresi, G (1985) *Ideals, Beliefs, Attitudes, and the Law: Private Law Perspectives on a Public Law Problem*, New York: Syracuse University Press.

Callahan, D (1995) *Setting Limits: Medical Goods in an Aging Society with a Response to My Critics*, Washington: Georgetown University Press.

Callahan, S (1996) 'A feminist case against euthanasia. Women should be especially wary of arguments for "the freedom to die"', *Health Progress*, 77(6): 21–29.

Cambridge Evening News (1990) 'Wife "killed MS victim out of love"', *Cambridge Evening News*, 20 June.

Campbell, A V (1998) 'Euthanasia and the principle of justice', in Gill, R (ed) *Euthanasia and the Churches*, pp 83–97, London: Cassell.

—— and Huxtable, R (2003) 'The Position Statement and its commentators: Consensus, compromise or confusion?' *Palliative Medicine*, 17: 180–183.

—— and Willis, M (2005) 'They stole my baby's soul: Narratives of embodiment and loss', *Medical Humanities*, 31: 101–104.

Campbell, C S, Hare, J and Matthews, P (1995) 'Conflicts of conscience: Hospice and assisted suicide', *Hastings Center Report*, 25(3): 36–43.

Cant, R (2002) 'Widow distraught as Dr keeps job; Anaesthetist reprimanded after hospital death', *South Wales Evening Post*, 21 February.

Capps, B (2006) 'Procedural ethics and the European stem cell debate', *Jahrbuch für Wissenschaft und Ethik*, 11: 42–66.

Capron, A (2001) 'Brain death – Well settled yet still unresolved', *New England Journal of Medicine*, 344: 1244–1246.

Carroll, L (1982) *The Complete Illustrated Works of Lewis Carroll*, London: Chancellor Press.

Carter, H and Khaleeli, H (2004) 'Husband, 100, spared jail for "act of love" killing', *The Guardian*, 9 July.

Chapman, C (2006) 'Swiss hospital lets terminally ill patients commit suicide in its beds', *British Medical Journal*, 352: 7.

Chittenden, M (1992) 'Ordeal of the caring doctor who killed', *The Sunday Times*, 20 September.

—— and Furbisher, J (1992) 'Tears as mercy doctor found guilty', *The Sunday Times*, 20 September.

Clough, S (1989) 'Pensioner smothered sister', *Western Mail* (Cardiff), 25 July.

Clouston, E (1996) 'Man who killed incurable brother freed', *The Guardian*, 15 October.

Coggon, J (2006) 'Could the right to die with dignity represent a new right to die in English law?' *Medical Law Review*, 14: 219–237.

Cohen-Almagor, R (2000) 'Language and reality at the end of life', *Journal of Law, Medicine and Ethics*, 28: 267–278.

Cole, L (1992) *Let Me Die: A Study of Voluntary Euthanasia Containing Many Case Studies*, Maidenhead: Lloyd Cole.

Coleman, C H (2002) 'The "disparate impact" argument reconsidered: Making room for justice in the assisted suicide debate', *Journal of Law, Medicine and Ethics*, 30: 17–23.

Committee on the Penalty for Homicide (1993) *Report*, London: Prison Reform Trust.

Craig, P (1997) 'Formal and substantive conceptions of the rule of law: An analytical framework', *Public Law*, 467–487.

Criminal Law Revision Committee (1976) *Working Paper on Offences against the Person*, London: Her Majesty's Stationery Office.

—— (1980) *Fourteenth Report: Offences against the Person*, Cmnd 7844, London: Her Majesty's Stationery Office.

Crook, A (2003) 'GMC lifts sanctions on doctor', *The Journal (Newcastle)*, 22 July.

CPS (Crown Prosecution Service) (2004) *The Code for Crown Prosecutors*, London: Crown Prosecution Service.

Daily Express (1975) 'Husband of mercy goes free to see dying wife', *Daily Express*, 12 December.

Daily Mail (1979) 'Mercy Killer is Told: Go Home' *Daily Mail*, 4 December.

Daily Telegraph, The (1985) 'Mercy-killing husband, 75, walks free', *The Daily Telegraph*, 2 July.

—— (2000) 'Mother helped son to kill himself', *The Daily Telegraph*, 27 October.

Daube, D (1972) 'The linguistics of suicide', *Philosophy and Public Affairs*, 1(4): 387–437.

Davies, J (1997) 'The case for legalising voluntary euthanasia', in Keown, J (ed) *Euthanasia Examined: Ethical, Clinical and Legal Perspectives*, pp 83–95, Cambridge: Cambridge University Press.

Davies, M (1998) *Textbook on Medical Law*, 2nd edn, London: Blackstone.

Davies, M R (1992) 'Letters: Facing up to legal and ethical dilemmas of euthanasia', *The Times*, 26 September.

Davis, A (1998) *Euthanasia: Questions and Answers*, London: Society for the Protection of Unborn Children Handicap Division.

—— (2002) 'Living with dignity' *The Observer*, 10 November.

De Bruxelles, S (1997) 'Son goes free after helping mother to die', *The Times*, 11 October.

De Cruz, P (2005) 'The terminally ill adult seeking assisted suicide abroad: The extent of the duty owed by a local authority', *Medical Law Review*, 13: 257–267.

De Haan, J (2002) 'The ethics of euthanasia: Advocates perspectives', *Bioethics*, 16(2): 154–172.

De Ionno, P (1991) 'Wife aided husband in car suicide', *The Times*, 15 May.

Dell, S (1984) *Murder into Manslaughter: The Diminished Responsibility Defence in Practice*, Oxford: Oxford University Press.

—— (1986) 'The mandatory sentence and section 2', *Journal of Medical Ethics*, 12: 28–31.

Department of Health and Social Security (1984) *Report of the Committee of Inquiry into Human Fertilisation and Embryology*, Cmnd 9314, London: Her Majesty's Stationery Office.

Derbolowsky, U (1983) 'Medical law in the light of fundamental human rights', *Medicine and Law*, 2: 193–197.

Derse, AR (2000) 'Is there a *lingua franca* for bioethics at the end of life?' *Journal of Law, Medicine and Ethics*, 28: 279–284.

Devlin, P (1962) *Samples of Lawmaking*, London: Oxford University Press.

—— (1985) *Easing the Passing: The Trial of Dr Bodkin Adams*, London: Bodley Head.

Dodd, V (1999) 'QC refuses to quit over "mongol" row', *The Guardian*, 30 April.

Donchin, A (2000) 'Autonomy, interdependence, and assisted suicide: Respecting boundaries/crossing lines', *Bioethics*, 14(3):187–204.

Downing, A B (ed) (1969) *Euthanasia and the Right to Death: The Case for Voluntary Euthanasia*, London: Peter Owen.

Doyal, L (1990) 'Medical ethics and moral indeterminacy', *Journal of Law and Society*, 17(1): 1–16.

—— (2001) 'Clinical ethics committees and the formulation of health care policy', *Journal of Medical Ethics*, 27 (Suppl. I): i44–i49.

—— (2006) 'Dignity in dying should include the legalisation of non-voluntary euthanasia', *Clinical Ethics*, 1: 65–67.

—— and Doyal, L (2001) 'Why active euthanasia and physician assisted suicide should be legalised', *British Medical Journal*, 323: 1079–1080.

Dray, M and Kirker, J (1985) 'Mercy killing husband is freed', *Birmingham Evening Mail*, 21 October.

Dubler, N N (2005) 'Conflict and consensus at the end of life', *Improving End of Life Care: Why Has It Been So Difficult? Hastings Center Report Special Report*, 35(6): s19–s25.

Dunstan, G R (1997) 'Commentary 2: Thesis correct: Argument unconvincing', *Journal of Medical Ethics*, 23: 160.

Durham, M (2001) 'Euthanasia: Man who helped daughter commit suicide walks free from court', *The Independent*, 9 June.

Dworkin, G (1988) *The Theory and Practice of Autonomy*, Cambridge: Cambridge University Press.

Dworkin, R (1993a) *Life's Dominion: An Argument about Abortion and Euthanasia*, London: HarperCollins.

Dyer, C (1992) 'Doctor in mercy killing case faces Medical Council discipline', *The Guardian*, 2 November.

—— (1996) 'Mercy killing of mother prompts inquiry', *British Medical Journal*, 312: 1055–1056.

—— (1997) 'Dying woman wins right to end life in dignity', *The Guardian*, 29 October.

—— (1999a) 'All I tried to do was relieve his agony, his distress and suffering', *The Guardian*, 12 May.

—— (1999b) 'Doctors as Gods', *British Medical Journal*, 319: 64.

—— (2000) 'Police question medical MP over "euthanasia"', *British Medical Journal*, 320: 464.

—— (2002) 'Pretty's legal battle for dignity in death', *The Guardian*, 13 May.

—— (2003) 'Swiss Parliament may try to ban "suicide tourism"', *British Medical Journal*, 326: 242.

—— (2005) 'GP is disciplined for willingness to help friend commit suicide', *British Medical Journal*, 331: 717.

—— (2006) 'Police question former GP about assisted suicide', *British Medical Journal*, 332: 256.

Eastbourne Gazette (1990) 'Pensioner's lethal cocktail for tragic wife', *Eastbourne Gazette*, 20 June.

Editorial (1981) 'Life comes first', *The Times*, 10 August.

Engelhardt Jr, H T (1996) *The Foundations of Bioethics*, 2nd edn, New York: Oxford University Press.

Epstein, M (2007) 'Legitimizing the shameful: End-of-life ethics and the political economy of death', *Bioethics*, 21(1): 23–31.

Farsides, B (1998) 'Guest Editorial: Palliative care – A euthanasia-free zone?' *Journal of Medical Ethics*, 24: 149–150.

Fenigsen, R (1990) 'A case against Dutch euthanasia', *Ethics and Medicine*, 6(1): 11–18.

Fenton, B (1995) 'Doctor admits "mercy killing" of two babies', *The Daily Telegraph*, 15 February.

Fenwick, A J (1998) 'Applying best interests to persistent vegetative state – A principled distortion?' *Journal of Medical Ethics*, 24: 86–92.

Finlay, I (2005) '"Assisted suicide": Is this what we really want?' *British Journal of General Practice*, 55(518): 720–721.

Finn, G (1999) 'Graduate in mercy killing bid freed', *The Independent*, 21 August.

Finnis, J (1986) *Natural Law and Natural Rights*, Oxford: Clarendon Press.

—— (1993) 'Bland: Crossing the Rubicon?' *Law Quarterly Review*, 109: 329–337.

—— (1997a) 'A philosophical case against euthanasia', in Keown, J (ed) *Euthanasia Examined: Ethical, Clinical and Legal Perspectives*, pp 23–35, Cambridge: Cambridge University Press.

—— (1997b) 'The fragile case for euthanasia: A reply to John Harris', in Keown, J (ed) *Euthanasia Examined: Ethical, Clinical and Legal Perspectives*, pp 46–55, Cambridge: Cambridge University Press.

—— (1999) 'Natural law and the ethics of discourse', *Ratio Juris*, 12(4): 354–373.

Fisher, A (1997) 'Theological aspects of euthanasia', in Keown, J (ed) *Euthanasia Examined: Ethical, Clinical and Legal Perspectives*, pp 315–332, Cambridge: Cambridge University Press.

Fisher, J (1999) 'Re-examining death: Against a higher brain criterion', *Journal of Medical Ethics*, 25(6): 473–476.

Fleet, M (1996) 'Home help cleared of "mercy killing"', *The Daily Telegraph*, 28 March.

Fletcher, D (1997) 'GP gives patients "an easy death"', *The Electronic Telegraph*, 12 September.

Fletcher, G P (1969) 'Prolonging life: Some legal considerations', in Downing, A B (ed) *Euthanasia and the Right to Death: The Case for Voluntary Euthanasia*, pp 71–84, London: Peter Owen.

—— (1978) *Rethinking Criminal Law*, Boston: Little, Brown and Company.

Flew, A (1969) 'The principle of euthanasia', in Downing, A B (ed) *Euthanasia and the Right to Death: The Case for Voluntary Euthanasia*, pp 30–48, London: Peter Owen.

Foot, P (1977) 'Euthanasia', *Philosophy and Public Affairs*, 6: 85–112.

Forbes, K (2006) 'RE: Richard Huxtable – via new email (Hello!)'. Email (16 October 2006).

—— and Huxtable, R. (2006) 'Editorial: Clarifying the data on double effect', *Palliative Medicine*, 20(4): 395–396.

Forrester, J (1993) 'Review: Splitting the difference: compromise and integrity in ethics and politics, by Martin Benjamin', *Noûs*, 27(1): 85–89.

Foster, C (2004) 'Rapid response: Time to test the law', *British Medical Journal*, 16 June. HTTP: <http://www.bmj.com> (accessed 12 December 2006).

Fraser, S I and Walters, J W (2000) 'Death – whose decision? Euthanasia and the terminally ill', *Journal of Medical Ethics*, 26: 121–125.

Freeman, M (1999) 'Death, dying and the Human Rights Act 1998', *Current Legal Problems*, 52: 218–238.

—— (2002) 'Denying death its dominion: Thoughts on the Dianne Pretty case', *Medical Law Review*, 10: 245–270.

Frey, R G (1981) 'Suicide and self-inflicted death', *Philosophy*, 56: 193–202.

—— (1998) 'The fear of a slippery slope', in Dworkin, G, Frey, R G and Bok, S *Euthanasia and Physician-Assisted Suicide: For and Against*, pp 43–63, Cambridge: Cambridge University Press.

Fuller, L L (1969) *The Morality of Law*, revised edn, New Haven: Yale University Press.

Gay-Williams, J (1979) 'The wrongfulness of euthanasia', in White, J E (ed) (1991) *Contemporary Moral Problems*, 3rd edn, pp 99–102, St Paul: West Publishing Company.

Gaylin W and Jennings B (2003) *The Perversion of Autonomy: Coercion and Constraints in a Liberal Society*, Washington: Georgetown University Press.

Gelfand, G (1984) 'Euthanasia and the terminally ill', *Nebraska Law Review*, 63: 741–762.

GMC (General Medical Council) (2002) *Withholding and Withdrawing Life-prolonging Treatments: Good Practice in Decision-making*, London: General Medical Council.

Gewirth, A (1978) *Reason and Morality*, Chicago: University of Chicago Press.

Gibb, F (1990) 'Landmark euthanasia trial may be stopped', *The Times*, 15 March.

Gibbs, G (1997) 'Dying surgeon in plea for compassion', *The Guardian*, 14 June.

Gillett, G (1988) 'Euthanasia, letting die and the pause', *Journal of Medical Ethics*, 14: 61–67.

—— (1994) 'Euthanasia from the perspective of hospice care', *Medicine and Law*, 13: 263–268.

Gillon, R (1969) 'Suicide and voluntary euthanasia: Historical perspective', in Downing, A B (ed) *Euthanasia and the Right to Death: The Case for Voluntary Euthanasia*, pp 173–192, London: Peter Owen.

—— (1997) '"Futility" – Too ambiguous and pejorative a term?' *Journal of Medical Ethics*, 23: 339–340.

—— (1999) 'When doctors might kill their patients: Foreseeing is not necessarily the same as intending', *British Medical Journal*, 318: 1431–1432.

—— (2003) 'Ethics needs principles – four can encompass the rest – and respect for autonomy should be "first among equals"', *Journal of Medical Ethics,* 29: 307–312.

Glazebrook, P R (1960) 'Criminal omissions: The duty requirement in offences against the person', *The Law Quarterly Review*, 76: 386–411.

Glover, J (1977) *Causing Death and Saving Lives*, London: Penguin Books.

Goff, R (1995) 'A matter of life and death', *Medical Law Review*, 3: 1–21.

Goldring, J and Hunt, J (1997) 'The case of Beverley Allitt', *Medical Science Law*, 37(3): 189–197.

Gooch, A (1998) 'Man's TV suicide fuels Spanish euthanasia debate', *The Guardian*, 6 March.

Gordon, L M (1966) 'The range of application of "voluntary", "not voluntary" and "involuntary"', *Analysis*, 26: 149–152.

Gormally, A J L (1978a) 'Prolongation of life: The principle of respect for human life', *Linacre Centre Papers*, 1: 1–28.

—— (1978b) 'Prolongation of life: Is there a morally significant difference between killing and letting die?' *Linacre Centre Papers*, 2: 1–20.

—— (1979) 'Prolongation of life: Ordinary and extraordinary means of prolonging life', *Linacre Centre Papers*, 3: 1–36.

Gormally, L (1994) 'The BMA Report on euthanasia and the case against legalization', in Gormally, L (ed) *Euthanasia, Clinical Practice and the Law*, 177–192, London: The Linacre Centre for Health Care Ethics.

—— (1997) 'Walton, Davies, Boyd and the legalization of euthanasia', in Keown, J (ed) *Euthanasia Examined: Ethical, Clinical and Legal Perspectives*, pp 113–140, Cambridge: Cambridge University Press.

—— (2002) 'Commentary on Skene and Parker: The role of the church in developing the law', *Journal of Medical Ethics*, 28: 224–227.

—— and Keown, J (1999) 'Human dignity, autonomy and mentally incapacitated patients: A critique of who decides?' *Web Journal of Current Legal Issues*, 4. HTTP: <http://webjcli.ncl.ac.uk/1999/issue4/keown4.html> (accessed 4 April 2007).

Gorman, E (1993) 'Teenager cleared of aiding suicide', *The Times*, 23 September.

Griew, E (1986) 'Reducing murder to manslaughter: Whose job?' *Journal of Medical Ethics*, 12: 18–23.

—— (1988) 'The future of diminished responsibility', *Criminal Law Review*, 75–87.

Griffiths, J (1995a) 'Recent developments in the Netherlands concerning euthanasia and other medical behavior that shortens life', *Medical Law International*, 2: 347–386.

—— (1995b) 'Assisted suicide in the Netherlands: The Chabot case', *Modern Law Review*, 58: 232–248.

Grubb, A (1993) 'Attempted murder of terminally ill patient', *Medical Law Review*, 1: 232–234.

—— (2001) 'Editorial: Euthanasia in England – A law lacking compassion?' *European Journal of Health Law*, 8: 89–93.

Guardian, The (1984) 'Devoted husband helped crippled wife kill herself', *The Guardian*, 31 July.

—— (1993) 'Man jailed for killing gay lover dying of Aids', *The Guardian*, 31 July.

—— (1995) 'Man jailed for threats to "mercy death" consultant', *The Guardian*, 5 August.

—— (1997) 'Pensioner who killed wife in "emotional collapse" freed', *The Guardian*, 19 November.

—— (1999) 'No headline', *The Guardian*, 5 November.

—— (2000) 'Euthanasia claim MP clear', *The Guardian*, 25 August.

Gunn, M (1994) 'The meaning of incapacity', *Medical Law Review*, 2: 8–29.

Gunn, M J and Smith, J C (1985) 'Arthur's Case and the right to life of a Down's syndrome child', *Criminal Law Review*, 705–715.

Habermas, J (1990) *Moral Consciousness and Communicative Action*, Cambridge: MIT Press.

Hagelin J, Nilstun T, Hau J and Carlsson H-E (2004) 'Surveys on attitudes towards legalisation of euthanasia: Importance of question phrasing', *Journal of Medical Ethics*, 30: 521–523.

Halliday, R (1997) 'Medical futility and the social context', *Journal of Medical Ethics*, 23: 148–153.

Hamilton, J R (1981) 'Diminished responsibility', *British Journal of Psychiatry*, 138: 434–436.

Hanks, G W and Twycross, R G (1984) 'Letter: Pain, the physiological antagonist of opioid analgesics', *The Lancet*, 30 June: 1477–1478.

Hardwig, J (1997) 'Is there a duty to die?' *Hastings Center Report*, 27(2): 34–42.

Hare, R M (1973) 'Survival of the weakest', in Gorovitz, S, Jameton, A L, Macklin, R, O'Connor, J M, Perrin, E V, St Clair, B P and Sherwin, S (eds) (1976) *Moral Problems in Medicine*, pp 364–369, New Jersey: Prentice-Hall.

—— (1975) 'Euthanasia: A Christian view', in Hare, R M (1992) *Essays on Religion and Education*, pp 72–85, Oxford: Oxford University Press.

—— (1994) 'Utilitarianism and deontological principles', in Gillon, R and Lloyd, A (eds) *Principles of Health Care Ethics*, pp 149–157, Chichester: John Wiley & Sons.

Harrington, J A (1996) 'Privileging the medical norm: Liberalism, self-determination and refusal of treatment', *Legal Studies*, 16: 348–367.

Harris, J (1980) *Violence and Responsibility*, London: Routledge and Kegan Paul.

—— (1985) *The Value of Life: An Introduction to Medical Ethics*, London: Routledge and Kegan Paul.

—— (1997a) 'Euthanasia and the value of life', in Keown, J (ed) *Euthanasia Examined: Ethical, Clinical and Legal Perspectives*, pp 6–22, Cambridge: Cambridge University Press.

—— (1997b) 'The philosophical case against the philosophical case against euthanasia', in Keown, J (ed) *Euthanasia Examined: Ethical, Clinical and Legal Perspectives*, pp 36–45, Cambridge: Cambridge University Press.

—— (1997c) 'Final thoughts on final acts', in Keown, J (ed) *Euthanasia Examined: Ethical, Clinical and Legal Perspectives*, pp 56–61, Cambridge: Cambridge University Press.

—— (2003) 'Consent and end of life decisions', *Journal of Medical Ethics*, 29: 10–15.

Harry, J (2007) 'Death probe Doc in clear', *Wales on Sunday*, 11 February.

Hart, H L A (1970) *Punishment and Responsibility: Essays in the Philosophy of Law*, Oxford: Clarendon Press.

Haslam, J (1980) 'Letter', *The Times*, 24 October.

Hendrick, J (2001) 'Legal aspects of clinical ethics committees', *Journal of Medical Ethics*, 27 (Suppl. I): i50–i53.

Hewson, B (1999) 'The law on managing patients who deliberately harm themselves and refuse treatment', *British Medical Journal*, 319: 905–907.

Hill, S (1978) 'A mercy killer's nightmare', *Ilford (Redbridge) Recorder*, 20 July.

Hill Jr, T E (1991) *Autonomy and Self-Respect*, Cambridge: Cambridge University Press.

Hinchliffe, M (1996) 'Vegetative state patients', *New Law Journal*, 146: 1579–1580, 1585.

Hodgkinson, N (1986) 'Euthanasia: A judge warns doctors must not "play God"', *The Sunday Times*, 30 November.

Hohfeld W N (1964) *Fundamental Legal Conceptions as Applied in Judicial Reasoning*, Cook, WW (ed) New Haven and London: Yale University Press.

Hollis, C (1964) *The Homicide Act*, London: Victor Gollancz.

Home Office, Department of Health and Social Security (1975) *Report of the Committee on Mentally Abnormal Offenders*, Cmnd 6244, London: Her Majesty's Stationery Office.

Horder, J (1988) 'Mercy killings – Some reflections on Beecham's case', *Journal of Criminal Law*, 52: 309–314.

Hornett, S I (1991) 'The sanctity of life and substituted judgement: The case of Baby J', *Ethics and Medicine*, 7(2): 2–5.

Horsnell, M (2006) 'Husband helped wife with MS to die', *The Times*, 20 October.

House of Keys (2006) *Report of the Select Committee of the House of Keys on Voluntary Euthanasia*, PP12/06, Isle of Man: House of Keys.

House of Lords Select Committee (1989) *Report of the Select Committee on Murder and Life Imprisonment*, HL 78 I–III, London: Her Majesty's Stationery Office.

—— (1994a) *Report of the Select Committee on Medical Ethics*, HL Paper 21, London: Her Majesty's Stationery Office.

—— (1994b) *Select Committee on Medical Ethics*, Vol II – Oral Evidence, London: Her Majesty's Stationery Office.

—— (1994c) *Select Committee on Medical Ethics*, Vol III – Written Evidence, London: Her Majesty's Stationery Office.

—— (2005a) *Assisted Dying for the Terminally Ill Bill [HL]*, Vol I – Report, HL Paper 86-I, London: Her Majesty's Stationery Office.

—— (2005b) *Assisted Dying for the Terminally Ill Bill [HL]*, Vol II – Evidence, HL Paper 86-II, London: Her Majesty's Stationery Office.

Hughes, D (1991) 'The reorganisation of the National Health Service: The rhetoric and reality of the internal market', *Modern Law Review*, 54: 88–103.

Hughes, J (2000) 'Consequentialism and the slippery slope: A response to Clark', *Journal of Applied Philosophy*, 17(2): 213–219.

Humphry, D (1978) *Jean's Way*, New York: Quartet Books.

—— (1991) *Final Exit: The Practicalities of Self-Deliverance and Assisted Suicide for the Dying*, Oregon: The Hemlock Society.

—— and Wickett, A (1986) *The Right to Die: Understanding Euthanasia*, London: The Bodley Head.

Hurst, S A and Mauron, A (2003) 'Assisted suicide and euthanasia in Switzerland: Allowing a role for non-physicians', *British Medical Journal*, 326: 271–273.

Husak, D (2005) 'On the supposed priority of justification to excuse', *Law and Philosophy*, 24: 557–594.

Huxtable, R (1999) 'Withholding and withdrawing nutrition/hydration: The continuing (mis)adventures of the law', *Journal of Social Welfare and Family Law*, 21(4): 339–356.

—— (2000a) '*Re M (Medical Treatment: Consent)*: Time to remove the "flak jacket"?' *Child and Family Law Quarterly*, 12(1): 83–88.

—— (2000b) 'The Court of Appeal and conjoined twins: Condemning the unworthy life?' *Bulletin of Medical Ethics*, 162: 13–18.

—— (2001) 'Logical separation? Conjoined twins, slippery slopes and resource allocation', *Journal of Social Welfare and Family Law*, 23(4): 459–471.

—— (2002a) 'Separation of conjoined twins: Where next for English law?' *Criminal Law Review*, 459–470.

—— (2002b) '*Re B (Consent to Treatment: Capacity)*: A right to die or is it right to die?' *Child and Family Law Quarterly*, 14(3): 341–355.

—— (2004) 'Get out of jail free? The doctrine of double effect in English law', *Palliative Medicine*, 18: 62–68.

—— (2005a) 'Fatal purposes: A Gewirthian analysis of the "right to die" in English law', *Contemporary Issues in Law* 8(2): 242–263.

—— (2005b) 'Drawing the line at the end of life?' *The Lancet* 366: 625–626.

—— (2007) 'Euthanasia and principled health care ethics: From conflict to compromise?' in Ashcroft, R E, Dawson, A, Draper, H and McMillan, J R (eds) *Principles of Health Care Ethics*, pp 489–495, 2nd edn, Chichester: John Wiley & Sons.

—— and Forbes, K (2004) '*Glass v UK*: Maternal instinct vs medical opinion', *Child and Family Law Quarterly*, 16(3): 339–354.

—— and Möller, M (2007) '"Setting a principled boundary"? Euthanasia as a response to 'life fatigue', *Bioethics*, 21(3): 117–126.

Independent, The (1989) 'Probation for parents who watched their daughter die', *The Independent*, 18 November.

Irwin, M (2004a) 'Am I breaking the law again?' *British Medical Journal*, 328: 1440.

—— (2004b) 'Arrested for showing compassion'. HTTP: <http://www.worldrtd.net> (accessed 4 December 2006).

Jack, D (1985) 'Mercy for husband who killed dying wife', *Daily Express*, 22 October.

Jackson, E (2004) 'Whose death is it anyway? Euthanasia and the medical profession', *Current Legal Problems*, 57: 415–442.

—— (2006) *Medical Law: Text, Cases, and Materials*, Oxford: Oxford University Press.

Jackson, L and Huxtable, R (2005) 'The doctor-parent relationship: As fragile as *Glass?' Journal of Social Welfare and Family Law*, 27(3–4): 369–381.

Jankiewicz, A (2001) 'Woman walks free after mercy killing case', *The Independent*, 29 September.

Jansen, A and Sulmasy, D P (2002) 'Sedation, alimentation, hydration, and equivocation: Careful conversations about care at the end of life', *Annals of Internal Medicine*, 136: 845–849.

Janssen, A (2002) 'The new regulation of voluntary euthanasia and medically assisted suicide in the Netherlands', *International Journal of Law, Policy and the Family*, 16: 260–269.

Jenkins, L (1995) 'Student chose death after prank led to paralysis', *The Times*, 16 December.

Jennett, B (1997) 'Letting vegetative state patients die', in Keown, J (ed) *Euthanasia Examined: Ethical, Clinical and Legal Perspectives*, pp 169–188, Cambridge: Cambridge University Press.

Jochemsen, H (1994) 'Euthanasia in Holland: An ethical critique of the new law', *Journal of Medical Ethics*, 20: 212–217.

Johnson, P and Bunyan, N (1999) '"Caring" GP cleared of murdering patient', *The Electronic Telegraph*. HTTP: <http://www.telegraph.co.uk/htmlContent.jhtml? html=/archive/1999/05/12/ndoc12.html> (accessed 4 April 2007).

Jones, J (1992) 'Convicted doctor offered new terms considering offer can resume work', *The Independent*, 21 November.

Jones, M (1991) '"Mercy killing" wife goes free', *Bristol Evening Post*, 14 May.

Jones, T (1995) 'Crippled graduate chooses death to spare family's pain', *The Times*, 26 May.

—— (1997) 'Suicide woman warned off rescuers', *The Times*, 8 May.

Kadish, S H (1994) 'Letting patients die: Legal and moral reflections', in Coleman, J L and Buchanan, A (eds) *In Harm's Way: Essays in Honor of Joel Feinberg*, pp 290–323, Cambridge: Cambridge University Press.

Kalven, H (1956) 'A special corner of civil liberties: A legal view I' *New York University Law Review*, 31: 1223–1237.

Kamisar, Y (1957) 'Euthanasia legislation: Some non-religious objections', in Downing, A B (ed) (1969) *Euthanasia and the Right to Death: The Case for Voluntary Euthanasia*, pp 85–133, London: Peter Owen.

—— (1997) 'Physician-assisted suicide: The last bridge to active voluntary euthanasia', in Keown, J (ed) *Euthanasia Examined: Ethical, Clinical and Legal Perspectives*, pp 225–260, Cambridge: Cambridge University Press.

Kamm, F M (1998) 'Physician-assisted suicide, euthanasia, and intending death', in Battin, M P, Rhodes, R and Silvers, A (eds) *Physician-Assisted Suicide: Expanding the Debate*, pp 28–62, New York and London: Routledge.

Kant, I (1991) *The Moral Law: Groundwork of the Metaphysic of Morals*, translated and analysed by Paton, H J, London: Hutchinson & Co.

Kass, L (1989) 'Neither for love nor money: Why doctors must not kill', *Public Interest*, 94: 25–36.

Katz, L (2004) 'GP jailed for giving lethal morphine overdose', *The Guardian*, 6 April.

Keenan, J F (1996) 'The concept of sanctity of life and its use in contemporary bioethical discussion', in Bayertz, K (ed) *Sanctity of Life and Human Dignity*, pp 1–18, 52 Philosophy and Medicine, Dordrecht: Kluwer Academic Publishers.

Kelso, P (2000) 'He only wanted to end his wife's pain. He ended up in court, at 84', *The Guardian*, 7 June.

Kennedy, I (1976a) 'The Karen Quinlan case: Problems and proposals', *Journal of Medical Ethics*, 2: 3–7.

—— (1976b) 'The legal effect of requests by the terminally ill and aged not to receive further treatment from doctors', *Criminal Law Review*, 217–232.

—— (1977) 'Switching off life support machines: The legal implications', *Criminal Law Review*, 443–452.

—— (1992a) 'Emerging problems of medicine, technology and the law', in Kennedy, I *Treat Me Right: Essays in Medical Law and Ethics*, pp 1–18, Oxford: Clarendon Press.

—— (1992b) '*R v Arthur*, *Re B*, and the severely disabled new-born baby', in Kennedy, I *Treat Me Right: Essays in Medical Law and Ethics*, pp 154–174, Oxford: Clarendon Press.

—— (1997) 'Commentary 3: A response to Lowe', *Journal of Medical Ethics*, 23: 161–163.

—— and Grubb, A (1993) 'Withdrawal of artificial hydration and nutrition: incompetent adult', *Medical Law Review*, 1: 359–370.

—— (1994) *Medical Law: Text with Materials*, 2nd edn, London: Butterworths.

Keown, D and Keown, J (1995) 'Killing, karma and caring: Euthanasia in Buddhism and Christianity', *Journal of Medical Ethics*, 21: 265–269.

Keown, J (1997a) 'Euthanasia in the Netherlands: Sliding down the slippery slope?' in Keown, J (ed) *Euthanasia Examined: Ethical, Clinical and Legal Perspectives*, pp 261–296, Cambridge: Cambridge University Press.

—— (1997b) 'Restoring moral and intellectual shape to the law after *Bland*', *The Law Quarterly Review*, 113: 481–503.

—— (ed) (1997c) *Euthanasia Examined: Ethical, Clinical and Legal Perspectives*, Cambridge: Cambridge University Press.

—— (2000) 'Beyond Bland: A critique of the BMA guidance on withholding and withdrawing medical treatment', *Legal Studies*, 20(1): 66–84.

—— (2001) 'Dehydration and human rights', *Cambridge Law Journal*, 60(1): 53–56.

—— (2002a) *Euthanasia, Ethics and Public Policy: An Argument Against Legalisation*, Cambridge: Cambridge University Press.

—— (2002b) 'The case of Ms B: Suicide's slippery slope?' *Journal of Medical Ethics*, 28(4): 238—239.

—— (2003) 'European Court of Human Rights: Death in Strasbourg – Assisted suicide, the *Pretty* case, and the European Convention on Human Rights', *International Journal of Constitutional Law*, 1(4): 722–730.

—— (2005) 'A futile defence of Bland: A reply to Andrew McGee', *Medical Law Review*, 13(3): 393–402.

—— (2006) 'Restoring the sanctity of life and replacing the caricature: A reply to David Price', *Legal Studies*, 26(1): 109–119.

Kevorkian, J (1991) *Prescription: Medicide – The Goodness of Planned Death*, Buffalo: Prometheus Books.

Khan, M and Robson, M (1995) 'What is a responsible group of medical opinion?' *Professional Negligence*, 11(4): 121–123.

Kinnell, H G (2000) 'Serial homicide by doctors: Shipman in perspective', *British Medical Journal*, 321: 1594–1597.

Koch, T (2005) 'The challenge of Terri Schiavo: Lessons for bioethics', *Journal of Medical Ethics*, 31: 376–378.

Kuhse, H (1987) *The Sanctity-of-Life Doctrine in Medicine: A Critique*, Oxford: Clarendon Press.

—— (1991) 'Euthanasia', in Singer, P (ed) *A Companion to Ethics*, pp 294–302, Oxford: Blackwell.

Lamb, D (1988) *Down the Slippery Slope: Arguing in Applied Ethics*, Kent: Crook Helm.

Lancet, The (1927) 'Medicine and the law: Euthanasia', *The Lancet*, 2: 986.

Lanham, D J (1973) 'Euthanasia', *Criminal Law Review*, 201–202.

Laurance, J (2005) 'Families furious after doctor is cleared of murder patients', *The Independent*, 15 December.

Law Commission (2005) *A New Homicide Act for England and Wales? A Consultation Paper*, Consultation Paper No 177, London: Law Commission.

—— (2006) *Murder, Manslaughter and Infanticide. Project 6 of the Ninth Programme of Law Reform: Homicide*, Law Com No 304, London: Law Commission.

Lawton, Lord Justice (1979) 'Do we need a new offence of "mercy killing"? Mercy killing: the judicial dilemma', *Journal of the Royal Society of Medicine*, 72: 460–461.

Lecky, W E H (1924) *History of European Morals: From Augustus to Charlemagne*, Honolulu: University Press of the Pacific.

Leicester Mercury (1986) '"Act of mercy" by pensioner who killed wife', *Leicester Mercury*, 11 November.

Leng, R (1982a) 'Mercy killing and the CLRC', *New Law Journal*, 132: 76–78.

—— (1982b) 'Death and the criminal law', *Modern Law Review*, 45: 206–211.

Lewis, P (2006) 'Medical treatment of dementia patients at the end of life: Can the law accommodate the personal identity and welfare problems?' *European Journal of Health Law*, 13: 219–234.

Liddell, K and Hall, A (2005) 'Beyond Bristol and Alder Hey: The future regulation of human tissue', *Medical Law Review*, 13(2): 170–223.

Linacre Centre (The Linacre Centre for Health Care Ethics) (1982) 'Euthanasia and clinical practice: Trends, principles and alternatives. A Working Party report', in Gormally, L (ed) (1994) *Euthanasia, Clinical Practice and the Law*, 1–107, London: The Linacre Centre for Health Care Ethics.

—— (1993) 'Submission to the Select Committee of the House of Lords on Medical Ethics', in Gormally, L (ed) (1994) *Euthanasia, Clinical Practice and the Law*, pp 111–165, London: The Linacre Centre for Health Care Ethics.

Liverpool Daily Post (1982) 'Man in suicide case is freed' *Liverpool Daily Post*, 22 June.

Lo, B, Dornbrand, L, Wolf, L E and Groman, M (2002) 'The Wendland case – Withdrawing life support from incompetent patients who are not terminally ill', *New England Journal of Medicine*, 346(19): 1489–1493.

Lowe, S L (1997) 'The right to refuse treatment is not a right to be killed', *Journal of Medical Ethics*, 23: 154–158.

Lowman, J and Palys, T (2000) 'Ethics and institutional conflict of interest: The research confidentiality controversy at Simon Fraser University', *Sociological Practice – A Journal of Clinical and Applied Sociology*, 2(4): 245–264.

Macaskill, M and Ungoed-Thomas, J (2000) 'Elderly are helped to die to clear beds, claims doctor', *The Sunday Times*, 2 April.

McCall Smith, A (1990) 'Committee ethics? Clinical ethics committees and their introduction in the United Kingdom', *Journal of Law and Society*, 17(1): 124–139.

—— (1999) 'Euthanasia: The strengths of the middle ground', *Medical Law Review*, 7: 194–207.

MacDonald, N and Roy, D J (1998) 'Ethical issues in palliative care', in Doyle, D, Hanks, G W C and MacDonald, N (eds) *Oxford Textbook of Palliative Medicine*, pp 97–138, 2nd edn, Oxford: Oxford University Press.

McGleenan, T (1995) 'Human gene therapy and slippery slope arguments', *Journal of Medical Ethics*, 21: 350–355.

McLean, S A M (1994) 'Letting die or assisting death: How should the law respond to the patient in persistent vegetative state?' in Peterson, K (ed) *Law and Medicine: A Special Issue of Law in Context (Volume 11(2) 1993)*, 3–16, La Trobe University: La Trobe University Press.

—— (1996) 'Law at the end of life: What next', in McLean, S A M (ed) *Death, Dying and the Law*, pp 49–66, Aldershot: Dartmouth.

—— and Britton, A. (1996) *Sometimes a Small Victory*, Institute of Law and Ethics in Medicine, University of Glasgow: Scottish County Press Ltd.

—— (1997) *The Case for Physician Assisted Suicide*, London: Pandora Soap Box, Harper Collins.

—— and Maher, G (1983) *Medicine, Morals and the Law*, Aldershot: Gower.

Macklin, R (2003) 'Dignity is a useless concept' *British Medical Journal*, 327: 1419–1420.

Magnusson, R (1996) 'The future of the euthanasia debate in Australia', *Melbourne University Law Review*, 20(4): 1108–1142.

Manninen, B A (2006) 'A case for justified non-voluntary active euthanasia: Exploring the ethics of the Groningen Protocol', *Journal of Medical Ethics*, 32: 643–651.

Martel, J (2001) 'Examining the foreseeable: Assisted suicide as a herald of changing moralities', *Social and Legal Studies*, 10(2): 147–170.

Mason, J K (1988) *Human Life and Medical Practice*, Edinburgh: Edinburgh University Press.

—— (1995) *Forensic Medicine for Lawyers*, 3rd edn, London: Butterworths.

—— and Laurie, G T (2006) *Mason and McCall Smith's Law and Medical Ethics*, 7th edn, Oxford: Oxford University Press.

May, W F (1991) *The Patient's Ordeal*, Indiana: Indiana University Press.

—— (2003) 'Oral evidence to President's Council on Bioethics'. HTTP: <http://bioethics.gov/transcripts/oct03/oct17full.html> (accessed 28 March 2007).

Meakin, R G (1988) 'Diminished responsibility: Some arguments for a general defence', *Journal of Criminal Law*, 52: 406–413.

Menikoff, J A, Sacks, G A and Siegler, M (1992) 'Beyond advance directives – Health care surrogate laws', *New England Journal of Medicine*, 327(16): 1165–1169.

Meyers, D W (1970) *The Human Body and the Law: A Medico-Legal Study*, Edinburgh: Edinburgh University Press.

—— (1990) *The Human Body and the Law*, 2nd edn, Edinburgh: Edinburgh University Press.

Mill, J S (1962a) 'On liberty', in Warnock, M (ed) *Utilitarianism, On Liberty, Essay on Bentham (by John Stuart Mill), together with selected writings of Jeremy Bentham and John Austin*, pp 126–250, London: Collins, The Fontana Library.

—— (1962b) 'Utilitarianism', in Warnock, M (ed) *Utilitarianism, On Liberty, Essay on Bentham (by John Stuart Mill), together with selected writings of Jeremy Bentham and John Austin*, pp 251–321, London: Collins, The Fontana Library.

Miller, F K and Brody, H (2001) 'The internal morality of medicine: An evolutionary perspective', *Journal of Medicine and Philosophy*, 26(6): 581–599.

Mills, P and Winsper, K (1991) 'New life for tragic husband', *Evening Argus* (Brighton), 24 July.

Minelli, L A (2006) 'Some information about DIGNITAS'. HTTP: <http://www.dignitas.ch> (accessed 4 December 2006).

Mitchell, B (1990) *Murder and Penal Policy*, Basingstoke: MacMillan.

Momeyer, R (1995) 'Does physician assisted suicide violate the integrity of medicine?' *Journal of Medicine and Philosophy*, 20: 13–24.

Montgomery, J (1991) 'Rights, restraints and pragmatism: The Human Fertilisation and Embryology Act 1990', *Modern Law Review*, 54: 524–534.

Moor, D (2001) *Allowing Dignity in Death*, private publication (ISBN: 0 9540799 0 6).

Moore, M S (1993) *Act and Crime: The Philosophy of Action and its Implications for Criminal Law*, Oxford: Clarendon Press.

Moreno, J D (1995) *Deciding Together: Bioethics and Moral Consensus*, New York: Oxford University Press.

Morgan, D (1992) 'The greatest danger', *New Law Journal*, 142: 1652.

—— (2001) *Issues in Medical Law and Ethics*, London: Cavendish Publishing.

Morning Telegraph (1975) '"Kill me" plea by sick wife', *Morning Telegraph* (Sheffield), 21 November.

Morris, A (2000) 'Easing the passing: End of life decisions and the Medical Treatment (Prevention of Euthanasia) Bill', *Medical Law Review*, 8: 300–315.

Mumford, E and Mumford, D (1999) 'Rapid response: Competence and deliberate self-harm: A little legal knowledge can be dangerous', *British Medical Journal*, 11 July. HTTP: <http://www.bmj.com/cgi/eletters/319/7202/107#3846> (accessed 28 March 2007).

Murray, I (1997a) 'Euthanasia doctors accused of executing patients', *The Times*, 21 July.

—— (1997b) 'Motor neurone victim dies with dignity at home', *The Times*, 3 December.

Murphy, P (ed) (2007) *Blackstone's Criminal Practice 2007*, Oxford: Oxford University Press.

Nash, E (2005) 'Lover confesses to mercy killing that inspired film', *The Independent*, 12 January.

Nelson, D and Murphie, J (1994) 'No charges over "mercy killing"', *The Observer*, 4 December.

Nolan, W F and Johnson, G C (1967) *Logan's Run*, New York: Dial Press.

Norrie, A (1993) *Crime, Reason and History: A Critical Introduction to Criminal Law*, London: Weidenfeld and Nicolson.

Norton, C (1998) 'Doctor, will you help me die?' *The Sunday Times, Focus* supplement, 15 November.

Nursing Times (1994) 'CPS says no charge against mother-in-pain nurse', *Nursing Times*, 14 December.

—— (1995) 'Back to work for euthanasia nurse', *Nursing Times*, 26 April.

Nys, H (1999) 'Physician involvement in a patient's death: A continental perspective', *Medical Law Review*, 7: 208–246.

O'Connell, M and Whelan, A (1996) 'Taking wrongs seriously: Public perceptions of crime seriousness', *British Journal of Criminology*, 36: 299–318.

O'Connor, M, Kissane, D W and Spruyt, O (1999) 'Sedation in the terminally ill – A clinical perspective', *Monash Bioethics Review*, 18(3): 17–27.

Ogden, R (1995) 'Out of the closet – AIDS and euthanasia', *Voluntary Euthanasia Society*. HTTP: <http://www.ves.org.uk/library/ogden.htm> (accessed 28 July 1999).

Ognall, H (1994) 'A right to die? Some medico-legal reflection', *Medico-Legal Journal*, 62: 165–179.

Oldfield, S (1984) 'Loving wife tried to kill husband', *The Daily Mail*, 15 May.

Oliver, D (1997) 'Letter: Easing pain for the terminally ill', *The Times*, 11 November.

O'Neill, O (2002) *Autonomy and Trust in Bioethics*, Cambridge: Cambridge University Press.

—— (2003) 'Some limits of informed consent', *Journal of Medical Ethics*, 29: 4–7.

Osman, A, Ferriman, A and Timmins, N (1981) 'Women cry "Thank God" as Dr Arthur is cleared', *The Times*, 6 November.

Ost, S (2005) 'Euthanasia and the defence of necessity: Advocating a more appropriate legal response', *Criminal Law Review*, 355–370.

Otlowski, M F A (1997) *Voluntary Euthanasia and the Common Law*, Oxford: Clarendon Press.

Palmer, H (1957) 'Dr. Adams' trial for murder', *Criminal Law Review*, 365–377.

Paris, N (2007) '"Right to die" fight abandoned', *The Daily Telegraph*, 20 April.

Parker, M (2005) 'End games: Euthanasia under interminable scrutiny', *Bioethics*, 19(5–6): 523–536.

Parks, J A (2000) 'Why gender matters to the euthanasia debate', *Hastings Center Report*, 30(1): 30–36.

Pellegrino, E D (2001) 'The internal morality of medicine: A paradigm for the ethics of the helping and healing professions', *Journal of Medicine and Philosophy*, 26(6): 559–579.

Polack, C (2001) 'Is a tattoo the answer?' *British Medical Journal*, 323: 1063.

Policy Council (2004) *Billet D'État: Voluntary Euthanasia (Death with Dignity)*. HTTP: <http://www.gov.gg/ccm/general/billets/2004/billet-dtat---xvi-2004.en> (accessed 10 April 2007).

Poole, D (1986) 'Arthur's Case: (1) A comment', *Criminal Law Review*, 383–387.

Pratt, C (1974) 'For beloved Emma, a painless death', *Daily Express*, 26 October.

Price, D (1997) 'Euthanasia, pain relief and double effect', *Legal Studies*, 17(2): 323–342.

—— (2001) 'Fairly Bland: An alternative view of a supposed new "death ethic" and the BMA guidelines', *Legal Studies*, 21: 618–643.

Price, D P T (1996) 'Assisted suicide and refusing medical treatment: Linguistics, morals and legal contortions', *Medical Law Review*, 4: 270–299.

Purvis, J (2005) *Dying with Dignity Consultation*. HTTP: <http://www.jeremypurvis. org/consultation1.htm> (accessed 10 April 2007).

Quick, O (1999) 'Disaster at Bristol: Explanations and implications of a tragedy', *Journal of Social Welfare and Family Law*, 21(4): 307–326.

—— (2006) 'Prosecuting "gross" negligence: Manslaughter, discretion and the Crown Prosecution Service', *Journal of Law and Society*, 33(3): 421–450.

Quill, T E and Byock, I R (2000) 'Responding to intractable terminal suffering: The role of terminal sedation and voluntary refusal of food and fluids', *Annals of Internal Medicine*, 132: 408–414.

Rachels, J (1979) 'Euthanasia, killing, and letting die', in Ladd, J (ed) *Ethical Issues Relating to Life and Death*, pp 146–163, Oxford: Oxford University Press.

—— (1986) *The End of Life: Euthanasia and Morality*, Oxford: Oxford University Press.

—— (1993) 'Euthanasia', in Regan, T (ed) *Matters of Life and Death: New Introductory Essays in Moral Philosophy*, pp 30–68, New York: McGraw Hill.

Radin, M J (1989) 'Reconsidering the rule of law', *Boston University Law Review*, 69(4): 781–819.

Ramsey, J H R (1994) 'A King, a doctor, and a convenient death', *British Medical Journal*, 308: 1445.

Ramsey, P (1956) 'Freedom and responsibility in medical and sex ethics: A Protestant view', *New York University Law Review*, 31: 1189–1204.

Randell, T (2004) 'Medical and legal considerations of brain death', *Acta Anaesthesiologica Scandinavica*, 48(2): 139–144.

Raphael, D D (1988) 'Handicapped infants: Medical ethics and the law', *Journal of Medical Ethics*, 14: 5–10.

Ravenscroft, A J and Bell, M D D (2000) '"End-of-life" decision making within intensive care – Objective, consistent, defensible?' *Journal of Medical Ethics*, 26: 435–440.

Rawls, J (1972) *A Theory of Justice*, Oxford: Oxford University Press.

Raymond, D (1999) '"Fatal practices": A feminist analysis of physician-assisted suicide and euthanasia', *Hypatia*, 14(2): 1–25.

Rayner, M (1997) 'Letter: Doctors have right to help patients to die', *The Sunday Times*, 27 July.

Raz, J (1977) 'The rule of law and its virtue', *The Law Quarterly Review*, 93: 195–211.

Reiter-Theil, S (2001) 'The Freiburg approach to ethics consultation: Process, outcome and competencies', *Journal of Medical Ethics*, 27 Suppl I: i21–i23.

Richmond, P (1998) 'Response', in Gill, R (ed) *Euthanasia and the Churches*, pp 103–109, London: Cassell.

Robertshaw, P (1998) *Summary Justice: Judges Address Juries*, London and Washington: Cassell.

Robertson, D (1996) 'The withdrawal of medical treatment from patients: Fundamental legal issues', *Australian Law Journal*, 70: 723–746.

Rodgers, M E (2003) 'Human bodies, inhuman uses: Public reactions and legislative responses to the scandals of bodysnatching', *Nott LJ*, 12(2): 1–17.

Roland, J (1989) 'Manslaughter son is jailed', *Evening Post* (Nottingham), 20 January.

RCPCH (Royal College of Paediatrics and Child Health) (1997) *Withholding or Withdrawing Life Saving Treatment in Children: A Framework for Practice*, London: Royal College of Paediatrics and Child Health.

Rozenberg, J (2004) 'Dying woman free to commit suicide', *The Daily Telegraph*, 1 December.

Royal Commission (1953) *Royal Commission on Capital Punishment 1949–1953: Report*, Cmnd 8932, London: Her Majesty's Stationery Office.

Rusbridger, A (1981a) 'Exit helper "a vulture" says suicide candidate', *The Guardian*, 16 October.

—— (1981b) 'Exit man's "abuse on the telephone"', *The Guardian*, 17 October.

—— (1981c) '"Puppet master" controlled EXIT', *The Guardian*, 22 October.

—— (1981d) 'EXIT campaigner gaoled', *The Guardian*, 31 October.

Ryan, J (1979) 'Mercy killing man freed', *Daily Mail*, 4 October.

Sacks, J (2003) 'Power and responsibility: Science, humanity and religion in the 21st century'. HTTP: <http://www.st-edmunds.cam.ac.uk/faraday/CIS/sacks/> (accessed 28 March 2007).

Sacred Congregation for the Doctrine of the Faith (1980) *Declaration on Euthanasia*, London: Catholic Truth Society.

Saini, P (1998) 'Sanctity of life and the law: Annie Lindsell's case', *Voluntary Euthanasia Society*. HTTP: <http://www.ves.org.uk/DpA_Sanctity.html> (accessed 30 November 1999).

—— (1999) 'The doctrine of double effect and the law of murder', *Medico-Legal Journal*, 67(3): 106–120.

St John-Stevas, N (1961) *Life, Death and the Law: A Study of the Relationship Between Law and Christian Morals in the English and American Legal Systems*, London: Eyre and Spottiswoode.

Sanders, A (1985) 'Prosecution decisions and the Attorney-General's guidelines', *Criminal Law Review*, 4–19.

Sanders, J (1969) 'Euthanasia: None dare call it murder', *The Journal of Criminal Law, Criminology, and Police Science*, 60(3): 351–359.

Saunders, C (1995) 'In Britain: Fewer conflicts of conscience', *Hastings Center Report*, 25(3): 44–45.

Schauer, F (1985) 'Slippery slopes', *Harvard Law Review*, 99: 361–383.

Seale, C (2006a) 'National survey of end-of-life decisions made by UK medical practitioners', *Palliative Medicine*, 20(1): 3–10.

—— (2006b) 'Characteristics of end-of-life decisions: Survey of UK medical practitioners', *Palliative Medicine*, 20(10): 653–659.

Shand, J (1997) 'A reply to some standard objections to euthanasia', *Journal of Applied Philosophy*, 14: 43–47.

Shaw, T (1998) 'Mother is cleared of killing disabled daughter', *The Electronic Telegraph*, 19 May. HTTP: <http://www.telegraph.co.uk/htmlContent.jhtml?html=/archive/1998/05/19/nwat19.html> (accessed 28 March 2007).

Shipman Inquiry (2002) *First Report: Death Disguised*. HTTP: <http://www.the-shipman-inquiry.org.uk> (accessed 28 March 2007).

Singer, P (1993) *Practical Ethics*, 2nd edn, Cambridge: Cambridge University Press.

—— (1994) *Rethinking Life and Death: The Collapse of Our Traditional Ethics*, New York: St Martin's Press.

—— (1995) 'Presidential address: Is the sanctity of life ethic terminally ill?' *Bioethics*, 9: 327–343.

Skegg, P D G (1974) 'A justification for medical procedures performed without consent', *The Law Quarterly Review*, 90: 517–530.

—— (1978) 'The termination of life-support measures and the law of murder', *Modern Law Review*, 41: 423–436.

—— (1988) *Law, Ethics and Medicine: Studies in Medical Law*, revised edn, Oxford: Clarendon Press.

Skene, L and Parker, M (2002) 'The role of the Church in developing the law', *Journal of Medical Ethics*, 28: 215–218.

Smith, J C (1979) 'Case and comment: *R v Smith*', *Criminal Law Review*, 251–253.

—— (1993) 'Case and comment: *Airedale NHS Trust v Bland*', *Criminal Law Review*, 877–880.

—— (2000) 'A comment on Moor's case', *Criminal Law Review*, 41–44.

Smith, K J M (1983) 'Assisting in suicide – The Attorney General and the Voluntary Euthanasia Society', *Criminal Law Review*, 579–586.

Smith, S W (2005) 'Fallacies of the logical slippery slope in the debate on physician-assisted suicide and euthanasia', *Medical Law Review* 13(2): 224–243.

Smith, T V (1942) 'Compromise: Its context and limits', *Ethics*, 53(1): 1–13.

Solum, L (1998) 'Euthanasia at the intersection of law and morality', *Loyola of Los Angeles Law Review*, 31: 1115–1122.

South Wales Echo (1989) '"Loving" daughter helped "Mum" to die', *South Wales Echo* (Cardiff), 15 July.

Steinbock, B and Norcross, A (eds) (1994) *Killing and Letting Die*, 2nd edn, New York: Fordham University Press.

Stirrat, G M and Gill, R (2005) 'Autonomy in medical ethics after O'Neill', *Journal of Medical Ethics*, 31: 127–130.

Stokes, P (1998) 'Daughter who helped mother to die is freed', *The Daily Telegraph*, 30 June.

—— (2005) 'Jury clears widow accused of letting ME husband die', *The Daily Telegraph*, 28 April.

Stone, J (1994) 'Withholding life-sustaining treatment: The ultimate decision', *New Law Journal*, 144: 205–206.

Sullivan, M D, Ganzini, L and Youngner, S J (1998) 'Should psychiatrists serve as gatekeepers for physician-assisted suicide?' *Hastings Center Report*, 28(4): 24–31.

Sykes, N and Thorns, A (2003a) 'Sedative use in the last week of life and the implications for end-of-life decision making', *Archives of Internal Medicine*, 163: 341–344.

—— (2003b) 'The use of opioids and sedatives at the end of life', *The Lancet Oncology*, 4: 312–318.

Tallis, R (1996) 'Is there a slippery slope? Arguments for and against the various definitions of euthanasia', *Times Literary Supplement*, 12 January.

Tännsjö, T (2007) 'Why no compromise is possible', *Metaphilosophy*, 38(2–3): 330–343.

Tata, C (1997) 'Conceptions and representations of the sentencing decision process', *Journal of Law and Society*, 24(3): 395–420.

Teeman, T (2002) 'Son who tried to aid suicide is freed', *The Times*, 12 January.

Thomas, D A (1984) 'Case and comment: *R v Wallis*', *Criminal Law Review*, 46.
—— (1985) 'Case and comment: *R v Hough*', *Criminal Law Review*, 248–249.
Thompson, T, Barbour, R and Schwartz, L (2003) 'Adherence to advance directives in critical care decision making: Vignette study', *British Medical Journal*, 327: 1011–1014.
Thornton, R (1991) 'Wardship – Withholding medical treatment', *The Cambridge Law Journal*, 50: 238–240.
Times, The (1934a) 'Invalid son's death', *The Times*, 2 October.
—— (1934b) 'Invalid son's death', *The Times*, 3 December.
—— (1934c) 'Mrs Brownhill's reprieve recommended', *The Times*, 4 December.
—— (1935) 'Release after reprieve', *The Times*, 4 March.
—— (1946a) 'News in brief', *The Times*, 23 November.
—— (1946b) 'News in brief', *The Times*, 29 November.
—— (1953) 'Attempted murder of husband', *The Times*, 16 October.
—— (1957) 'Dr. Adams acquitted on murder charge', *The Times*, 10 April.
—— (1975) 'Suicide case spinster is cleared', *The Times*, 22 July.
—— (1980) 'Man who aided wife's suicide put on probation', *The Times*, 15 May.
—— (1983) 'Doctor was a mass murderer, former police Chief says', *The Times*, 11 July.
—— (1984) 'Novelist jailed for nine months after helping woman to commit suicide', *The Times*, 15 December.
—— (1985) 'Parents cleared of son's murder', *The Times*, 15 May.
—— (1988) 'Man aided daughter's suicide', *The Times*, 19 February.
—— (1990) 'Probation for aiding suicide', *The Times*, 17 March.
—— (1994) 'Euthanasia verdict makes legal history', *The Times*, 7 October.
Timmins, N (1981) 'Dr Jolly is not to be prosecuted', *The Times*, 6 October.
Tobias, J (2006) 'Letters: The ethics of euthanasia', *The Guardian*, 9 June.
Today (1986) 'Nurse admits mercy killing', *Today*, 27 December.
Tong, R (1997) 'A feminist interpretation of Engelhardt's bioethics: More a moral friend than a moral stranger', *Reason Papers* 60–74.
Tur, R H S (2003) 'Legislative technique and human rights: The sad case of assisted suicide', *Criminal Law Review*, 3–12.
Twycross, R G (1982) 'Euthanasia – A physician's perspective', *Journal of Medical Ethics*, 8: 86–91.
—— (1997) 'Where there is hope, there is life: A view from the hospice', in Keown, J (ed) *Euthanasia Examined: Ethical, Clinical and Legal Perspectives*, pp 141–168, Cambridge: Cambridge University Press.
Van der Burg, W (1991) 'The slippery slope argument', *Ethics*, 102: 42–63.
van Zyl, L (2000) *Death and Compassion: A Virtue-Based Approach to Euthanasia*, Aldershot: Ashgate.
VanDeVeer, D (1986) *Paternalistic Intervention: The Moral Bounds of Benevolence*, New Jersey: Princeton University Press.
Varelius, J (2007) 'Illness, suffering and voluntary euthanasia', *Bioethics*, 21(2): 75–83.
Veatch, R M (2001) 'The impossibility of a morality internal to medicine', *Journal of Medicine and Philosophy*, 26(6): 621–642.
Velleman, J D (2004) 'Against the right to die'. HTTP: http://homepages.nyu.edu/~dv26/Work/Against_the_Right.pdf> (accessed 4 April 2007).

Vickers, L (1997) 'Assisted dying and the laws of three European countries', *New Law Journal*, 147: 610–611.

Victor, P (1990) 'Brother and sister go free after trying to kill dying mother', *The Times*, 14 November.

Wainwright, M (2003) 'Arrested euthanasia society chief resigns', *The Guardian*, 15 December.

—— (2005a) 'Daughter's fears over morphine injections', *The Guardian*, 28 October.

—— (2005b) 'Jury clears former GP of murdering patients with morphine doses', *The Guardian*, 15 December.

—— (2005c) 'Doctor cleared of killing patients upsets relatives', *The Guardian*, 31 December.

Walker, N and McCabe, S (1973) *Crime and Insanity in England. Volume Two: New Solutions and New Problems*, Edinburgh: Edinburgh University Press.

—— Padfield, N (1996) *Sentencing: Theory, Law and Practice*, London: Butterworths.

Wall, P D (1997) 'The generation of yet another myth on the use of narcotics', *Pain* 73: 121–122.

Wells, C (1994) 'Patients, consent and the criminal law', *The Journal of Social Welfare and Family Law*, 16: 65–78.

Western Mail (1982) 'Man cut wife's throat to end her pain', *Western Mail* (Bristol), 7 September.

Wheat, K (2000) 'The law's treatment of the suicidal', *Medical Law Review*, 8: 182–209.

Wilkinson, P (1990) 'Doctor cleared of murdering patient with pain-killing jab', *The Times*, 16 March.

Williams, B (1995) *Making Sense of Humanity and Other Philosophical Papers 1982–1993*, Cambridge: Cambridge University Press.

Williams, G (1958a) *The Sanctity of Life and the Criminal Law*, London: Faber & Faber.

—— (1958b) 'Euthanasia legislation: A rejoinder to the non-religious objections', in Downing, A B (ed) (1969) *Euthanasia and the Right to Death: The Case for Voluntary Euthanasia*, pp 134–147, London: Peter Owen.

—— (1960) 'Diminished responsibility', *Medicine, Science and the Law*, 1: 41–53.

—— (1973) 'Euthanasia', *Medico-Legal Journal*, 41: 14–34.

—— (1977) 'Letters to the Editor: Switching off life support machines', *Criminal Law Review*, 635.

—— (1981) 'Letter: Life of a child', *The Times*, 13 August.

—— (1983) *Textbook of Criminal Law*, 2nd edn, London: Stevens and Sons.

—— (1991) 'Criminal omissions – The conventional view', *The Law Quarterly Review*, 107: 86–98.

—— (2001a) 'The principle of double effect and terminal sedation', *Medical Law Review*, 9: 41–53

—— (2001b) 'Provocation and killing with compassion', *Journal of Criminal Law*, 65(2): 149–160.

Wilson, W (1998) *Criminal Law: Doctrine and Theory*, London: Longman.

—— (1999) 'Doctrinal rationality after *Woollin*', *The Modern Law Review*, 62: 448–463.

Wolf, S (1996) 'Gender, feminism, and death: Physician-assisted suicide and euthanasia', in Wolf, S (ed) *Feminism and Bioethics: Beyond Reproduction*, pp 282–317, New York: Oxford University Press.

Wong, D B (1992) 'Coping with moral conflict and ambiguity', *Ethics*, 102(4): 763–784.

Woodcock, J (1984) 'Wife who could not face life after 50', *Daily Mail*, 31 July.

Woods, S (2007) *Death's Dominion: Ethics at the End of Life*, Berkshire: Open University Press.

Wootton, B (1960) 'Diminished responsibility: A layman's view', *The Law Quarterly Review*, 76: 224–239.

—— (1978a) *Crime and Penal Policy: Reflections on Fifty Years' Experience*, London: George Allen & Unwin.

—— (1978b) 'The right to die', in Bean, P and Seal, V G (eds) (1992) *Barbara Wootton: Selected Writings. Vol 3: Social and Political Thought*, pp 177–182, Hampshire: The Macmillan Press.

Wreen, M (1998) 'The definition of euthanasia', *Philosophy and Phenomenological Research*, 48(4): 637–653.

Zucker, M B and Zucker, H D (1997) *Medical Futility and the Evaluation of Life-sustaining Interventions*, New York: Cambridge University Press.

Index

Able 58–60
abortion
  Act 1967 18
  compromise, and 150, 155–156
  conscience, and 139
  slippery slope, and 18, 28–29
  value of life, and 155–156
absolutism 153–154
  vitalism and 11, 135
active euthanasia – *see* euthanasia
acts/omissions distinction
  criticism of 22, 148, 159
  defence of 12
  definition(s) of 6, 7, 12
  doctor's defence, as a 118, 123, 144
  law, in 108, 117–131, 136, 138, 160–
    162, 170
  See also duty; killing; withdrawing
    and withholding treatment
advance directive(s) 65, 88, 139, 161
  euthanasia and 15
  interpretation of 75, 161
  law, in 73, 75
  laypersons and 75
  Mental Capacity Act 2005 and 73
  paramedics and 75
  suicide note as 74
  tattoo as an 75
  verbal form of 75
Aids 68
Allitt, Ms 129
Ambrose, Mr 47
analgesic – *see* opioids
arthritis 33, 106
Arthur 26, 84, 86, 88, 108–109, 110,
  125–126, 128, 130
artificial nutrition and hydration
  medical treatment, as 124–125

'normal' feeding, contrasted with
    124–125
  refusal of 148
  See also withdrawing and withholding
    treatment
assault 30, 73, 124, 152
assisted suicide 18, 25, 34, 37, 47, 54,
    55–83, 94, 95, 142
  advice and 51, 58, 59, 81, 82, 168
  aiding, abetting, counselling and
    procuring, definitions 57–58, 59
  attempted 60
  charging lottery xv, 72
  complicity in suicide xv, 57, 60–61
  'death tourism' xv–xvi, 8, 55, 57,
    63–66, 78, 82, 167–168, 172
    intention and 64
    law-in-action and 55, 62, 64–66,
      82
    local authority's duty and 65
    location of death, relevance of, and
      65
  definition(s) of 9, 57, 58, 62–63
  doctors, by xvi, 67, 69
  duty to perform 25
  euthanasia 7, 25, 80, 150, 166
  'final act' test in 7, 15, 166
  human rights and 79–82
  intention and 58, 60
  murder 57, 61, 62–63, 82
  omission, by xvi, 7, 9, 57, 62, 68–77,
    161–162
    charging lottery 72
    criticism of legal status 70–71
    duty and 70–71, 73, 74, 173
    encouragement and 70
    law-in-action and 68–70, 72, 73
  physician 4, 10, 25, 83

presence insufficient for 70
prohibition on xiii, xv, 79
  challenges to 79–82
  relaxation of 57, 78
  providing the pills xvi, 66–68
  evidence of 66, 67
  intention in 66–67, 168
  law-in-action and 57, 62, 66–68,
    82
  doctors 67–68
  refusal of treatment, and 72–77
  sentencing and 77–79, 166
  Suicide Act 1961, aims of 76
  types of xvii, 56, 60–61
  See also duty; euthanasia; reform
    of the law, proposals for; suicide
attempted murder – see murder
Attorney General 50, 58–59, 87, 98,
  126
Australia
  Northern Territory 10, 59, 64
autonomy, respect for 2, 31, 73, 74, 82,
    142, 143, 146, 149, 151, 153,
    156, 160, 161, 166, 173
  appeal of 26
  consequentialist ethics and 13, 16, 24
  deontological ethics and 13, 24
  doctor, of 139
  feminist ethics and 13
  Greek derivation 13
  law, in 34, 73, 75, 80, 137, 138, 144
  liberal, as 14, 24–25, 138
  limits on 115, 116
  meaning of 14, 24–25, 145, 151, 174
  paternalism 14
  person performing euthanasia, of 14,
    25, 139
  sanctity of life v 137–139
  scope of 25, 139, 147, 151
  See also value of life
autopsy 87, 164

B, re 72–73, 76, 138, 139
barbiturates 8, 56, 64, 87, 95, 107
Basnyat, Dr 99
Belgium 10, 64
beneficence xv, 13, 16, 17, 112, 146,
  173
best interests
  consequentialist ethics and 16
  law, in 2, 46, 76, 103, 124–125, 133,
    135
  necessity and 76, 103

quality of life and 15, 16, 46, 134,
  135
proxy and 17
sanctity of life and 134
substituted judgement and 139
withdrawing treatment and 2, 103,
  124–125, 133, 135
See also medical profession;
    withdrawing and withholding
    treatment
Blakemore, Mrs 51
Bland 2, 3, 5, 6, 7, 8, 9, 13, 15, 16, 22,
    72, 88, 103, 108, 123–125, 129,
    130, 132, 134–135, 136, 137,
    138, 139, 140, 141, 150, 170,
    173
Bolam 103, 124, 128–129
Bouldstridge, Mr 36, 38, 52, 166
Brewer, Dr 94
Brownhill, Mrs 43

Canada 81–82
cancer 20, 49, 56, 85, 94, 96, 97
capacity – see competence
Carr, Dr 107, 109, 110, 112
causation
  assisted suicide, and 59, 63, 69, 73
  bias in attributing 100–101, 109, 140
  chain of 59, 100
  depression, of 37–39, 41
  double effect, and xvi, 86–87, 88,
    90–91, 92, 96, 100–102, 103,
    104, 113, 164
  euthanasia, and 6–7, 9, 86
  mercy killing, and 36–37, 169
  omissions, and 123, 134
cerebella ataxia 65
cerebral arteriosclerosis 87
Chabot 18
Chard, Mr 66–67, 168
children
  adults 71, 72
  attempted murder of 110–111,
    125–126
  best interests of 46, 115, 133–134
  competence and 138
  duty to 71, 122, 125, 128
  parents and 2, 16, 26, 38, 43, 69–71,
    108, 116, 122, 125, 135, 153,
    162
  quality of life of 16, 26, 46, 115,
    133–134
  sanctity of life and 134

See also incompetence; infanticide; withdrawing and withholding treatment
chronic illness – *see* illness
Cocker, Mr 36, 37, 38, 41, 42, 49
committees
  clinical ethics committees 148, 152, 155, 161
  compromise and 155–158, 161, 169, 172
  Criminal Law Revision Committee 38, 46, 53, 165
  Warnock Committee 155–156, 165
  See also House of Lords Select Committee
compassion 28, 42, 52, 76, 94, 137, 146, 160, 165, 167, 170
  See also mercy killing; quality of life; suffering
competence
  children and 138
  euthanasia and 1, 5, 14, 15, 49, 50
  mental capacity act 2005, and 76
  mental disorder, and 75
  rationality, and 75–76
  refusal of treatment, and 74, 76, 116, 118, 137, 146
  suicide and 65, 75–76
  test for 75
  See also incompetence; rationality
complicity in suicide – *see* assisted suicide
compromise
  committee, by 155–158
  conditions of 149–151, 157
  defence of 53, 143, 151–154
  democracy and 159, 174
  euthanasia, and xvii, 31, 53, 142–143, 144–145, 149, 155, 156–158, 158–174
    assisted suicide and 82–83, 165–168
    double effect and 112–114, 162–165
    mercy killing and 52–54, 165–171
    omissions and 160–162, 170
  integrity, and 151, 154, 156, 158
  problems with 143, 149–154, 158, 168
confidentiality
  euthanasia, and 68, 108
conflict
  ethical xiii, xiv, xv, xvi, xvii, 3, 4, 7, 9, 30–31, 57, 114, 117, 131,
    139–140, 141, 142, 145, 147, 148, 149, 151–154, 159, 161, 172–174
  law, in 3, 31, 114, 124, 125,131, 134, 139–140, 142, 144–145, 150
  tragic 53
conjoined twins 93, 104, 115, 116, 132, 135, 153
conscience 80, 153, 158
  conscientious objection 16, 139
consensus
  assisted suicide, and 59
  euthanasia, and xvii, 141, 142, 143, 146–149, 155, 160, 161, 162
consent
  absence of 58, 66, 78
  assisted suicide, and 61, 62
  death, to 62, 94, 95, 115, 122, 132
  informed 74, 75
  murder, no defence to 115, 122, 132
  prosecution, to 58, 66, 78
  See also assault; autonomy, respect for; euthanasia; refusal of treatment
consequentialist ethics 22, 146, 152
  acts/omissions distinction, and 22, 120
  autonomy, and 13, 16, 24
  conjoined twins and 136
  quality of life, and 16, 157
  slippery slope, and 18
Cooper, Mr 69, 70
coroners 37, 51, 58, 68, 69, 74, 86, 138
Cox 30, 52, 87, 99, 106–107, 108, 109, 110, 112, 113, 145, 152, 165
Crew, Mrs 64
criminal law
  fair labelling in 63, 165, 170, 171
  flexibility in 62, 144, 165
  See also assisted suicide; infanticide; manslaughter; murder
Crown Prosecution Service (CPS)
  Code for Crown Prosecutors 50–51, 95, 109, 110
  criticism of 52
  non/prosecution by 51–52, 56, 64, 67–68, 79, 95, 96, 97, 106, 108, 109

Davies, Dr 94
Dawson, Lord 95
Dean, Dr 69, 73

death
  ambivalence about 159, 168
  bad 13
  brain stem 7, 9
  certificates 174
  desire for 15, 20, 25, 76–77
  good 4–5, 24, 147, 174
  natural causes 4, 36, 51,63, 69, 85, 86,
      96, 101, 106, 109, 111, 127
  painless xiii, 20, 97
  penalty 43–44, 98
  threat 30, 152
  'tourism' xv–xvi, 57, 62, 63–66, 78,
      82, 124, 167, 168, 17264
  See also causation; dignity; dying
decision–making
  bilateral 128
  crisis situation, in a 149
  doctor, by 1, 113, 127, 162
  parent, by 153
  patient, by 3, 5, 8, 13, 14, 29, 65,
      75–76, 131, 137–138, 142, 149,
      150, 173
  proxy, by 1, 15, 17, 116, 139
  unilateral 128, 161, 165, 170, 173
defence(s)
  doctors' xvi, 83, 102–105, 121, 173
  double effect, as xvi, 102–105, 172,
      173,
  mercy killing as 39, 160, 165–166,
      172, 174
  self 5, 11, 135
  See also diminished responsibility;
      excuse; necessity; provocation
dementia 33, 85, 170
deontological ethics 145, 146, 151
  autonomy, and 13
  See also sanctity/inviolability of life
depression
  diminished responsibility, and 38, 39,
      41, 45
  euthanasia and 18, 20, 47, 63, 78
  grief and 39
  Netherlands 18
  reactive 38, 39, 41, 77
diamorphine – see opioids
Dignitas – see Switzerland
dignity 2, 11, 14, 25, 26
  death with 22, 107
Dignity in Dying 57, 157
dihydrocodeine (DF118) 108, 111
diminished responsibility
  abnormality of mind 37–38, 39

assisted suicide and 57, 63, 82, 144
  depression, and 38, 39, 41, 45
  infanticide, and 166
  jury finding 41
  mental responsibility, substantially
      impaired 38, 39–40
  psychiatric evidence 41
  stretching of xv, 34, 39, 40, 41, 42, 45,
      53, 165
  use in mercy killing trials 32–54
Director of Public Prosecutions (DPP)
      2, 51, 58, 66, 69, 78, 79–80, 108,
      126
doctors – see assisted suicide;
      defence(s); duty; euthanasia;
      guidelines; medical opinion;
      medical profession; opioids;
      paternalism
Doran, Mr 46
double effect 85–106, 112–113
  causation and 100–102
  clinical application of 12, 89–91, 101
  criticism of 22, 24, 85–106, 112–113
  defence, as a xvi, 83, 102–105, 172,
      173
  distress, relief of, and 12, 88, 90–91,
      103, 112, 169
  doctrine of xiv, xvi, 11–12
  euthanasia and 91–92, 94–96,
      105–106, 107
  hypocritical, as 94
  intention and 83, 92–100
  legal principle of xvi, 86, 87–88, 111,
      132, 144
  reform and 113, 159, 162–165, 172,
      174
  withdrawing treatment and 134
  See also causation; defence(s);
      foresight; intention; opioids
Down's syndrome 17, 26, 40, 108, 125,
      161
dualism, mind/body 11, 23, 134–135
duty
  autonomy, and 13, 73, 82
  care, of/rescue, to 70–71, 73, 74,
      118, 120–126, 124, 140, 160,
      162
  contractual basis of 122
  control behaviour, to 71
  die, to 17
  doctor, of 73, 112, 118, 120–126, 130,
      131, 140, 170, 174
  euthanasia, to perform 25, 82

friend, of 121, 122, 130, 161, 165, 170
intruder, of 120–123, 130, 170, 174
moral 121–122, 131, 154, 174
quality of life, and 82, 122, 125–126,
    146
relative, of 69, 71, 73, 120–123, 128,
    130, 170, 174
sanctity of life, and 14, 82, 151, 160
sentencing and 70
state (bodies), of 65, 74, 80, 136, 167
See also intruder; withdrawing and
    withholding treatment
dying
    ambivalence about 159
    medicalisation of 146
    well 4–5
    See also death; Dignity in Dying

Eisenmenger syndrome 88
ethics – *see* autonomy, respect for;
        morality; quality of life; sanctity/
        inviolability of life; value of life
European Convention on Human Rights
    European Commission of Human
        Rights 61, 81
    European Court of Human Rights 2,
        61, 80, 81
    margin of appreciation and 80, 81
    right to a fair trial (article 6) 81
    right to be free from inhuman and
        degrading treatment (article 3)
        80
    right to enjoy rights free from
        discrimination (article 14) 80
    right to freedom of thought,
        conscience and religion (article
        9) 80
    right to life (article 2) 80, 81, 131
    right to respect for private and family
        life (article 8) 80, 81
    See also human rights
euthanasia
    active xiii, 6, 9, 15, 16, 22, 27, 123,
        136, 138, 150, 159, 160, 162,
        170
    animals, of 16, 52
    autoeuthanasia 9
    beneficent 16
    categories of 6–9
    covert 91–92, 94–96, 105, 113, 162
    debate on 17, 21, 25, 30, 31, 138, 141,
        143, 148, 150, 152, 154, 155,
        156, 158, 159, 165

definition(s) of 4–9
evidence of 30, 91
Greek derivation 4
involuntary xiv, 5, 6, 9, 15, 17, 18, 27,
    34, 49, 61, 136, 147, 170, 171,
    172
murder, as 41, 86, 112
non–consensual 17, 28, 171
non–voluntary 5, 6, 9, 15, 16, 17, 19,
    27, 34, 49, 126, 145, 170
overt 105, 162, 163, 168
passive xiii, 6, 7, 9, 72, 130, 150
'practical' arguments surrounding 10,
    17–21, 27–30, 131, 145, 146,
    147, 171
pre–emptive 8
prohibition on xiii, xv, xvii, 10, 28, 41,
    57, 71, 81, 86, 87, 107, 112, 132,
    134, 136, 138, 142
public opinion on 26, 67, 110, 157,
    167, 171
voluntary xvii, 5, 7, 9, 10, 15, 16, 18,
    19, 20, 25, 26, 27, 28, 34, 36, 38,
    49, 50, 51, 59, 91, 65, 72, 79, 80,
    95, 105, 108, 110, 132, 138, 139,
    145, 148, 152, 157, 163, 166,
    170, 174
See also assisted suicide;
    autonomy, respect for; justice;
    motive; murder; quality
    of life; reform of the law,
    proposals for; sanctity/
    inviolability of life; slippery
    slope; value of life
excuse xv, xvii, 43, 119, 167, 171, 173,
    174
justification *v* 53, 113, 158–160, 165,
    174
partial defence, as xvii, 159–160
See also diminished responsibility;
    mercy killing
EXIT 57
Exit Deutsche Schweiz – *see*
    Switzerland

family members
    assisted suicide, by 56, 60–83
    best interests of patient, and 1, 76,
        128, 148
    duties of 69, 71, 73, 120–123, 128,
        130, 170, 174
    duties towards 153
    mercy killing, by xv, 31, 33–54, 113

proxies, as 1, 76
See also intruder; mercy killing
feminist ethics 13, 14
foresight
    double effect and xiv, 11–12, 22, 93,
        113
    intention and xiv, xvi, 7, 22, 66, 67,
        72, 73, 86, 92–93, 97, 113, 134,
        136, 168
    oblique/indirect intention 66, 92, 99
    side effects xiv, 11
    virtual certainty, of xvi, 7, 60, 66, 67,
        72, 73, 86, 89, 92–93, 97, 100,
        164
    See also double effect; intention
Fox, Mr 49, 170
Francis, Mr 60, 62
friend(s)
    assisted suicide, by 63, 66, 67, 82,
        168
    duty of 121, 122, 130, 161, 165,
        170
    mercy killing, by 35, 36, 63, 113,
        169
    See also family members; intruder;
        mercy killing
Friends at the End (FATE) 57
futility
    definition(s) of 12, 23
    criticism of 22–24, 147, 157, 160
    law, in 116, 132–133, 161
    See also inviolability/sanctity of life;
        ordinary/extraordinary means
        distinction

Gardner, Mr 44, 48
Garrow, Dr 108
General Medical Council (GMC)
    disciplinary proceedings and 56, 89,
        94, 99, 106, 112, 126
    See also guidelines; medical
        profession
General Practitioner(s) (GP)
    assisted suicide of 8
    expert evidence of 85
    non/prosecution of 55, 56, 67, 69,
        85–86, 87, 88, 94–95, 97, 98,
        99, 107, 108
    opioids, understanding of, by 99
Germany 30, 88
    mercy killing law in 165
    See also Nazism
Glass 89, 148

Guernsey 10
guidelines
    medical organisations, from 129, 136,
        157
    sentencing, on 33, 167
    See also Crown Prosecution Service
        (CPS)
Gustaffson, Dr 99

Heath, Ms 36, 52
Heginbotham, Mr 33–34, 37, 38, 44, 47,
        52, 141, 170, 171, 173
Hemlock Society 51
Hippocratic Oath 10, 19, 30
Hindley, Dr 95
Holden, Mr 60, 78
Holland – *see* Netherlands
homicide – *see* assisted suicide;
        defence(s); infanticide;
        manslaughter; murder; sentences
        and sentencing
hospice – *see* palliative care/medicine
Hough 36, 45, 55, 63
Houghton, Mr and Mrs 40, 41, 42–43,
        45
House of Lords Select Committee
    medical ethics, on 21, 51, 79, 88, 90,
        94, 140, 157
    murder and life imprisonment, on 37,
        136, 165
    Assisted Dying for the Terminally Ill
        Bill, on 79, 88, 107
    compromise, and 157–158
Hudson, Ms 66, 77
human rights
    assisted suicide, and 2, 61, 80–81
    autonomy, and 16, 116
    duties, and 24
    sanctity of life, and 10, 131, 134
    withdrawing treatment from patient in
        PVS, and 124, 136
    See also European Convention on
        Human Rights
Humphry, Mr 51, 58, 74

illness 29, 70, 75
    chronic 8
    terminal 8, 89, 141
    See also depression; dementia;
        suffering
incompetence
    autonomy, and 16
    best interests, and 17, 76, 123, 139

euthanasia, and 16–17, 49, 50, 130,
    134, 136, 139
  necessity, and 74, 76
  proxy decision–makers, and 17, 116,
    139
  sanctity of life, and 133–136
  substituted judgement, and 116, 139
  suicide, and 74
  See also advance directive(s); best
    interests; children; negligence;
    withdrawing and withholding
    treatment
infanticide 35, 166
inheritance 22, 47, 60, 78, 98, 163, 169
insanity 39, 45
intention
  acts/omissions distinction, and 13, 22,
    72, 124
  assisted suicide, and 1, 58, 59, 60,
    64, 65, 66, 72, 73, 74, 168
  definition of 21
  direct 7, 67, 73, 92, 93, 99, 168, 169
  double effect, and xvi, 22, 55–56,
    83, 87, 88, 91, 92–100, 113,
    164
  euthanasia, and 6, 7, 8, 9, 32, 36, 91,
    94–96, 106, 107, 115, 123, 129,
    132, 145, 165, 168
  foresight, and 60, 64, 66–67, 72, 73,
    88, 93, 97, 101
  inconsistent application of 101, 104,
    173
  intruder, and 121
  Jehovah's Witnesses in refusing
    treatment 72
  motive, and 46–47, 98–99, 106
  objective evidence and 164
  oblique/indirect 7, 66, 92, 99
  responsibility, and 22
  sanctity of life, and xiii, xiv, 3, 10, 11,
    12, 134, 137
  subjectivity of 163, 164
  suicide, and 9, 69
  withdrawing treatment, and 23
  See also double effect; foresight;
    refusal of treatment
interests
  critical 14
  social 14, 82
  state 116, 135, 137
  See also best interests; public interest
intruder 120–123, 126–128, 130, 161,
    165, 170

inviolability of life – see sanctity/
    inviolability of life
involuntary euthanasia – see euthanasia
Irwin, Mr 55–57, 63, 64, 65, 67, 68, 94,
    95, 96, 97, 142, 145, 173
Isle of Man 10, 56

Jackson, Mr 60, 62, 63
Jennison, Mrs 60, 62, 66
Johnson, Mr 40, 44
Johnson, Mr and Mrs 69–77, 161, 162
Jolly, Dr 108
Jones, Mr 35, 40, 44, 49
Jordan, Dr 69, 73
judges
  condemnation of euthanasia by 35,
    42–43, 107, 112, 127
  conservatism of 118
  criticism of prosecutors by 52
  directions to jury from 107, 109,
    110–112, 126, 127
  lenient sentencing by 33, 42–51, 52,
    63, 77–79, 112, 144
  stretching of diminished responsibility
    by 39–42
  sympathy for defendant expressed by
    33, 46, 52, 112
juries
  assisted suicide trials, in 62, 67
  diminished responsibility, and 41
  euthanasia/mercy killing trials, in 35,
    41, 43, 53, 55, 86, 95, 97, 98, 99,
    100–101, 103, 106, 107, 109,
    110, 111, 112, 127, 164, 168, 169
  inquests, in 69
  intention, and 93, 106, 108
  See also judges
justice
  euthanasia, and 17–18, 29, 145–146
  resource allocation, and 17, 145–146
justification
  acts/omissions distinction, and
    122–123, 130, 140, 170
  double effect, and xiv, xvi, 90, 101,
    102–105, 106, 113
  euthanasia, of xvii, 15, 16, 17, 18, 22,
    25, 130, 138, 140, 170
  excuse 53, 113, 158–160, 165, 171,
    174
  See also intruder

Karapetian, Mr 126–127, 128, 170
Killick, Mr 49, 170, 171

killing
    See acts/omissions distinction;
        manslaughter; murder;
        withdrawing and withholding
        treatment
King, Mrs 35, 36
Kneen, Mrs 56

law
    action-guiding function 140, 144,
        150
    bias/deference towards medical
        profession in 19, 51, 68–77, 83,
        84–114, 115–131, 144, 169, 172,
        173
    clarity in xvi, xvii, 36, 53, 57, 58, 61,
        62, 63, 64, 66, 67, 69, 75, 82, 88,
        92, 103, 105, 114, 117, 118, 133,
        138, 150, 163, 171
    contradiction in 3, 57, 113, 117, 139,
        142, 144, 150, 172
    enforcement 98, 162, 173
    in-action v. on-books 34, 39, 41–42,
        53, 67, 81–82, 83, 99, 164
    inconsistency in law 34, 49, 68, 82,
        86, 138, 139, 142, 144, 147, 162,
        164, 171
    See also conflict; law commission;
        legal fiction
law commission
    double effect, and 104–105
    mercy killing proposal of xvii, 42, 53,
        165, 167, 171
Lawson, Mr 68–69
legal fiction 37, 102, 105
letting die – *see* acts/omissions
        distinction; withdrawing and
        withholding treatment
liberty – *see* autonomy
life – *see* life support, withdrawal
        of; quality of life; sanctity/
        inviolability of life; value of life;
        wrongful life
life support, withdrawal of – *see*
        withdrawing and withholding
        treatment
Lindsell, Ms 88, 103, 105, 163
living will – *see* advance directive(s)
Lodwig, Dr 96, 98, 101, 108, 109
Long, Mr 43
Loughran, Mr 66
Lyons, 'Dr' 61, 62, 67, 78
Lyons, Mrs 63, 167

malpractice – *see* negligence
manslaughter – s*ee* provocation;
        diminished responsibility
March, Mr 60, 78
Marshall, Mrs 35, 42, 43, 48
Martin, Dr 85–86, 87, 98, 108, 109, 113,
        142, 150, 173
Masters, Mr 49
Maurice, Dr 94, 108
McAuley, Mr 45
McGranaghan 77, 78, 166
McShane 47, 60, 63, 66, 78, 169
media
    reporting of crime 48
    sources xv
    surveys on euthanasia 91, 94–95
mediation 148, 161, 172
medical opinion
    accepted practice 91, 103, 118, 122,
        125, 128, 129
    divergent 125, 129
    evidence, as 85, 88, 103, 133, 163,
        164
    proper treatment 103
    reasonable/responsible body of 88,
        103, 129, 163, 164
    See also guidelines
medical profession
    attitudes to assisted suicide/euthanasia
        of xiii, 105
    bias/deference towards 19, 51, 68–77,
        83, 84–114, 115–131, 144, 169,
        172, 173
    non/prosecution of members of xvi,
        67, 84–114
    values of 118, 119, 129
    See also assisted suicide; conscience;
        defence(s); doctors; duty;
        euthanasia; guidelines; medical
        opinion; paternalism
medical treatment
    demand for 133, 137
    See also artificial nutrition and
        hydration; best interests; futility;
        medical opinion; medical
        profession; negligence; refusal
        of treatment; withdrawing and
        withholding treatment
mental states – *see* depression; dementia;
        diminished responsibility;
        incompetence
mercy killing
    assisted suicide, and 55–83

attempted murder, and 36–37, 44, 49, 50, 51, 52, 63, 127, 166
charging lottery, and 62–63, 82, 171
defence, as 39, 41, 45, 50–52, 79, 165–171, 172
definition(s) of xiii, xv, 8, 34, 44–48, 170
diminished responsibility, and 32–54, 144, 165
exceptional, as 42–46, 62
murder, as xv, 34–37, 44, 45, 50, 52, 53, 63
provocation, and 36, 38, 41
public opinion on 167, 171
sentencing
    leniency in 33, 42–46, 51, 52, 63, 77–79, 112, 144
    lottery, and 48–50
    patterns 78
See also assisted suicide; diminished responsibility; euthanasia; motive; reform of law, proposals for
misdiagnosis 20, 29, 103
Monaghan, Mrs 37, 44, 50
Moor, Dr 55, 83, 85, 86, 97, 98, 100, 101, 103, 108, 109, 110, 111, 164
moral
    agency 119
    ambivalence about death/dying 158–159
    cloaking moral issues 23, 123, 125, 139–140
    complexity 150, 154
    conflict xiv, xvi, 3, 8, 21, 87, 114, 117, 131–140, 142, 150, 151–154
    creativity 145
    discomfort 158–159, 161
    indeterminacy, and 148, 151
    language 4, 146, 159, 161
    'pause' 159, 172
    responsibility 22
    status 150, 155–156
    strangers 130
    See also morality
morality
    law and 115–140
    law, internal xvii, 3, 142, 144
    medicine, internal 128
    See also autonomy, respect for; conflict; compromise; pluralism; quality of life; sanctity/ inviolability of life; value of life

morphine – see opioids
Morris, Mr 45
Morrison, Mr 38, 44
motive
    absence of 85
    acts/omissions distinction, and 22
    doctor, of 85, 98, 106, 112, 121, 127
    euthanasia, in 6, 7, 8
    intention, and 46–47, 98–99, 106
    intruder, of 121, 127
    merciful 6, 7, 8, 38, 40, 47, 48, 49, 53, 77, 112, 169, 173
    mixed 47, 78, 169
    murder, and 36, 98, 106, 121, 171
    reason, as 6, 7, 8, 98
    sentencing, and 45–50, 112
    unmerciful 47, 121
    See also intention; intruder; mercy killing
motor neurone disease xiii, 2, 8, 27, 79, 98
multiple sclerosis 36, 68, 69, 75
murder
    assisted suicide 57, 61, 62–63, 82
    attempted 36–37, 44, 49, 50, 51, 52, 63, 110–111, 125–126, 127, 166
    consent, and 115, 122, 132
    euthanasia as 41, 86, 112
    mercy killing as xv, 34–37, 44, 45, 50, 52, 53, 63
    motive, and 36, 98, 106, 121, 171
    necessity, and 104
    sanctity of life and 132, 136
    status, and 87, 120, 127
    See also causation; consent; euthanasia; intention; sentences and sentencing

Nazism 4, 19, 28
necessity
    best interests and 74, 76, 103
    conjoined twins and 104
    double effect and 102–105
    euthanasia and 20, 105, 163
    murder and 104
    See also best interests; defence(s)
negligence
    manslaughter, gross 86, 99, 107, 127, 163, 164, 173
    suicide prevention and 74
    tort of 103, 124, 129
Netherlands
    Chabot 18–19

euthanasia
  defined 5
  law and procedure 5, 10, 64, 158, 169
  necessity in 105, 163
  non/prosecution in 19
  slippery slope argument in 19, 21, 28
  Sutorius 25
non–maleficence 13
non–voluntary euthanasia – *see* euthanasia
Northern Territory – *see* Australia

O'Donohoe, Mrs 60
omission(s) – *see* acts/omissions distinction; duty; withdrawing and withholding treatment
opiate – *see* opioids
opioids 12, 88, 89–92, 93, 94, 96, 98, 99, 101, 102, 103, 104, 105, 108, 113, 129, 160, 162
  See also palliative care/medicine
ordinary/extraordinary means distinction
  burdens/benefits and xiv, 12
  criticism of 22–24, 147, 157, 160, 161
  definition(s) of 12, 23
  futility and xiv, 12, 21, 23
  law, in 116, 132–133
  See also futility; withdrawing and withholding treatment
organ retention 128
Oregon 10, 64
Osborne 66, 77
overdose 9, 47, 60, 63, 66, 67, 69, 77, 85, 90, 94, 99, 107
  See also opioids

pain – *see* suffering
pain-killing drugs/medication – *see* opioids
palliative care/medicine xiii, xiv, 12, 13, 80, 89, 147, 148, 157, 162
  availability of 19, 93
  definition of 89
  euthanasia and 5, 19–20, 26, 148, 163
  expert opinion in 85, 90–91, 93, 95, 101
  hospices 19, 68, 86, 88

philosophy 113
  training in 107, 146
  World Health Organisation and 90
  See also double effect; opioids
passive euthanasia – *see* euthanasia
paraplegia 64
parentalism – *see* paternalism
paternalism 14, 167
patient(s) – *see* autonomy; best interests; consent; treatment; withdrawing and withholding treatment
persistent vegetative state – *see* permanent vegetative state (PVS)
permanent vegetative state (PVS)
  dying, distinguished from 2, 116
  home care of patient in 121
  withdrawing treatment from patient in 2, 116
persons
  personhood, and 16, 150
  respect for 14, 16
  responsibility and 22
  See also assault
Peugh, Mrs 94
Pitman, Mr 61, 62, 63, 78
pluralism
  compromise, and 153–158
  moral 151, 153–154
  society, and 21, 131, 153
pneumonia 69, 90, 101
police xv, 33, 35, 36, 51, 56, 64, 67, 68, 74, 86, 94, 96, 97, 98, 106, 108, 127, 167
potassium chloride 96, 99, 106
Pratten, Mrs 60, 63
Pretty xiii, xiv, xvii, 1, 2, 3, 8, 9, 10, 12, 13, 14, 16, 18, 21, 25, 26, 34, 50, 57, 58, 71, 79–82, 105, 115, 117, 137, 141, 143, 145, 168, 173
principles of biomedical ethics – *see* principlism
principlism
  criticism of 151, 152
  four principles approach 13, 17, 146, 152
prisoners
  duty owed to 74
  suicide of 74, 77, 166
progressive supranuclear palsy 8
prosecution – *see* Crown Prosecution Service (CPS); Netherlands

provocation 35, 36, 38, 41
proxy – *see* decision–making
public interest
    disclosing confidential information in
        68
    non/prosecution and 50, 51, 52, 67,
        78, 79, 110
    preserving life in 81
    sentencing and 45, 112
public opinion – *see* assisted suicide;
        euthanasia

quadriplegia 133
quality of life
    appeal of 26–27
    autonomy *v* 15, 17, 49, 170
    compromise and 156, 160, 161, 169,
        170
    criticism of 18, 26–27, 31, 143, 157,
        160
    law, in 53, 116, 118, 120, 122, 126,
        131, 142
    meaning of 15–17, 26
    mercy 8, 15
    sanctity of life *v* 12, 13, 22–24,
        133–136, 147, 157
    scope of 26–27, 29, 126, 169
    See also suffering; value of life
Quinlan 116, 117, 118, 122, 131, 139,
        141, 147

Raheem, Dr 99
rationality
    competence, and 74, 75, 138
    law, in xvii, xviii, 44, 100, 123, 133,
        136, 138, 144–145, 164, 173
    reflection, and 149
    suicide, and 75
Rayner, Dr 94
Reed, Mr 57, 58, 61, 78, 81
reform of the law, proposals for
    assisted suicide 10, 79, 105, 145, 159,
        161–162, 165, 166–167, 168,
        172, 173
    double effect 113, 159, 162–165, 172,
        174
    mandatory life sentence 165
    mercy killing xvii, 42, 53, 165–171,
        172
    non–voluntary euthanasia 27, 145,
        170
    voluntary euthanasia 10, 145, 159
    withdrawing treatment 13, 160–162

refusal of treatment
    assisted suicide, and 72–73
    competence to issue 74, 75–76,
        137–138
    intention and 72–73, 173
    predicted legal status 118
    right to 1, 72–73, 137–138
    suicide, and 72, 75–76
    See also advance directive(s);
        autonomy, respect for; intention;
        suicide
relativism 153
religious perspectives 1, 10, 11, 20, 24,
        80, 131, 132, 135
    See also sanctity/inviolability of life;
        vitalism
resources – *see* justice
resuscitation
    'do not attempt' 69, 74, 75, 128
Ridler, Mr 61
right(s) – *see* autonomy, respect for;
        duty; European Convention on
        Human Rights; human rights;
        refusal of treatment
Robey 62, 63, 77, 78, 167
Rodriguez 81–82, 169
rule of law 144
    See also morality

Sampedro 81–82
sanctity/inviolability of life
    absolute/not 134
    appeal of 24
    autonomy 13, 136–139, 156
    compromise, and 53, 82, 113, 149,
        156, 159, 160, 161, 162, 164,
        166, 170
    criticism of 21–24
    law, in 58, 72, 115, 117, 131–133,
        136, 137
    meaning of 10–13, 21–22
    principle of xiv, 10–13
    quality of life 21–24, 133–136
    revolution against 134, 136
    scope of 23–24
    secular version(s) of 10, 11, 24
    suicide, and 137
    theological version(s) of 10, 11, 24,
        132
    vitalism *v* 11, 24, 135
    See also double effect; ordinary/
        extraordinary means distinction;
        value of life

Sawyer, Mr 35, 47
Scotland 56
    assisted suicide in 59
    reform proposed in 10
    Voluntary Euthanasia Society of 59
    See also Friends at the End (FATE)
Scott-Moncrieff, Dr 94–95
sedatives – *see* sedation
sedation
    sedative drugs and xiv, 19, 56, 88,
        90–91, 101, 102, 106, 160, 164
    terminal 148
    See also double effect; opioids
self-determination – *see* autonomy,
        respect for
sentences and sentencing
    aggravating factors 46, 78
    community order 33, 167, 172
    conditional discharge 44, 49, 78
    death penalty 43–44
    deterrent, as 167
    guidance on 33, 167, 172
    imprisonment 30, 42–43, 44, 46, 47,
        48, 49, 57, 63, 77, 78, 127, 171,
        173
        life xv, 34, 35, 36, 43, 63,
            109, 115, 132, 165, 166,
            172
    leniency in 33, 42–51, 52, 63,
        77–79, 112, 144
    licence 35
    lottery 48–50, 166
    mitigating factors 35, 45, 46
    nominal penalty 44, 51, 52
    non–custodial 34, 44, 53, 167, 172
    patterns 33, 49, 77, 78, 172
    probation 43, 44, 45, 46, 47, 49, 50,
        69, 70, 78, 166, 167
    psychiatric treatment 44, 45, 49, 167
    public interest and 45, 79, 112
    suspended 46, 47, 48, 78, 99, 106,
        112
Shipman, Dr 87, 98, 113, 129, 163
Simpson 43
Sinha, Dr 99
slippery slope xiv, 17–21, 27–30, 31, 50,
        82, 131, 146, 149
Spain 81–82
spina bifida 16, 20
status
    doctor, as 87, 120–123, 128–130
    mercy killer, as 45–48, 171
    moral 150, 155–156, 165

murder and 87, 120, 127
    See also family members; intruder
substituted judgement 15, 139, 116
    See also incompetence
suffering
    assisted suicide, and xvi, 2, 47, 64, 75,
        79–80
    benefit of 20, 29
    double effect, and 12, 87, 106, 112,
        162, 164, 169, 173
    euthanasia, and xiii, xv, 3, 5, 8, 9,
        26–27, 29, 32, 33, 48, 56, 105,
        107, 136, 138, 142, 146, 147,
        148, 160, 163, 169, 172
    goal of medicine, and 29
    life fatigue, and 8, 25
    mental 47, 75
    pain, pain-relief and 12, 19, 20, 55,
        56, 67, 69, 83, 85, 88, 89–92, 93,
        94, 95, 96, 97, 98, 99, 102, 103,
        105, 106, 107, 112, 113, 123,
        129, 162
    palliative care/medicine, and 19, 26,
        128, 162
    quality of life, and xiv, 3, 15–17, 21,
        26–27, 53, 82, 115, 117, 131,
        133, 134, 136, 142, 146, 147,
        148, 150, 155, 163, 166, 169, 174
    See also competence; depression;
        illness; quality of life
suicide
    Act 1961 xvi, 35, 55, 58, 63, 70, 79,
        82, 165, 166
    attempted 33, 38, 58, 77, 173
    autoeuthanasia, as 5, 9
    'committing' 58, 73
    decriminalisation of 58
    definition(s) of 9, 61
    duty to prevent/rescue 73, 74, 76
    entitlement/liberty to commit 58, 76,
        137
    intention and 72
    manual 51, 58, 59, 74, 82, 168
    notes 74
    omission, by 72, 82
    pacts 77
    pills 168
    prisoners, by 74, 77, 166
    refusal of treatment, and 72–73
    right to commit 1, 58, 80, 137
    See also assisted suicide; duty;
        rationality
surrogate – *see* decision–making

Sutorius 25–26
Sweeney 45, 47
Switzerland
  'death tourism' xvi, 8, 63–66
  Dignitas 56, 64
  Exit Deutsche Schweiz 64
  mercy killing law in 64, 165

Taylor 36
Taylor, Dr 126
Taylor, Mrs Karen 69
Taylor, Mrs Kelly 88
terminal illness – *see* illness
thanatology 29
Thompson, Mr and Ms 36
treatment – *see* medical treatment
trust 19, 50, 107, 168
Turner, Dr 8

utilitarian ethics 16, 22, 152, 156
  See also consequentialist ethics

value of life xiii–xiv, xvi, 3, 130, 144,
    147, 149, 150, 151–152, 158
  compromise on 31, 53, 82, 113,
    158–159, 168, 173, 174
  intrinsic xiv, xv, 3, 10–13, 21–24, 53,
    82, 116, 131–133, 140, 142, 143,
    144, 145, 156, 174
  instrumental xiv, 3, 15–17, 26–27,
    53, 116, 131, 133–136, 140, 142,
    143, 144,145, 156, 174
  self-determined xiv, 3, 10, 13–15,
    24–26, 116, 131, 136–139, 140,
    142, 143, 144,145, 156, 174
  undermining 18, 19
  See also autonomy, respect for; quality
    of life; sanctity of life
ventilation 7, 72–73, 116, 120, 133–134,
    138
  See also withdrawing and withholding
    treatment
virtual certainty, foresight of – *see*
    double effect; foresight; intention
virtue ethics 13, 146
vitalism 11, 24, 135
voluntary euthanasia – *see* euthanasia

Voluntary Euthanasia Society (VES)
    10, 36, 55, 56, 58–59, 61, 65, 94,
    97, 169
  Scotland, of 59
vulnerable persons 50
  euthanasia and 2, 18, 20, 24, 58, 76,
    80, 81, 137
  local authority and 65

Wallis 47, 66, 78
Walters, Dr 94
Watts, Mrs 127, 128
'whistle–blowing' 68, 108
Whiteley, Prof 69
Wise, Mrs 56, 50
withdrawing and withholding treatment
  act, as 6, 117, 120–123, 127, 130,
    136, 150
  artificial nutrition and hydration, of 2,
    6, 88, 103, 123–125, 127, 148
  causation and 100
  definitions of and distinctions between
    6, 118, 119
  intention in 121, 134
  law, in xvi, 103, 108, 116, 123–128,
    148
  omission, as 6, 117, 118, 119,
    120–123, 150
  predicted legal status 117–123
  reform and 13, 159, 160–162, 165,
    173
  selective non–treatment 6
  See also acts/omissions distinction;
    artificial nutrition and hydration;
    best interests; duty; futility;
    intruder; ordinary/extraordinary
    means distinction; refusal of
    treatment
withholding treatment – *see* withdrawing
    and withholding treatment
Woollin 60, 64, 66, 72, 93, 97, 99, 101,
    164, 168, 173
wrongful life 133

Young, Mr 61

Z, re 65, 76, 78, 124, 167